MW01438581

THE YEARBOOK OF LANGLAND STUDIES

THE YEARBOOK OF LANGLAND STUDIES

Editors
Alastair Bennett, Royal Holloway, University of London
Katharine Breen, Northwestern University
Eric Weiskott, Boston College

Editorial Assistants
Eliza H. Feero, Charlotte Goddu, Northwestern University

Editorial Board
Michael Calabrese, California State University, Los Angeles
Cristina Maria Cervone, University of Memphis
Andrew Cole, Princeton University
Rita Copeland, University of Pennsylvania
Isabel Davis, Natural History Museum, University of London
Andrew Galloway, Cornell University
Simon Horobin, Magdalen College, University of Oxford
Traugott Lawler, Emeritus, Yale University
Adin Lears, Virginia Commonwealth University
Jill Mann, Emerita, University of Notre Dame and Girton College, University of Cambridge
Linne R. Mooney, University of York
Ad Putter, University of Bristol
Elizabeth Robertson, University of Glasgow
Wendy Scase, University of Birmingham
D. Vance Smith, Princeton University
Thorlac Turville-Petre, Emeritus, University of Nottingham
Nicholas Watson, Harvard University
Nicolette Zeeman, King's College, University of Cambridge

The Yearbook of Langland Studies

37 (2023)

Edited by
ALASTAIR BENNETT, KATHARINE BREEN,
AND ERIC WEISKOTT

BREPOLS

YLS welcomes submissions dealing with *Piers Plowman* and related poetry and prose in the traditions of didactic and allegorical alliterative writing. Papers concerning the literary, historical, religious, intellectual, codicological, and critical contexts of these works are also invited. Submissions are doubleblind peer reviewed. In preparing their manuscripts for review, authors should avoid revealing their identity within the essay itself and follow the MHRA Style Guide (available at https://www.mhra.org.uk/Publications/Books/StyleGuide/download.shtml). The editors are Alastair Bennett (Royal Holloway, University of London), Katharine Breen (Northwestern University), and Eric Weiskott (Boston College); please send submissions to yls.submissions@gmail.com.

Individual subscriptions are included in membership in the International *Piers Plowman* Society. To become a member, visit our website (www.piersplowman.org). Information on institutional subscriptions should be sought from Brepols Publishers (periodicals@brepols.net). Back issues of volumes 1–19 may be ordered from Medieval Institute Publications, Western Michigan University, 1903 W. Michigan Avenue, Kalamazoo, MI 49008–5432 (http://www.wmich.edu/medieval/mip/). Back issues starting with volume 20 can be acquired from Brepols. The complete run of YLS, from the first issue in 1987, is available online to those whose institutions subscribe to the e-journal through Brepols (see https://www.brepolsonline.net/loi/yls).

© 2023, Brepols Publishers n.v., Turnhout, Belgium.

All rights reserved. No part of this publication may be reproduced, stored in a retrieval system, or transmitted, in any form or by any means, electronic, mechanical, photocopying, recording, or otherwise without the prior permission of the publisher.

D/2023/0095/273
ISBN 978-2-503-60425-1
DOI 10.1484/J.YLS.5.135589
ISSN 0890-2917
eISSN 2031-0242

Printed in the EU on acid-free paper.

Contents

Commentary 7

Further Remarks on the Audience and Public of *Piers Plowman*
Michael JOHNSTON 11

Langland's Rhythm and the Clock in the Brain
Thomas CABLE and Noriko INOUE 69

The Commercialization of *lechecraft* in *Piers Plowman*
Patrick OUTHWAITE 97

'Meddling with Making'. Speech, Poetic Craft, and the Spectre of Imaginatif in *Piers Plowman* A
Grace Catherine GREINER 137

Reviews 155

Annual Bibliography, 2022
Patrick OUTHWAITE 193

Commentary

This issue of *YLS* presents four new essays on different aspects of *Piers Plowman*, alongside ten reviews of recent books, and the annual biography of scholarship on Langland. In 'Further Remarks on the Audience and Public of *Piers Plowman*', Michael Johnston takes up Anne Middleton's invitation to consider the relationship between the poem's real and projected readership. Johnston offers a fresh examination of every surviving manuscript of *Piers* produced before 1500, combining insights from existing scholarship with new archival findings of his own to present a striking picture of what we know about the readers and owners of these books. He shows that the poem reached a conspicuously diverse audience, with readers drawn from across the different estates and social strata of late medieval England, in both urban and rural locations. *Piers Plowman*'s exhortations to these different groups and its address to their various concerns are not just literary conceits, Johnston argues, but rather reflect the scope and breadth of the poem's actual readership. Johnston's essay is notable both for its detailed account of the individual manuscripts where evidence for ownership and circulation can be established, and in its ambition to characterize the whole corpus of surviving copies. Where studies of individual manuscripts might lead us to prioritize the concerns of particular readers, aristocrats or Londoners or secular clergy for example, a consideration of the manuscript record as a whole demands that we reckon with the rich diversity of Langland's readership.

In 'Langland's Rhythm and the Clock in the Brain', Thomas Cable and Noriko Inoue propose new avenues for research into the metre of *Piers Plowman* and other poems in the alliterative tradition. Stepping back from debates about the number of beats in the alliterative long line, they seek to ask new questions about the role of rhythm in Langland's work, drawing insights from recent research in cognitive science and musicology and placing these in dialogue with the more familiar methodologies of metrical analysis. To understand rhythm as the product of such linguistic features as semantic emphasis or alliteration is to confuse cause and effect, Cable and Inoue argue. Rather, rhythm originates in human anatomy and physiology, in what cognitive scientists have called the 'clock in the brain', and gives shape, in turn, to those features of language that are susceptible to metrical analysis. This is an approach that calls for new attention to the embodied experience of composing, reading, and performing alliterative verse. (Eric Weiskott recused himself from evaluating this essay, as is our policy when a submission engages substantially with one of the editors' own.)

In 'The Commercialization of *lechecraft* in *Piers Plowman*', Patrick Outhwaite considers the representations of 'leches' and physicians in *Piers Plowman* and related texts such as *Mum and the Sothsegger*, asking what these can tell us about late medieval attitudes to the practice of medicine. Outhwaite describes the complex account of 'lechecraft' that emerges from these poems, where healers who are motivated by charity effect cures for the soul as well as the body, while those who seek to profit from their work are treated with suspicion, often alongside other urban tradespeople engaged in dubious practices. Outhwaite reads these poems as sources for the social history of medicine, showing that their sceptical account of practices like uroscopy, and of practitioners like cobblers, echoes and supplements the concerns expressed by London civic authorities, as well as by other late medieval writers. *Piers Plowman*, he argues, reflects a broader late medieval resistance to the professionalization of medicine, and a preference for the amateur healer who offers his services for free.

Grace Catherine Greiner turns to the A text in '"Meddling with Making": Speech, Poetic Craft, and the Spectre of Imaginatif in *Piers Plowman* A'. Greiner discerns the 'spectre' or 'pre-memory' of Imaginatif, a personification first introduced in the B text, in this earlier version of Langland's poem, showing how the A text anticipates Imaginatif's inquiries into the value of Will's poetic 'makynge' in several scenes where the dreamer and his interlocutors consider different kinds of speech in relation to various forms of productive labour, craft, and creativity. In these A-text scenes, she writes, we find that Langland is already working out a theory of poetic composition that draws on contemporary understandings of the imagination, and that reflects his concern with the ethical value of labour. Greiner also considers the work of John But, who echoes Imaginatif's B-text phrase 'And þow medlest þee wiþ makynge' (B.12.16) in his own conclusion to the A text. But reveals himself to be an astute reader of *Piers* in its multiple versions, recognizing the continuities between the treatments of poetic craft in A and B.

This issue of *YLS* goes into production not long after the eighth International *Piers Plowman* Society conference, which was held at Senate House in London, from 6 to 8 July 2023. The programme committee, chaired by Rebecca Davis, put together a rich and rewarding schedule of events, including plenary lectures from Katharine Breen and Emily Steiner, plenary panels on Langland's London and celebrating the work of Derek Pearsall, a panel with the poets Bernard O'Donoghue and Keston Sutherland, who presented translations of *Piers* and new work in response to the poem, and concurrent sessions on all aspects of *Piers Plowman*, its contexts, traditions, and legacy. The excellent work we heard presented at this conference attests to the good health of *Piers Plowman* studies today. The editors look forward to publishing the plenary lectures in the next issue of this journal, and we warmly encourage scholars who presented papers at the conference to consider submitting their work to *YLS*.

Finally, we invite submissions for *YLS* 38 and beyond on the topic of Langland and disability studies. This is for an ongoing series of studies spread over multiple issues of *YLS*, guest-edited by Rick Godden.

Alastair Bennett
Katharine Breen
Eric Weiskott

MICHAEL JOHNSTON

Further Remarks on the Audience and Public of *Piers Plowman**

▼ **ABSTRACT** Building upon Anne Middleton's work on Langland's audience and public, this essay offers a fresh examination of all pre-1500 manuscripts of *Piers Plowman*. This examination demonstrates that Langland's poem reached a nationwide audience, with attested readers among the aristocracy, the lay commons, the secular clergy, and the regular clergy. This circulation also represents distribution among both rural and urban readers. This essay also puts such manuscript evidence into dialogue with *Piers Plowman* itself, suggesting that Langland's poem, by its various appeals to nearly every social group from late medieval England, envisioned the wide readership that its manuscripts achieved.

▼ **KEYWORDS** manuscripts, illumination, dialect, scribe, provenance, audience, public, reception, readership

---

* I am grateful to Taylor Cowdery and H. M. Cushman for the chance to present an early version of this material at the University of North Carolina's Medieval and Renaissance Colloquium in Spring 2021. I also gratefully acknowledge Purdue University for naming me a University Faculty Scholar, and the College of Liberal Arts for several ASPIRE Grants for Research Travel, all of which helped to defray the costs of visits to libraries. Finally, I thank the National Humanities Center for the Kent R. Mullikin Fellowship, which enabled me to begin sorting through the copious notes that eventually resulted in this essay.

Michael Johnston is an Associate Professor of English at Purdue University (West Lafayette, IN, USA).

The Yearbook of Langland Studies, 37 (2023), 11–68
BREPOLS ❦ PUBLISHERS   10.1484/J.YLS.5.136475

Two of the ghosts that *Piers Plowman* scholars — of the historicist bent — find ourselves perpetually chasing: whom did Langland imagine as his readers? And who actually read this most baffling and confounding poem? Anne Middleton influentially distinguishes the poem's *audience* from its *public*, defining the former as 'that readership actually achieved by the work'. The poem's audience, she writes, 'may be attested by such evidence as the date and location of copies, their place in books and collections, their ownership and transmission by bequest, gift, or purchase, and by comments on the text and references and allusions to it, and uses of it'. Middleton defines the text's public as the 'readership imagined and posited by the composer as a necessary postulate in the practical process of bringing the work into being, for a certain effect within certain perceived historical conditions'.[1] In other words, the public consists of those whom the text constructs as its imaginative readers.

Approaches to both questions have varied. Elucidating what Middleton calls the 'audience', some have looked at early evidence of the poem's readership, primarily from wills and external allusions, while others have scoured manuscript evidence.[2] Scholars extrapolating from evidence internal to the poem itself have posited a bewildering range of publics for *Piers Plowman*, from the way the poem might have inspired John Ball and the leaders of the 1381 rising, to the way it invokes the world of secular clerics and civic administrators, to its affiliations with Wycliffite thought, to its appeals to the aristocracy or various classes of clergy.[3] In this essay, I do not wish to adjudicate between these competing claims about the poem's audience or public — though I do intend to build upon them. Instead, I will here argue that the poem's manuscript record, if looked at comprehensively, can usefully complicate notions of Langland's audience. In particular, I will argue that a consideration of the social circumstances surrounding the manuscripts' likely places of production and early circulation belies attempts to limit Langland's vision and reach to any one

---

1 Middleton, 'Audience and Public', pp. 101–02. Middleton's work is heavily indebted to Burrow, 'The Audience'. See also Burrow, 'Postscript', appended to the 1984 reprint of his 1957 essay (which appeared in *Anglia*), in which Burrow largely concurs with Middleton's argument.

2 For a succinct overview of the poem's attested and likely readers, see Kerby-Fulton, 'Langland and the Bibliographic Ego', pp. 110–22. See also Hudson, 'Epilogue'; Robert A. Wood, 'A Fourteenth-Century London Owner'; and Turville-Petre, *The Alliterative Revival*, pp. 45–46. On the manuscript evidence, see Doyle, 'Remarks on Surviving Manuscripts'; Horobin, 'Manuscripts and Readers'; Eyler and Benson, 'The Manuscripts of *Piers Plowman*'; and Uhart, 'The Early Reception of *Piers Plowman*'. There are also numerous studies of individual manuscripts of *Piers Plowman*, reference to which will recur frequently below.

3 For a general overview of the broad public that Langland's poem envisions, see Benson, *Public 'Piers Plowman'*, passim, but particularly chapters 2 and 3. For references to specific publics, see the various sections, below.

segment of the late medieval English reading classes. Langland's audience, that is, was as diverse as the English reading classes themselves were.

But this argument also has implications for our understanding of Langland's public. As a result of the diversity of Langland's audience, I will argue, the diversity of critical takes on Langland's public begins to make sense. Middleton insisted, quite convincingly, that questions of audience and public are not so distinct as they might at first seem:

> Specifying what I shall call the audience might appear at the outset to be a matter of 'objective' information, while determining its public will seem an exercise in 'subjective' interpretation. Yet the more closely one approaches either question in detail, the more spurious does this way of formulating the distinction between them become. They are, rather, complementary and reciprocal processes. Both the audience and the public of the poem are capable of some objective specification, which in both cases requires interpretation. [...] [S]tudies of the audience and the public of a work are complementary, in methods as well as ends. The history of its reception and transmission gives an account of its readers' accommodations; examination of the public implied by, and formally included within, the work and its revisions traces its writer's accommodations to the conditions of composition as he perceives them.[4]

Taking my cue from Middleton, I will, in discussing various manuscript traditions, also refer to moments in the poem likely to have appealed to particular sets of readers. And while my argument aims to produce a more comprehensive understanding of Langland's audience than she offered, I certainly concur with Middleton that *Piers Plowman*'s wide reach is no accident: this wide reach precisely accords with Langland's expansive social vision, a vision which yielded a concomitantly expansive public. Langland's audience and public, that is, should not be treated as discrete categories.

Hints of the diversity of the poem's audience can be found in the attested owners of *Piers* manuscripts from wills and inventories. Covering the years 1396–1465, Ralph Hanna identifies six medieval owners of *Piers*: one cathedral canon (Walter de Brugge), two parish priests (William Palmere, John Wyndhill), one merchant (Thomas Roos), one lawyer (Thomas Stotevyle), and one MP (Sir Thomas Charleton).[5] I would note here that even this limited sample of six owners attests to a great diversity of readership, ranging across distinct types of clergy and distinct types of lay readers. But now, as we turn from the archival record to the surviving manuscripts themselves, and as we organize those very manuscripts

---

4 Middleton, 'Audience and Public', pp. 101–02.
5 Hanna, *William Langland*, pp. 35–36.

along some of the major cultural fault lines of late medieval England, we will see that this diversity is amplified further yet. That is, I will here show that Langland's poem was produced for, and read by, nearly every conceivable type of late medieval reader. To demonstrate this, I offer new examinations of each pre-1500 manuscript of *Piers Plowman*; but rather than repeating the manuscript-survey approaches that previous scholars like A. I. Doyle and Simon Horobin have so carefully utilized, and rather than the meticulous reconstruction of scribal engagement with Langland's poem that Sarah Wood has recently offered, instead here I will approach the manuscripts afresh by centring cultural history.[6]

In this analysis, I will consider how the manuscripts arrayed themselves with respect to some of the main divisions marking late medieval English society: urban vs. rural, laity vs. clergy, and commons vs. aristocracy.[7] I here sidestep questions of gender, for Kathryn Kerby-Fulton has already shown that Langland's poem has some surprising moments of appeal to a female readership, but also that the poem actually achieved a remarkably wide readership among women. Beyond Middleton's insights, then, my methodology here is also much indebted to Kerby-Fulton's.[8] Looking at the audience and public together, in light of the major divisions within late medieval English society, is, I hope to show, a fruitful approach that affords us an appreciation of the diverse social imaginary of Langland's poem. This is a poem that both envisioned and reached a remarkably diverse range of readers.

The analyses to follow rely upon my own examination of every surviving complete, or substantially complete, pre-1500 manuscript of the poem. The discussion to follow will thus encompass these forty-six manuscripts:[9]

1 Aberystwyth, National Library of Wales, MS 733B
   (A Text MS *N + C-Text MS N²)
2 Cambridge, Corpus Christi College, MS 293 (C Text MS S)

---

[6] Sarah Wood, *'Piers Plowman' and Its Manuscript Tradition*. For Doyle's and Horobin's surveys, see above, n. 2.

[7] Note that I studiously pass over questions of textual criticism, treating each manuscript, regardless of its place in the textual tradition, as *Piers Plowman* simpliciter. My aim here is to investigate the history of Langlandian production and reception, not to establish anything about Langland's processes of composition or the authenticity of various textual traditions.

[8] Kerby-Fulton, 'The Women Readers'.

[9] Cambridge, Gonville and Caius College MS 669/46; Cambridge, Pembroke College MS 312 C/6; Oslo, Schøyen Collection, MS 1953; and *olim* Cambridge, John Holloway (bifolium) are incomplete or fragmentary copies, and thus I omit them. Cambridge, University Library MS Gg.4.31; London, British Library MS Sloane 2578; London, British Library MS Royal 18.B.xvii; New Haven, Yale University, Beinecke Library MS Takamiya Deposit 23; Oxford, Bodleian Library MS Digby 145; Oxford, Bodleian Library MS James 2, part 1; Oxford, Bodleian Library MS Wood donat. 7 are post-1500 copies, and thus I omit them.

THE AUDIENCE AND PUBLIC OF *PIERS PLOWMAN*: FURTHER REMARKS   15

3   Cambridge, Newnham College, MS 4 (B Text MS Y)
4   Cambridge, Trinity College, MS B.15.17 (B Text MS W)
5   Cambridge, Trinity College, MS R.3.14
    (A Text MS*T + C-Text MS T)
6   Cambridge, Cambridge University Library, MS Add. 4325
    (C Text MS Q) (hereafter **CUL Add. 4325**)
7   Cambridge, Cambridge University Library, MS Dd.1.17
    (B Text MS C) (hereafter **CUL Dd.1.17**)
8   Cambridge, Cambridge University Library, MS Dd.3.13
    (C Text MS G)
9   Cambridge, Cambridge University Library, MS Ff.5.35 (C Text MS F)
    (hereafter **CUL Ff.5.35**)
10 Cambridge, Cambridge University Library, MS Ll.4.14 (B Text MS C^2)
11 Dublin, Trinity College, MS 212 (C Text MS V) (hereafter **TCD 212**)
12 Dublin, Trinity College, MS 213 (A Text MS E) (hereafter **TCD 213**)
13 Liverpool, University Library, MS F.4.8
    (A Text MS Ch + C Text MS *Ch)
14 London, British Library, MS Additional 10574
    (B Text MS Bm + A-Text + C Text MS *L) (hereafter **BL Add. 10574**)
15 London, British Library, MS Additional 34779 (C Text MS P^2)
    (hereafter **BL Add. 34779**)
16 London, British Library, MS Additional 35157 (C Text MS U)
    (hereafter **BL Add. 35157**)
17 London, British Library, MS Additional 35287 (B Text MS M)
    (hereafter **BL Add. 5287**)
18 London, British Library, MS Cotton Caligula A.xi
    (B Text MS Cot + A Text + C Text MS O) (hereafter **BL Cotton Caligula A.xi**)
19 London, British Library, MS Cotton Vespasian B.xvi (C Text MS M)
    (hereafter **BL Cotton Vespasian B.xvi**)
20 London, British Library, MS Harley 875 (A Text MS H)
    (hereafter **BL Harley 875**)
21 London, British Library, MS Harley 2376 (C Text MS N)
    (hereafter **BL Harley 2376**)
22 London, British Library, MS Harley 3954
    (B Text MS H + A Text MS H^3) (hereafter **BL Harley 3954**)
23 London, British Library, MS Harley 6041
    (A Text MS H^2 + C Text MS *H^2) (hereafter **BL Harley 6041**)
24 London, Lincoln's Inn, MS 150 (A Text MS L)
25 London, Society of Antiquaries, MS 687 (A Text MS M)
    (hereafter **Antiquaries 687**)
26 London, University of London, MS S.L.V.17 (C Text MS A)
    (hereafter **Clopton MS**)
27 London, University of London, MS S.L.V.88 (C Text MS J)

(hereafter **Ilchester MS**)
28 New York, J. P. Morgan Library, MS M.818 (A Text MS J)
29 Oxford, Bodleian Library, MS Ashmole 1468 (A Text MS A)
(hereafter **BodL Ashmole 1468**)
30 Oxford, Bodleian Library, MS Bodley 814
(B Text MS Bo + A Text + C Text MS B)
(hereafter **BodL Bodley 814**)
31 Oxford, Bodleian Library, MS Digby 102 (C Text MS Y)
(hereafter **BodL Digby 102**)
32 Oxford, Bodleian Library, MS Digby 171 (C Text MS K)
(hereafter **BodL Digby 171**)
33 Oxford, Bodleian Library, MS Douce 104 (C Text MS D)
(hereafter **BodL Douce 104**)
34 Oxford, Bodleian Library, MS Douce 323 (A Text MS D)
(hereafter **BodL Douce 323**)
35 Oxford, Bodleian Library, MS Eng. poet. a.1 (A Text MS V)
(hereafter **Vernon MS**)
36 Oxford, Bodleian Library, MS Laud misc. 581 (B Text MS L)
(hereafter **BodL Laud misc. 581**)
37 Oxford, Bodleian Library, MS Laud misc. 656 (C Text MS E)
(hereafter **BodL Laud misc. 656**)
38 Oxford, Bodleian Library, MS Rawlinson poet. 38 + London, British Library MS Lansdowne 398 (B Text MS R)
39 Oxford, Bodleian Library, MS Rawlinson poet. 137 (A Text MS R)
(hereafter **BodL Rawlinson poet. 137**)
40 Oxford, Corpus Christi College, MS 201 (B Text MS F)
41 Oxford, Oriel College, MS 79 (B Text MS O)
42 Oxford, University College, MS 45 (A Text MS U)
43 San Marino, Huntington Library, MS HM 114
(B Text MS Ht + A and C Text Materials) (hereafter **HM 114**)
44 San Marino, Huntington Library, MS HM 128 (B Text MS HM)
(hereafter **HM 128**)
45 San Marino, Huntington Library, MS HM 137 (C Text MS P)
46 San Marino, Huntington Library, MS HM 143 (C Text MS X)
(hereafter **HM 143**)[10]

---

10 Of these forty-six manuscripts, I examined thirty-one in situ, while relying on digital surrogates, microfilms or paper facsimiles for these fifteen: Aberystwyth, National Library of Wales MS 733B; Cambridge, Corpus Christi College, MS 293; Cambridge, Trinity College MSS B.15.17 and R.3.14; CUL Add. 4325; TCD 212 and TCD 213; London, Lincoln's Inn MS 150; Ilchester MS; BodL Douce 104, BodL Laud misc. 581 and BodL Rawlinson poet. 38 (+ BL, MS Lansdowne 398 [originally one manuscript]); Oxford, Corpus Christi College, MS 201; Vernon; and HM 143.

A few words are in order, at the outset, about the limits of the corpus I have chosen. First, because I am exclusively concerned with the production and readership of Langland's poem, I exclude the Z text, which is, for large swaths, almost certainly not Langlandian, and which would thus more naturally merit inclusion within a study of the production and readership of texts from, in C. David Benson's formulation, '*the workshop of William Langland* or *the school of Langland*'.[11] I also omit extracts from my consideration here, for — while I recognize that they have much to tell us about what particular scribes did with Langland's poem for particular readers — I am primarily concerned with the copying and production of Langland's poetic output as Langland himself envisioned it (that is, A, B and C as complete texts), not whether particular passages in isolation attracted copyists.[12] And I omit manuscripts surviving fragmentarily, because the evidence they offer is almost always too exiguous to tell us anything substantial about their production or circulation. Additionally, because I am interested in how Langland's poem was produced within manuscript culture — that is, within the culture of the book that Langland himself inhabited — I selected 1500 as a rough cut-off date. Of course, manuscript copying in general continued long after 1500, but its numbers were increasingly diminishing and by then it existed alongside, and was dwarfed by, print.[13] But I do trace *Piers Plowman*'s readers and owners a bit further, up to *c.* 1600, simply because on numerous occasions, reliable evidence of sixteenth-century ownership survives, showing that a given manuscript had remained in a particular locale for many years and can thus shed light on the life of *Piers* manuscripts closer to the time of Langland's life. Of course, one could theoretically examine all provenance evidence in

---

11 Benson, *Public 'Piers Plowman'*, p. 65 (emphasis in original). The case for the authorial status of Z was first made in William Langland, *Piers Plowman: The Z Version*, ed. by Rigg and Brewer, and subsequently gained influential support by being included in A. V. C. Schmidt's Parallel-Text edition. For refutations of Z's authenticity, see Kane, 'The "Z Version" of *Piers Plowman*'; and Hanna, *Pursuing History*, chapter 12. Also important to note is recent scholarship that reads Z as a unique poem in its own right, but which simultaneously shows that Z departs from Langlandian thought in some essential ways. For example, Kerby-Fulton, 'Confronting the Scribe-Poet Binary', pp. 500–10, connects Z to the world of scriveners, while Fuller, 'The Craft of the "Z-Maker"', suggests that Z softens Langland's anticlericalism and therefore might have arisen from within the clerical ranks.
12 For particularly insightful analyses of extracts from *Piers Plowman*, see Horobin, 'John Cok'; and Warner, 'An Overlooked *Piers Plowman* Excerpt'.
13 Although there are fascinating sixteenth-century manuscripts, I do not here take them into consideration. In positing 1500 as a terminus for my investigations, I follow the periodization of book history espoused by Gillespie and Wakelin, 'Introduction'. And for a more detailed exposition of my thoughts about such periodization, see the Introduction and Conclusion to Johnston, *The Middle English Book: Scribes and Readers*. For particularly insightful studies of post-1500 manuscripts, see Turville-Petre, 'Sir Adrian Fortescue'; and Fuller, 'Langland in the Early Modern Household'.

these manuscripts, up to the present day, but the farther removed one gets from a manuscript's original production, the less telling those results are about the manuscript's early life and circulation.[14] And thus I have settled on 1600 as a rough terminus for my investigations of readership here. So, while I am not pursuing questions of the production of Langland's text in early modern England, I do consider somewhat later provenance evidence when it offers insight into the circulation of *Piers Plowman*.

These analyses come from my own examination of the manuscripts, as well as original archival research shedding new light on the readership of several. I will, of necessity, have to repeat much from previous scholarship. Rodney M. Thomson frames his study of the Bury Bible as 'Judicious synthesis and commentary, rather than the eliciting of new facts or the offering of fresh interpretations'.[15] With such a large manuscript corpus, I will, on occasion, likewise have recourse to collating previous scholarship and signalling where I agree. But I also offer much that is new. And, most importantly, I hope to offer original insights into the diversity of readership that formed the audience of *Piers Plowman*.

A Rural Public and Audience

Langland's poem is inarguably conversant with the rhythms and practices of rural English life, and certainly agriculture is central to the poem's social imaginary.[16] Christopher Dyer, for example, has carefully catalogued all of the references to agricultural practices, demonstrating that Langland was no stranger to life outside the metropolis.[17] Following the trial of Lady Meed, almost the entirety of the Visio takes place in a location that is clearly agricultural. But even prior to this, in the 'fair feeld ful of folk' — what one might call Langland's ethnographic taxonomy of his society — agricultural labourers are the first specific group of people we meet:

---

14 On the movement of *Piers* manuscripts in recent years, see Edwards, 'The Selling of *Piers Plowman* Manuscripts'.
15 Thomson, *Bury Bible*, p. 1.
16 A point made persuasively by O'Neill, 'Counting Sheep in the C Text'; Pigg, 'Life on the Manor'; Rentz, 'Half-Acre Bylaws'; and Rhodes, 'Medieval Political Ecology'. See also Johnston, 'The Clerical Career of William Rokele', pp. 119–21, where I note the concentration of rural imagery in the A text. The comments I make there are part of a larger set of speculations on the possibility that William Rokele, who was priest in three subsequent parishes in Essex and Suffolk, may have been the author of *Piers Plowman* and thus the A text would have arisen soon after his experience in these rural locations, before relocating to London. It is the later B and C texts that have a much more detailed engagement with life in the capital.
17 Dyer, '*Piers Plowman* and Plowmen'.

A fair feeld ful of folk fond I þer bitwene —
Of alle manere of men, þe meene and þe riche,
Werchynge and wandrynge as þe world askeþ.
Somme putten hem to þe plouȝ, pleiden ful selde,
In settynge and sowynge swonken ful harde.

(B.Prol.17–21; emphasis mine)[18]

The Seven Deadly Sins likewise have more than a passing rural/agricultural tinge to them. As Benson remarks of Langland's depiction of the sins, 'Their portraits often do not even pretend to describe individual lives, [and] thus sexes and professions are mixed together'.[19] To 'sexes and professions' we might add 'rural and urban dwellers', for there are plenty of references to the personified sins dwelling in agricultural spaces.[20] And, of course, immediately following the confession of the Seven Deadly Sins, Piers himself conflates pilgrimage, penance and ploughing, transmuting the accoutrement of a pilgrim into that of an agricultural labourer:

And heng his hopur on his hales in stede of a scryppe;
A buschel of breed corn brouht was þerynne:
'For Y wol sowen hit mysulf, and sethe wol Y wende
To pilgrimages as palmeres doen, pardon to wynne.
My plouh-pote shal be my pyk-staff, and pyche a-to þe rotes,
And helpe my coltur to kerue and clanse þe forwes'.

(C.8.60–65)

Here, then, one of the central rituals of the late medieval Church is reimagined using metaphors of rural food production. Thus, Rosemary O'Neill's remark that 'Many scholars have explored the way that Langland turns, throughout the poem, to the manor in search of solutions to the complex social problems that vex his work' makes eminent sense.[21]

But such rural imagery is not confined to the Visio, for the Vita has a squarely agricultural metaphor near its conclusion, as well: the division of the graces in B.19/C.21 is explicitly figured through the medium of ploughing. In this scene, Grace gives to Piers four oxen, which are the

---

18 All citations of *Piers Plowman* are from William Langland, *Piers Plowman: A Parallel-Text Edition*, ed. by Schmidt.
19 Benson, *Public 'Piers Plowman'*, p. 98.
20 Wrath, for example, confesses that he is slow to do his penance and quick to blame God when the harvest is poor (C.6.110–14). Couetyse confesses that he is frequently envious of his neighbour's animals and will slowly extend the boundaries of his property onto theirs (C.6.262–71). Sloth then confesses that he prefers hunting and managing manorial estates to reading hagiography (C.7.30–34).
21 O'Neill, 'Counting Sheep in the C Text', p. 91.

four Evangelists; four horses, which are the four major patristic authors; two harrows, which are the Old and New Testaments; and grains to plant, which are the cardinal virtues. Langland has chosen to figure what is certainly a pivotal moment in the Vita in agricultural terms: having just witnessed the Harrowing of Hell — the pinnacle of salvation history — we now find ourselves back in the material world. As several critics have noted, the end of B.18/C.20, when Will had crept to the cross after the Harrowing of Hell, felt like a moment of resolution and narrative stasis.[22] This moment of ploughing, which immediately follows, marks our re-entry into history, fraught with economic pressures. But Langland leavens that return with heavy theological allegorization. In the place of the very human form of agricultural labour that had marked the Visio's ploughing scene, this second ploughing scene turns to a more abstract allegory, grounding the society in theological ideals, thus offering a brief, fleeting hope for that society — figured as an idealized agricultural field — to be ordered and righteous.[23] As Robert Worth Frank puts it, this moment 'reveals a fundamental tenet in the poet's thought, his belief that labor is God-given. The divinity of labor, the concept which creates the figure of Piers, is here expressed in the identification of the divisions of grace and the divisions of labor. The curse of Adam has become a blessing.'[24]

So, given *Piers Plowman*'s intense focus on rural economics, one might expect the poem to have found an audience among readers in a similarly rural setting. In making the argument that this following set of manuscripts indeed circulated in such a setting, I do not make any claims about the social class of such rural readers — this is a topic I treat separately, below. Some were distinctively middling, while others were comparatively wealthy, and yet others were members of the clergy. But what unites all of these manuscripts is the evidence that they were located in social settings akin to that envisaged by large swaths of Langland's poem. So, when compared to manuscripts attributable to the capital (to be discussed below), an almost equal number were produced away from London, from as far afield as Northumberland and the south-west Midlands. I count eleven in this category.[25]

The evidence suggests that these eleven were produced and circulated in areas that did not boast a concentration of urban dwellers, and thus these books were most likely made by local scribes for local readers in

---

22 Bloomfield, *'Piers Plowman' as a Fourteenth-Century Apocalypse*, p. 125; Barney, *Penn Commentary*, pp. 97–98.
23 On the theological and allegorical significance of the differences between the Visio's and Vita's ploughing scenes, see Aers, *'Piers Plowman' and Christian Allegory*, pp. 120–30.
24 Frank, *'Piers Plowman' and the Scheme of Salvation*, p. 102.
25 CUL Add. 4325; BL Cotton Vespasian B.xvi; TCD 212; Clopton MS; Oxford, University College MS 45; BodL Ashmole 1468; Antiquaries 687; New York, J. P. Morgan Library, MS M.818; BL Harley 3954; TCD 213; and the Vernon MS.

a rural setting. This number of rural manuscripts should not come as a surprise, since the vast majority of England's inhabitants — witness Maurice Keen's suggestion that late medieval England was 'a kingdom in which nine out of ten people lived on and by the land'[26] — resided outside of even small boroughs. As J. C. Russell notes, 'The boroughs were the largest of the inhabited places of England, but in percentage of the total population, and even less in number, they formed but a small part of the people'.[27] As Russell further reveals, in 1377 even Norfolk, the most densely populated English county, had but 65.5 inhabitants per square mile.[28] As a result, the majority of the English lived in an environment not unlike the rural settings depicted in *Piers Plowman*.

Of course, London was not the only urban centre in late medieval England and was not the only city where books were made, and thus we cannot justifiably equate all non-London productions with rural England. Although no convincing evidence has ever been offered, it remains a possibility that some of these manuscripts could have been made in any of England's smaller cities or boroughs, such as Oxford or York, or even Bury St Edmunds, where we know there was active manuscript production.[29] However, many of these manuscripts were produced and owned in areas that demonstrably lacked the sorts of organized manuscript production we know took place in London and a few other cities. So this group of codices, as I will argue, likely points to a vibrant tradition of non-metropolitan production and circulation of *Piers Plowman*. It seems most likely, that is, that most of these were commissioned by local readers, tapping into local networks of documentary copyists. The range of trained writers throughout late medieval England, available to copy documents and literary texts, has been underscored recently by scholars such as Richard Beadle, Andrew Prescott, Kathryn Kerby-Fulton, and myself.[30] Such a model best accounts for most of these rural copies of *Piers* — made in remote locales for readers residing in such remote locales. And even if any of the manuscripts I discuss in this section was to have been produced in a small borough for an owner in the proximity of that borough, such could still justifiably be

---

26 Keen, *English Society*, p. 48.
27 Russell, *British Medieval Population*, p. 306.
28 Russell, *British Medieval Population*, p. 313.
29 On production in Oxford, see Donovan, *The de Brailes Hours*, pp. 9–21; Pollard, 'The University and the Book Trade in Mediaeval Oxford'; and Parkes, 'The Provision of Books'. On York, see Friedman, *Northern English Books*; and Gee, 'The Printers, Stationers and Bookbinders of York'. On Bury St Edmunds, see Scott, 'Lydgate's "Lives of St Edmund and Fremund"'.
30 Beadle, 'Prolegomena to a Literary Geography'; and 'Middle English Texts and Their Transmission'; Prescott, 'Administrative Records'; Kerby-Fulton, *The Clerical Proletariat*; Johnston, 'Copying and Reading *The Prick of Conscience*'; Johnston, 'The Household and Literary Production in England'; and Johnston, *The Middle English Book*, chapters 6 and 7.

called a rural manuscript, for England's smaller boroughs were contiguous to, and heavily imbricated with, rural agricultural practices. It was only in England's comparatively large cities where residents might have led a life more or less divorced from the country.

In all of the cases I discuss here, I rely upon a combination of dialectal and early provenance evidence to determine where the manuscript was produced, for dialect alone does not tell us where a manuscript was copied.[31] To that end, I here only account manuscripts as rural copies if evidence of both production and early use points to a relatively sparsely inhabited area. But as I will also argue here, dialect evidence can be helpful in locating manuscripts. This is so simply because, outside of London, scribes were unlikely to be living and working far from where they were born. As Merja Stenroos and Kjetil Thengs remark, 'Given that *most* people in virtually any historical period will not tend to move very far from their origins [...], the majority of the scribes working in a given area at a given time are likely to have had a local background (unless we have good reason to think otherwise); the largest cities, to which migration was considerable, may to some extent form an exception.'[32] And as *The Linguistic Atlas* notes, multiple-scribe manuscripts typically show 'that the scribes were either (a) local, or (b) had migrated from a surrounding catchment-area within a radius of, on average, some ten or fifteen miles'.[33] This fits with what historians have demonstrated about migration patterns in late medieval England: it was not uncommon for people to leave their village in search of better economic opportunities elsewhere, but such migration tended to be limited to a circumscribed area: '[i]mmigrants to Nottingham, Leicester, Norwich, even York were primarily drawn from a local zone of under forty miles. Small town migration, such as that into Stratford on Avon, had a field comparable to that of rural migration — i.e. of about seven to eight miles'.[34] Thus, in what follows, I trust scribal

---

31 In spite of how useful the map in Samuels, 'Dialect and Grammar', p. 207, is, we must proceed with caution when applying dialectal evidence in isolation. For example, many C-text manuscripts exhibit a south-west Midlands dialect, which for a long time had led scholars to believe that these testify to Langland returning to Malvern, where he was born, late in his life and sending out manuscripts of the latest version of his poem from there. However, as Horobin, '"In London and opeland"', has shown, the i-group of C-text manuscripts were copied in London, likely by scribes copying literatim, thereby preserving their exemplars' regional dialects.
32 Stenroos and Thengs, 'The Geography of Middle English', p. 91.
33 *Linguistic Atlas*, vol. I, p. 23. For further comments in a similar vein, see Lewis and McIntosh, *Descriptive Guide*, pp. 16–17; Manly and Rickert, eds, *The Text of 'The Canterbury Tales'*, vol. I, pp. 545–57; and Johnston, 'Copying and Reading *The Prick of Conscience*', pp. 745–56.
34 Hovland, 'Apprenticeship in Later Medieval London', p. 61. See also Poos, *Rural Society*, pp. 159–79; Dyer, 'Were Late Medieval Villages "Self-Contained"?'; and Whittle, 'Population Mobility'.

dialect, when confirmed by provenance evidence, to offer a reliable guide to where any given manuscript was copied.

Four manuscripts have demonstrable, secure connections to the southwest Midlands. This is a region for which we have no substantial evidence of centralized book production on a wide scale, and thus these books are likely made by rural scribes for rural readers. **CUL ADD. 4325** is in a dialect that M. L. Samuels puts in north-west Gloucestershire,[35] while an *ex libris* in a hand of sec. xv/xvi notes, 'Iste lyber partenth ad magyster [*sic*] Thome [*sic*] lovell' (fol. 83ᵛ), a man hitherto unidentified. I have found two Thomas Lovells of the right period, but this owner is almost certainly the doctor of Canon Law who held the prebendaries of Buckland Dinam and Wormenstre in the diocese of Bath and Wells in the 1510s, was a subdean of Bath and Wells Cathedral from 1516, and died 1518/19. Given that his ex libris in **CUL ADD. 4325** titles Lovell 'magyster', this Lovell is much more likely the owner of the manuscript than the other candidate — the Thomas Lovell who was a prominent lawyer, Speaker of the House of Commons, and close affiliate of Henry VII and VIII.[36] Second, also from this region is **BL COTTON VESPASIAN B.XVI**, from the first half of the fifteenth century, whose scribal dialect the electronic *Linguistic Atlas* (hereafter, *eLALME*) locates to Warwickshire.[37] This manuscript likely remained in this region, for fol. 95ᵛ, which was originally left blank, was filled in by a contemporary scribe with notes about the Blood of Hailes, a famous relic at Hailes Abbey, which lies just over the Warwickshire border.

The third manuscript with ties to this south-western area is **TCD 212**. This manuscript is a reminder that London did not enjoy a monopoly on high-end book decoration, for its opening leaf contains a full-page blue and red bar border that looks to have been professionally executed. But both its scribe and early ownership point to Gloucestershire and, at the conclusion of the manuscript's copy of the C text, there are a number of indicators of continued circulation in that same region.[38] Immediately following *Piers* is a chronicle, in a separate but roughly contemporary hand, focusing on events along the Welsh–English border.[39] The ascription to follow may well make this the most consequential manuscript of *Piers Plowman*: on fol. 89ᵛ, in a hand contemporary with, and possibly identical to, that of the annals, a note reads, 'Memorand*um* q*uo*d Stacy de Rokayle pat*er* Will*el*mi de Langlond qui Stacius fuit generosus & morabatur in

---

35 Samuels, 'Langland's Dialect', p. 239.
36 On Lovell, see Baildon, 'Escheator's Accounts', pp. 237–43; and *Fasti*, pp. 11–12, 20–21, 78–79.
37 Benskin and others, *An Electronic Version*: LP 4686, Grid 415 255.
38 *eLALME* analyses the dialect as LP 7190, located to Grid 369 230.
39 Brooks, 'The *Piers Plowman* Manuscripts', suggests the manuscript may have originated in the priory at Abergavenny, while Pates, '*Piers Plowman*', suggests Tewkesbury.

Schipton under Whicwode tenens do*mi*ni le Spenser in co*mi*tatu Oxon' qui pre*dictus* Wille*lmus* fecit librum qui vocatur Perys Ploughman' (Let it be remembered that Stacey de Rokayle, the father of William of Langland, was of the gentry and dwelt in Shipton-under-Wychwood, a tenant of the lord le Spenser, in the county of Oxfordshire, which aforementioned William made the book that is called Perys Ploughman). The veracity of this note is part of a long and complex history of the Rokele family and questions about the authorship of *Piers Plowman*, which need not detain us here.[40] The key point to note is simply that the Despensers held both Shipton-under-Wychwood, where the note would place the poet's father, and the area around Malvern, where the poet likely grew up, indicating this note's veracity.[41] But it also indicates that the manuscript has ties to the south-west, for the note clearly signals an investment in, and knowledge of, the local area.

The fourth and final manuscript from the south-west Midlands is the **Clopton MS**, which contains the C text, the Middle English *La Estoire del Euangelie* and *The Assumption of Our Lady*. However, it was originally part of a larger, rather impressive collection of Middle English devotional literature. What are now today Princeton, Princeton University Library MS Taylor 10 and Washington, DC, Folger Shakespeare Library MS V.b. 236 were originally a single codex with **Clopton**, containing *Mandeville's Travels*, *Handlyng Synne* and *Meditations on the Supper of the Lord and Hours of the Passion*. Though all three manuscripts are clearly in a single hand, *eLALME* analyses **Clopton**'s copy of *La Estoire* and *Piers Plowman* separately, putting them both quite near one another in Worcestershire.[42] Complicating this localization is Ryan Perry's observation that, although most of the texts reflect a south-west Midlands dialect, the two texts in the Folger Library portion of the manuscript reflect an East Midlands dialect.[43] Note, however, that Perry presents a persuasive case that the entire manuscript was compiled in the south-west Midlands. And the armorial devices in the manuscript show that it was owned by the Clopton family, a prominent gentry family from the south-west region.[44]

Scholars have long recognized that a group of A-text manuscripts exhibits dialectal features of the East Midlands, and thus that Langland may have published the first iteration of his poem in that region, or at least early versions may have been sent there and then circulated there in

---

40 For a thorough discussion, see Adams, *Langland and the Rokele Family*.
41 Hanna, *William Langland*, pp. 2–3.
42 For *La Estoire*: LP 7650, Grid 382 266; for *Piers*: LP 7780, Grid 380 243.
43 Perry, 'Clopton Manuscript', pp. 136–47.
44 Ker, *Medieval Manuscripts*, I, pp. 376–77; Turville-Petre, 'The Relationship', pp. 35–42; Perry, 'Clopton Manuscript'; and the entry for this MS at the *Manuscripts of the West Midlands* database <https://www.dhi.ac.uk/mwm/browse?type=ms&id=88> [accessed 16 Aug. 2023].

a particularly concentrated way.[45] Indeed, in my examinations, the largest group of non-London manuscripts clusters around East Anglia. This group is, moreover, entirely composed of A-text manuscripts. Among these, **OXFORD, UNIVERSITY COLLEGE MS 45** brings together a scribe from Cambridgeshire with a scribe nearby, from the Norfolk–Suffolk border.[46] Both scribes are from the first half of the fifteenth century, and although Scribe 1 works on parchment and Scribe 2 on paper, it otherwise seems likely that they coordinated their copying efforts to achieve uniformity, for both have the same size leaf (213 × 145 mm) and writing block (175 × 110 mm), and both scribes execute the Latin text and passus titles in red ink. So, we must be dealing with scribal collaboration, likely somewhere in the area where Suffolk, Norfolk, and Cambridgeshire meet. The manuscript also shows ownership in this region: as Thomas Kittel notes, guards around the paper bifolia are recycled documents, pointing to a landowner who had holdings in Norfolk, Suffolk, and Essex.[47] Of course, binding could always be a later addition and does not, *prima facie*, tell us anything definitive about the circulation of a manuscript's texts prior to its last binding. But in this case, the binding is tawed leather, making it likely to pre-date 1475.[48] Thus, these guards can be taken as evidence that the manuscript circulated somewhere near where it was produced.

eLALME puts the scribe of **BODL ASHMOLE 1468** in Suffolk,[49] and my own analysis of the manuscript shows intriguing provenance evidence connecting the ownership of the manuscript to the same region. In its current state, the manuscript is a composite, comprising three discrete production units. The first unit, in a hand of sec. xv^{med}, contains medical treatises in Middle English. And though the opening 171 pages are in a single hand, on blank leaves at the unit's end (pp. 172–79), subsequent scribes have jotted down additional recipes. The second unit, perhaps a bit later (sec. xv$^{2/2}$ seems a reasonable approximation of the script), contains two medical treatises in Latin (pp. 180–306). The third unit contains the A text of *Piers Plowman* (pp. 307–78), in a hand of sec. xv$^{2/2}$. Each of these three units is on a different stock of paper, and, given that the binding is clearly post-medieval, the codicological evidence is insufficient to conclude that the unit containing *Piers* was, in late medieval England,

---

45 This is explored most fully in Madrinkian, 'Producing *Piers Plowman*', chapter 3. See also Hanna, *Pursuing History*, pp. 200–01, 235–36; Adams, *Langland and the Rokele Family*, pp. 25–28.
46 Scribe 1: Cambs. (LP 698, Grid 549 271), Scribe 2: 'Language of S central Norfolk on Suffolk border'. Madrinkian, 'Producing *Piers Plowman*', p. 133, independently affirms this localization, finding that the scribe's forms demonstrate 'a consistent affiliation to East Anglia and the East Midlands, especially west Norfolk'.
47 Kittel, 'History of Contact', p. 77.
48 See Pearson, *English Bookbinding*, p. 41.
49 LP 4568, Grid 567 283.

read alongside the other two units. To this end, George Kane asserts that this is 'a composite volume assembled in the seventeenth century', without offering any evidence for his dating.[50]

But, *pace* Kane, I am convinced that the manuscript's constituent units were at least in physical proximity to one another by the late fifteenth century, and thus provenance evidence from any one of the units will apply to all of the units. There are marginal comments throughout the manuscript, most of them in hands of the second half of the fifteenth century. One of the scribes who wrote a marginal comment on *Piers* at p. 351 also copied out one of the medical recipes in the manuscript's first unit, on p. 174. Several distinguishing features of his hand license the conclusion that this is the same scribe, adding to the text proper in the first unit and adding a marginal comment to *Piers* in the third unit: the descender on his -y curves 90 degrees to the right at the base of the letter; he employs the single-chambered Secretary -a in medial position and the double-chambered Anglicana -a in initial position; he uses an exaggerated loop on the ascender of his -h, while the descenders of this letter curve sharply to the left; and he uses a sigma-shaped -s with a long tail running parallel to the base-line. These are all distinctive features, present in both the medical recipe and the marginal comment on *Piers*, meaning at the time of this scribe's work, both units were likely bound together or were, at the least, in the same location as one another.

This palaeographical detail is of significance to placing the manuscript, for the scribe who commented in the margins of *Piers* on p. 351, when he copied out a recipe earlier in the manuscript (p. 174), wrote in an identifiably East Anglian dialect. This dialect is close to that of the *Piers*-scribe, meaning **BodL Ashmole 1468** was likely copied and stayed in Suffolk. First, he employs several words with the distinctively East Anglian spelling feature of <qw> for an aspirated /w/: 'qwyt wyn' for 'white wine', 'qwylle' for 'while' and 'qwet' for 'white'. The recipes he copies alternate between <a> and <o> for OE /ā/ (e.g., ston, hald, langer, ald), which would indicate a scribe from the Midlands, where those two forms intersected. Further diagnostic forms include:

- When: quen (a form not found south of a line extending from East Anglia to the north-west Midlands)
- Each: ech (a southern form, not found north of the Midlands)
- Them: þam (a few scattered southern uses, but this is primarily a north Midlands and northern form, rarely employed south of Norfolk)

---

50 Kane, ed., *Piers Plowman: The A Version*, p. 1. Black, *Descriptive, Analytical, and Critical Catalogue*, cols 1275–77, attempts no guess about when the manuscript's constituent units were first joined together.

Admittedly, a single recipe is a small sample size to draw from, but given the prevalence of such markedly East Anglian features in this scribe's spelling, we can be relatively certain that he was from Suffolk or Norfolk, meaning **BodL Ashmole 1468** was an East Anglian production.

If my argument about **Ashmole 1468**'s dialect being a reliable indicator of where it was produced has merit, then it follows that **Antiquaries 687** (also containing the A text) was produced in the same region. This is so precisely because, as Michael Madrinkian notes, the two manuscripts share a paper stock, and thus they must have been made in proximity to one another.[51] Further underscoring their connections to East Anglia is Kittel's observation that the watermark common to these two manuscripts also appears in Oxford, Bodleian Library, MS Digby 87, a copy of *The Prick of Conscience* in the hand of a scribe from Ely.[52] So there was clearly some source of paper that was common to the scribes of all three manuscripts, and it would only make sense that it were located somewhere in East Anglia, or immediately nearby in Ely, where these scribes were all from.

Antiquaries 687 is a palaeographically complex manuscript. To my eye, almost the entirety of the manuscript, save for some pieces added to the end, is in a single hand. This scribe worked in four discrete production units, the first containing *The Prick of Conscience* (pp. 5–358); the second a Middle English prose form of confession (pp. 359–82); the third containing Richard of Lavenham's treatise on the Seven Deadly Sins, a treatise on the Ten Commandments in Middle English prose, and the Latin *Sancti Edwardi Confessoris visio de sacerdotibus pravis* (pp. 383–470); and the fourth containing *Piers Plowman* (pp. 471–549). What I see as the second scribe copies only pp. 552–58, a Middle English prose text about excommunication, appended to the end of *Piers*.

eLALME's analysis accords with mine in positing a unique scribe for the final seven pages, locating this scribe to Suffolk.[53] But what I see as a single scribe, they see as three scribes, the first of whom they locate to Norfolk, while locating the second and third to Suffolk.[54] Making an absolute determination of scribal stints is particularly difficult with this manuscript, since it consists of four discrete production units. This means it is possible the scribe worked on each unit seriatim, across an extended period of time, and thus his hand might be expected to have changed

---

51 Madrinkian, 'Producing *Piers Plowman*', p. 131.
52 Kittel, 'History of Contact', pp. 83–84. *eLALME* analyses the scribe of Digby 87 at LP 4565, which they locate to Grid 560 285.
53 LP 639, Grid 635 286.
54 *eLALME*'s Scribe 1: LP 638, Grid 552 316; *eLALME*'s Scribes 2 and 3 do not receive an LP number and are merely described as from Suffolk. For slightly variant assessments of the scribal stints, though agreeing in assigning the vast majority of the manuscript to a single scribe, see Madrinkian, 'Producing *Piers Plowman*', p. 122; Willetts, *Catalogue of Manuscripts*, pp. 293–94; and Kittel, 'History of Contact', p. 149.

between work on each unit. Regardless of the precise distribution of stints, *eLALME*'s analysis shows that this scribal collaboration took place among East Anglian scribes. Coupled with the fact that it shares a watermark with **BodL Ashmole 1468** — also East Anglian — we can be confident that **Antiquaries 687** was produced there. Finally, although this is beyond the chronological scope of my analyses, the manuscript has notes pertaining to Healing, Lincolnshire, in a hand of the late sixteenth or early seventeenth century (pp. 559–62), indicating that a future owner of this book had some interests in a nearby county.

From Norfolk or Lincolnshire — the evidence is mixed — is **New York, J. P. Morgan Library MS M.818**, the product of a single scribe who worked in two discrete production units, the first containing *The Pistill of Susan* and Rolle's *Form of Living*, the second containing *Piers Plowman*. Evidence for separate production of the two units abounds: the two units are on different sizes of paper, with unit I's leaf being 222 mm in height, and the opening three quires of unit II's being 216 mm, before it reverts to the 222 mm size of unit I for the remaining quires. Unit I has two quires, a 6 and a 10, while unit II comprises a bifolium, followed by regular 12s.[55] However, these units are now in a limp leather binding, likely of the fifteenth century, meaning they must have been joined relatively soon after their production.

The scribe of this manuscript was from Lincolnshire or Norfolk, as *eLALME*'s identification shows, and as early provenance evidence attests.[56] The earliest provenance evidence points to Lincolnshire: a note mentioning Boston and the nearby village of Swineshead.[57] Sixteenth-century evidence then points to Leicestershire, a contiguous county. These are two indentures in different mid-sixteenth-century hands: 'hic Indentura testatur Robert*us* Nashe' (fol. 33ᵛ); and 'hec inde*n*tura testat*ur* qu*o*d Robert*us* Whytell filius Johanes [*sic*] Whettell gen*er*osus in comitatu Leycestrie posuit see [*sic*] ippsu*m* [*sic*] apprenticiu*m*' (fol. 35ᵛ). I have not identified any of the men named here, but the second indenture points to a gentleman (generosus) in Leicestershire committing to an apprenticeship.

The final manuscript with East Anglian ties is **BL Harley 3954**. Not only does its scribe's dialect show him as a native of Norfolk, but, as Horobin notes,

---

55 Note that my collation differs from that in the library's online Corsair catalogue.
56 LP 510, Grid 507 345. *eLALME* only analyses the dialect from the scribe's copy of Rolle's *Form of Living* (which they mislabel *Mirour de l'Homme*). Assuming this reflects the scribe's native dialect, and thus could apply to his copy of *Piers* as well, this scribe would be from south-east Lincolnshire, roughly between Boston and Grantham. Madrinkian, 'Producing *Piers Plowman*', pp. 134–37, analyses the scribe's dialect from *Pistill of Susan* and *Piers Plowman*, concluding that the scribe shows definitive evidence of employing Norfolk forms.
57 As noted by Kittel, 'History of Contact', pp. 78–79.

A further indication of this provenance is the unique variant in Harley's text of *Piers* at A 5.119 which replaces a reference to Winchester with Sleaforth, a town in south Lincolnshire. Further evidence of the manuscript's Norfolk pedigree is shown by the appearance of the same sequence of religious lyrics in Cambridge University Library Ii.iv.9, a manuscript which also contains a fragment of a document connected with Norwich and Sedgeford.[58]

This manuscript's decoration may also point to Norfolk. In this case, *Piers*'s companion text, *Mandeville's Travels*, has a striking '99 pictures and 38 blanks for pictures'. Kathleen Scott suggests that, although these illustrations are far from ornate, 'the style of the Harley drawings bears some (distant) relationship to that of Harley 2278, also East Anglian', further speculating that both may have been East Anglian productions.[59]

But it was not only in East Anglia that Langland's A text circulated. The most far-flung copy of *Piers* is to be found in **TCD 213**, whose dialect is from the extreme north of England.[60] Much provenance evidence also points to Northumberland. For example, the front flyleaf records a play performed at Pittington (a village a few miles east of Durham). Moreover, several localizable references appear in the manuscript. A list of debts names 'Joh*annes* Tade de beall / Joh*annes* Watson de goswyk / Joh*annes* Waliarth de scrime*r*sto[n] / Willia*mus* [*sic*] sandson de bukton' (fol. 67^r). I have not managed to identify any of these men, but they are all from villages clustered around the coast of Northumberland, quite close to Lindisfarne. Later, we find the name 'Thomas foster of gyllega' (fol. 72^v, sec. xvi$^{1/2}$). There were numerous Thomas Fosters in the north in the sixteenth century, so this name cannot be positively identified, but the place name likely refers to *Gilesgate*, just outside of Durham, as Duggan and Thorlac Turville-Petre suggest. Finally, the name Cuthbert Emmerson appears on fol. 68^r, and Duggan and Turville-Petre note that the Emmersons were a Durham family.[61]

Finally, the splash **VERNON MS**, containing the A text (fols 394^v–401^v), has proven difficult to localize with any specificity. It is, however, almost certainly a product of the West Midlands. Its two scribes have

---

58 Horobin, 'Harley 3954', p. 69. *eLALME* analyses this scribe as LP 4103, Grid 583 305. Note, however, that the *eLALME* reports, 'The language of *Piers Plowman* differs from that of the rest of the MS', without explaining how. Perhaps this means that the scribe was from Norfolk but tended not to translate the dialect of his copy of *Piers Plowman*?
59 Scott, *Survey of Manuscripts ... vol. 6: Later Gothic Manuscripts*, II, pp. 209–10.
60 *eLALME* does not provide a full analysis, only noting that the language is from Durham or Northumberland, while adding that 'The language may derive in part from this area, but it is mixed with a more southerly element'. Duggan and Turville-Petre, eds, *Wars of Alexander*, pp. xxxi–xxxvi, affirm a localization to Durham.
61 Duggan and Turville-Petre, eds, *Wars of Alexander*, p. xi.

been localized to quite near one another in Worcestershire, and these two scribes also collaborated on **VERNON**'s sister manuscript, known as the Simeon Manuscript (London, British Library MS Additional 22283).[62] And although these two manuscripts contain many of the same texts, in this case the latter does not contain *Piers*. The scale of **VERNON** is staggering: the manuscript originally measured 544 × 393 mm, with more than 420 leaves, and weighing nearly 50 pounds. Something this size would have required over 200 animal skins and is estimated to have taken four years to produce.[63] But not only is **VERNON** large, it is lavishly decorated, with numerous bar borders, flourished initials, and miniatures. Different scholars have posited different numbers of artists, with possibly as many as nine at work on the borders and initials, and four illustrators completing the miniatures.[64] The only provenance evidence internal to the manuscript itself shows that it was owned in Staffordshire in the early modern period, before it was bequeathed to the Bodleian in 1677.[65] Regardless of the precise details, the **VERNON MS** was certainly a provincial production, originating somewhere in the West Midlands.

A London (and Dublin) Public and Audience

For every scholar who focuses on the rural affiliations of *Piers Plowman*, there is seemingly another attending to the poem's multiple London affinities. Hanna makes the strongest and most detailed case, but numerous others, such as James Simpson (who remarks unequivocally that 'I need not dwell on Langland as a Londoner; the fact that he lived in the City is not in question'), have also marshalled compelling evidence for the poem's situatedness in the capital.[66] The Visio, particularly in B and C, is full of references to bustling city life, with some specific nods to identifiable

---

62 *eLALME* analyses Scribe 1 of Vernon as LP 7630, Grid 389 270, and Scribe 2 as LP 7670, Grid 378 262. Smith, 'Mapping the Language', affirms the localization of Scribe 1. These scribes are connected to a series of textual productions in the north-west Midlands: see Horobin, 'The Scribes of the Vernon Manuscript'.
63 Robinson, 'The Vernon Manuscript'; and Doyle, 'Codicology, Palaeography, and Provenance'.
64 The most thorough studies are by Lynda Dennison, Kathleen Scott, A. I. Doyle, and Rebecca Farnham, whose various findings are summarized in tabular form in Scase, 'The Artists', pp. 227–28.
65 Quinn, 'Earlier Owners'.
66 Hanna, *London Literature*, chapter 6; Simpson, '"After Craftes Conseil"', p. 110. For further remarks on Langland's connection to urban, London life, see Barron, 'William Langland'; Clopper, 'Engaged Spectator', pp. 127–32; Galloway, 'Non-Literary Commentary'; Knapp, 'Towards a Material Allegory', pp. 95–101; and Warner, *The Myth of 'Piers Plowman'*, pp. 37–52. See also Pearsall, 'Langland's London', for remarks on how problematic the poet's relationship to the city was.

locales within London. The apologia in the C text is patent in its location, for our poet relates that he 'wonede in Cornehull [...] Amonges lollares of Londone' (C.V.1, 4). The famous line in B, thought to encode the poet's name ('"I haue lyued in londe", quod I, "my name is Longe Wille"' [B.XV.152]) has been changed in C, as the poet now says, 'Ich haue yleued in Londone monye longe ʒeres' (C.XVI.286). So there can be no doubt that the poet was presenting himself — by the time he wrote the C text, at least — as a Londoner. And thus it makes a certain amount of sense that scholars have suggested Langland's most immediate readership came from the bureaucratic civil servants of London.[67]

By the time Langland came to write his poetry, London was emerging as the nation's centre of literary production. The last quarter of the fourteenth century marked the first real growth in London book production.[68] Thus, were Langland residing in London, production of copies of his poem would have been happening right under his nose. Evidence for how Chaucer and Gower were themselves connected to manuscript production, though lacking for Langland, nonetheless holds out the tantalizing possibility that, as a London poet, Langland might have had some involvement with, or at least knowledge of, book production.[69] To whatever extent vernacular English books were made to deluxe standards, such were most often made in London, where the majority of book artisans congregated. The most prolific scribes of Middle English literature also congregated in London, and thus it makes sense to consider what portion of Langland's manuscripts arose in the capital.

Of the forty-six manuscripts under consideration here, I count thirteen with relatively secure evidence of production in London (with one further from Dublin, which I discuss below).[70] Several different forms of evidence can suggest metropolitan production. First, we might consider decoration. The most ornate forms of decoration were carried out in urban centres, and by the later Middle Ages, much of that had centralized in London. In any given manuscript, very basic elements of decoration — e.g., pen-flourished initials, paraphs — may well have been executed by the scribe

---

67 Hanna, *Pursuing History*, pp. 236–43; and Kerby-Fulton and Justice, 'Langlandian Reading Circles'.
68 For general remarks, see Hanna, *London Literature*, chapter 1. For a detailed analysis of the growth, see Christianson, 'Evidence for the Study', and Christianson, 'The Rise of London's Book Trade'.
69 On Chaucer's potential connections to London book production, see Mooney, 'Chaucer's Scribe' and Horobin, 'Adam Pinkhurst'. On Gower's potential connections, see Sobecki, *Last Words*, chapter 1.
70 Cambridge, Newnham College, MS 4; Cambridge, Trinity College, MS B.15.17; BL, Additional MSS 10574, 35157, 35287; BL, Cotton MS Caligula A.xi; Ilchester MS; Bodleian Library, MSS Bodley 814, Digby 102, Douce 104, Laud misc. 581; Oxford, Corpus Christi College, MS 201; HM 114, 143.

himself, and thus when considering manuscripts that are undecorated, or that have only the most basic decoration, one does not need to posit production in a metropole.[71] But when we find manuscripts with bar borders on the opening page, use of gold leaf, multiple-coloured initials, or historiated initials, we are likely looking at something produced by a professional book artist.[72] Such high-end decoration was not carried out exclusively in London, and several *Piers* manuscripts with such decoration are definitely not London productions, but absent evidence to the contrary, London remains the most likely place of origin for such books.[73]

Six *Piers* manuscripts — admittedly, a definite minority — seem to me to fit the description of professional decoration.[74] First is **CAMBRIDGE, NEWNHAM COLLEGE MS 4**, whose opening leaf contains a blue and gold full-page bar border.[75] With **CAMBRIDGE, TRINITY COLLEGE MS B.15.17**, although its opening has been damaged over time, it is clear that it was likewise in the hands of a professional artist: it opens with an 8-line initial -I, inside of which is ornate red and white checkering. Blue and gold vines grow out of the opening initial, encompassing 3/4 of the leaf.[76] Finally, **OXFORD, CORPUS CHRISTI COLLEGE MS 201** has the only historiated initial among *Piers* manuscripts. Here, inside the opening -I is a man who has fallen asleep with his head resting on his hand, with a background painted in gold leaf.[77]

---

[71] Scott-Fleming, *The Analysis of Pen Flourishing*; and Doyle, 'Penwork Flourishing'.

[72] Alexander, *Medieval Illuminators*, p. 16; Kaufmann, 'Decoration and Illustration', p. 57; and Michael, 'Oxford, Cambridge and London', p. 109.

[73] Case studies by James-Maddocks, 'The Peripatetic Activity'; and Dennison and Morgan, 'The Decoration of Wycliffite Bibles', pp. 288–303, demonstrate that in late medieval England, professional decoration did, on occasion, arise from outside of London.

[74] As I discussed above, TCD 212 also seems to have been decorated professionally, but it was likely produced in the south-west Midlands.

[75] Kane and Donaldson, eds, *Piers Plowman: The B Version*, p. 14; Benson and Blanchfield, *The Manuscripts of Piers Plowman*, pp. 50–54, 150–58. See also Hanna, *London Literature*, p. 246, who notes that this manuscript is one of five employing spacing instead of paraphs to mark section breaks. Because this feature is exhibited by Cambridge, Trinity College MS B.15.17 and BL Add. 35287 — both definitively London productions — Hanna contends that all five likely emanated from the capital.

[76] James, *The Western Manuscripts*, vol. I, pp. 480–81; Kane and Donaldson, eds, *Piers Plowman: The B Version*, pp. 13–14; Benson and Blanchfield, *The Manuscripts of Piers Plowman*, pp. 159–63. Digital images of this manuscript are available as part of the edition by Turville-Petre and Duggan for the *Piers Plowman Electronic Archive* <http://piers.chass.ncsu.edu/texts/W> [accessed 16 Aug. 2023]. Elaborate opening leaves are also found in HM 143, the Clopton MS and the Ilchester MS.

[77] For an image of this manuscript's opening leaf, see the *Electronic Archive* edition by Adams, Duggan, Eliason, Hanna, Price-Wilkin, and Turville-Petre <http://piers.chass.ncsu.edu/texts/F> [accessed 16 Aug. 2023]. This image is also reproduced on the cover of William Langland, *Piers Plowman*, trans. by Schmidt.

Textual affiliations between copies can also point to London. In this case, three copies of the B text (**BL ADD. 10574, BODL BODLEY 814**, and **BL COTTON CALIGULA A.XI**, known collectively as BmBoCot, based on their respective sigils) are so closely related that they must have been made in proximity to one another.[78] Scholarly opinion remains divided as to the precise genetic relationship between the three manuscripts, but there is unanimity that they were produced in some sort of collaborative fashion. Of course, collaboration across multiple manuscripts could take place anywhere, but such is most likely to occur in London, where there were the greatest number of scribes and exemplars concentrated in one place. The scribes' dialects show them to be from disparate places, further suggesting London, for the capital is the most likely place where scribes from far away from each other would meet up.[79]

Early sixteenth-century provenance evidence shows that **BL ADD. 10574** remained in London: 'brought from Kelsey xxvj octob[e]r amen xxxiiijo RH viijm per me Ion Thynne' (fol. 91^v). This is almost certainly the John Thynne who, at the date of this purchase, was serving as steward of Edward Seymour, Viscount Beauchamp (who would soon become the first Lord Protector during the minority of Edward VI), where Thynne was primarily based in London. This John Thynne would later be the founder of Longleat House, as well as its library. Given that this manuscript does not appear in Thynne's 1577 booklist, it seems that he did not incorporate this into his library at Longleat.[80] Thynne will re-appear in the discussion below, for his name is also associated with **BODL LAUD MISC. 581**.

There is tenuous evidence connecting the other two manuscripts of the BmBoCot triad to London, as well. It is possible that the script of **BL COTTON CALIGULA A.XI** reflects Chancery training, though this claim has not been widely accepted.[81] Regarding the language of **BL COTTON CALIGULA A.XI**, Carl Grindley concludes that this manuscript was 'probably the product of an elite London scribe' who engaged in 'progres-

---

78 Kane and Donaldson, eds, *Piers Plowman: The B Version*, p. 42 n. 61.
79 Samuels, 'Langland's Dialect', p. 241, argues that all three were likely copied in London but 'appear to derive certain of their dialectal features from a north Gloucestershire exemplar'. On London as the likeliest home of dialectal diversity, see Horobin and Mosser, 'Scribe D's SW Midlands Roots', pp. 301–04; and Carillo-Linares and Williamson, 'Linguistic Character'.
80 Girouard, 'Thynne, Sir John'; and Duggan and Hanna, 'Introduction', I.10.
81 Fisher, '*Piers Plowman* and the Chancery Tradition', p. 269, argues for a script based on the Chancery. Kerby-Fulton, 'Professional Readers of Langland', p. 109, dissents, offering instead that the scribe 'shows a more standard *anglicana formata* such as one sees, in its better moments, in London bookshops of the period (that is, first quarter of the fifteenth century), in its worse, in Exchequer records'.

sive de-translation' of the south-west Midlands relicts in his exemplars.[82] Regarding **BodL Bodley 814**, which is the work of two scribes, Brian Davis suggests that Scribe 1's 'spelling indicates that he learned to write in Cambridgeshire', while Scribe 2 'was trained in Warwickshire, perhaps near the border with Northamptonshire'.[83]

Other copies of *Piers Plowman* contain the work of scribes whose hands have been identified in additional literary manuscripts, pointing, once again, to London as a likely copying location. Above, I discussed the decoration of **Oxford, Corpus Christi College MS 201** as pointing to London. But its scribe does as well. There is evidence that this scribe was involved in several Middle English copying endeavours: his hand has been identified in a fragment of *The Prick of Conscience*, as well as in rubrics of the R Manuscript of the B Text.[84] Finally, the scribe of this manuscript may well have connections to Westminster bureaucracy, for, as with **BL Cotton Caligula A.xi**, the scribal hand of **Corpus Christi MS 201** may reflect training in the Chancery, which would put this scribe in London/Westminster.[85] Connections between the hand practised in government offices and the manuscripts of Middle English literary texts are in need of further palaeographical attention, for thus far the connections posited by scholars are, though provocative, rather gestural.[86]

Three of the five scribes who collaborated on Cambridge, Trinity College MS R.3.2, containing Gower's *Confessio amantis*, may have had a hand in copying manuscripts of *Piers*, as well.[87] It is universally agreed that this manuscript was made in London. The scribe whom Doyle and Malcolm Parkes named Scribe C has never been otherwise identified, though they note that this scribe 'wrote a small neat hand modelled on anglicana of a type found in some *de luxe* copies of the Statutes and in documents of some offices of state'.[88] Their Scribe E is Thomas Hoccleve who, so far as we know, never put his hand to a copy of Langland. Of the three remaining scribes, Scribe A has the most tendentious relationship to copying *Piers Plowman*: Grindley notes that two scribes provide interlinear

---

82 Grindley, 'The A-Version Ancestor', pp. 79–80.
83 Davis, 'The Rationale for a Copy of a Text', p. 145. Davis does not offer evidence for these analyses, nor does this manuscript appear in *eLALME*.
84 Doyle, 'Ushaw College, Durham, MS 50'; and Taylor, 'The F Scribe and the R Manuscript'.
85 Fisher, '*Piers Plowman* and the Chancery Tradition', p. 273; and Kerby-Fulton, 'Professional Readers of Langland', pp. 108–09, both concur on this point.
86 Sobecki's 'The Handwriting' and 'Communities of Practice', in their detailed attention to the palaeographical practices of government offices, both represent a promising methodological start in this direction.
87 For a discussion of this manuscript, see Doyle and Parkes, 'The Production of Copies of the *Canterbury Tales*'.
88 Doyle and Parkes, 'The Production of Copies of the *Canterbury Tales*', p. 174.

corrections to **BL Add. 35157**, the first of which he contends resembles Doyle and Parkes's Scribe A.[89] Since Grindley first offered it in 1996, no one else has taken up this suggestion, so it certainly would need further palaeographical analysis before being accepted. But there are further signs that **BL Add. 35157** may have been made in London, for its main scribe, who signs his name (Preston), may well also have been the scribe of the Litlyngton Missal, produced for Westminster Abbey.[90]

Doyle and Parkes's Scribe D was the scribe of the **Ilchester MS** of *Piers*. In addition to the Trinity Gower and **Ilchester**, his hand has been identified in eleven manuscripts. Linne R. Mooney and Estelle Stubbs suggest that Scribe D is John Marchaunt, Chamber Clerk and then Common Clerk at the London Guildhall, an identification that has proven controversial.[91] But regardless of the scribe's name, there has been no disagreement that this very prolific Middle English scribe both worked in London and was responsible for the **Ilchester MS**.[92] More controversy yet has swirled around whether Doyle and Parkes's Scribe B copied **Cambridge, Trinity College MS B.15.17**, the manuscript that supplies the copytext for both Kane and Donaldson's Athlone edition of the B text and A. V. C. Schmidt's Everyman edition. Doyle and Parkes noted that their Scribe B was also the scribe of the Hengwrt and Ellesmere manuscripts of *The Canterbury Tales*, while Horobin and Mooney extended this scribe's canon to include the copy of *Piers* in **Trinity B.15.17**.[93] Subsequently, Mooney identified Scribe B as Adam Pynkhurst, placing him in the same copying milieu as other guildhall clerks, like Scribe D.[94]

---

89 Grindley, 'Life of a Book', pp. 124–30.
90 Grindley, 'Life of a Book'. Mooney, 'Locating Scribal Activity', p. 192 n. 30, however, expresses hesitation about Grindley's identification. The scribe of the Litlyngton Missal was also named Preston. For a description of the Litlyngton Missal, see Sandler, *Survey of Manuscripts ... vol. 5: Gothic Manuscripts*, ii, pp. 172–75. Note that this is also one of the i-family of C-text manuscripts whose production Horobin, '"In London and opeland"', p. 263, would place in London.
91 On Marchaunt (?) and his oeuvre, see Mooney and Stubbs, *Scribes and the City*, chapter 3. For a critique of Mooney and Stubbs's identification, see Warner, *Chaucer's Scribes*, pp. 97–103.
92 There is some disagreement about whether Scribe D was a native Londoner or an immigrant: Samuels, 'Dialect and Grammar', p. 206, suggests this manuscript was 'copied in London from a S. W. Worcs. exemplar', while Smith, 'Studies in the Language', vol. 1, pp. 190–294, has argued that this scribe was a native of the south-west who emigrated to London. Horobin, '"In London and opeland"', pp. 256–67, suggests, instead, that the exemplar was not necessarily from the south-west, but rather that the scribe had a high tolerance for exotic spellings, leaving dialectal relicts intact. See also Horobin and Mosser, 'Scribe D's SW Midlands Roots', for a general discussion of Scribe D's habits of dialectal translation, in which they cast doubt on the notion that he was from the south-west.
93 Doyle and Parkes, 'The Production of Copies of the *Canterbury Tales*', pp. 184–92; Horobin and Mooney, 'A *Piers Plowman* Manuscript'.
94 Mooney, 'Chaucer's Scribe'.

This argument has not been universally accepted, so we cannot say for certain that the scribe of **TRINITY B.15.17** is Doyle and Parkes's Scribe B, but his hand is certainly quite close, and there is ample reason for thinking he worked in London.[95] It seems reasonable to assume that, whoever he was, he was copying in London, for his language was likely tailored to a London readership.[96] Horobin has offered yet further evidence of this scribe's ties to London by identifying his hand as corrector in another copy of *Piers*, **BL ADD. 35287**.[97]

The copyist of **HM 114** is yet another *Piers*-scribe whom Mooney and Stubbs connect to London's guildhall. Beyond **HM 114**, this scribe copied London, Lambeth Palace MS 491 (a compilation of Middle English prose and verse) and contributed to London, British Library MS Harley 3943, containing Chaucer's *Troilus and Criseyde*. Mooney and Stubbs identify him as Richard Osbarn, chamber clerk in London from 1400 to 1437.[98] Whether Mooney and Stubbs have correctly named this scribe or not, there is a general consensus that he produced **HM 114** in London. Since his copy of the B text is highly conflated with readings from other versions of the poem, it is justifiably assumed that this scribe must have had access to numerous copies of *Piers*, a condition most likely to hold in London.[99]

Two other manuscripts that I believe were London productions represent outliers, since it is neither their decoration nor their scribes' participation in multiple literary manuscripts that allows us to locate them to the capital. **BODL LAUD MISC. 581** is a puzzling manuscript: its dialect has eluded scholars, but Duggan and Hanna contend that 'Everything suggests that the manuscript is a London product'.[100] As further evidence of the London connections of this copy, I would note that the scribe has drawn the reader's attention to XIII.271 ('My wafres þere were gesen whan chichestre was maire', fol. 56ʳ) by boxing the words *chichestre* and *maire* in red, and adding a *nota* in the margin, also in red. This is one

---

95 For responses, see Roberts, 'On Giving Scribe B a Name'; and Warner, *Chaucer's Scribes*, chapters 2 and 3.
96 Eliason, Duggan, and Turville-Petre, 'Introduction'.
97 Horobin, 'Adam Pinkhurst and the Copying'. For further suggestions of London production, see Turville-Petre, 'Putting It Right'; and Wood, 'Two Annotated *Piers Plowman* Manuscripts', pp. 276–83.
98 Mooney and Stubbs, *Scribes and the City*, chapter 2. The scholarship on this scribe is vast: See Wood, *'Piers Plowman' and Its Manuscript Tradition*, chapter 6; Adams and Turville-Petre, 'The London Book Trade'; Bart, 'Intellect, Influence and Evidence'; Bowers, 'Two Professional Readers', pp. 129–45; Hanna, 'The Scribe of Huntington HM 114'; Kerby-Fulton, Hilmo and Olson, *Opening up Middle English Manuscripts*, pp. 75–79; Phillips, 'Compilational Reading'; and Warner, *Chaucer's Scribes*, chapter 4.
99 For a succinct summary, see Galloway, 'Uncharacterizable Entities', pp. 71–72.
100 Duggan and Hanna, 'Introduction', § III. See also n. 80, above: Laud misc. 581 is another manuscript with the distinctive use of spacing, which may provide further evidence of its London origin.

of only four red *nota*s in the manuscript.[101] This scribe regularly boxes proper nouns within the text in red, so the attention drawn to *chichestre* is not unusual. But drawing attention to the word *maire* and adding a *nota*, with neither part of his typical practice, suggest he or his patron had a particular interest in Chichester's mayoralty, or London history more generally. As I discussed above, sixteenth-century provenance shows that the book continued to live in London.

Two other manuscripts to note here: Horobin has shown that the scribe of **BodL Digby 102** was otherwise employed as a scribe for the Brewers' Company of London, thus placing the production of this manuscript firmly there.[102] Finally, the well-known copy of *Piers* in **BodL Douce 104** was certainly an urban production — though in this case, it was produced and circulated in Dublin. This manuscript has received a fair amount of scholarly attention due to its cycle of illustrations, which were most likely drawn by the scribe himself.[103] Thanks to a colophon on fol. 112^v, we know the manuscript dates from 1427. *eLALME* shows that this was an Irish scribe, from the Pale, where the manuscript remained for the first 150 years of its life, when it belonged to Sir James Ley, an English official in Ireland sec. xvi/xvii.[104] Also of note is the scribe's famous emendation of C.22.221–23, which in the *textus receptus* mocks an Irish priest for his drunkenness. The scribe of this manuscript alters these lines, making the priest a Welshman, suggesting that the manuscript was being copied in Ireland and the scribe wished to avoid upsetting the 'patriotic' sensibilities of the Irish reader.

A Lay, Aristocratic Public and Audience

Among those critics attentive to issues of social class in the poem, there has long been a tradition of reading *Piers Plowman* as fundamentally elegiac, lamenting the decline of feudalism and the stability such values offered the world. In John Alford's formulation, '*Piers Plowman* is partly an argument for turning back the clock'.[105] Others have seen the poem's

---

101 For an accounting of marginalia, see Benson and Blanchfield, *The Manuscripts of Piers Plowman*, p. 194.
102 Horobin, 'The Scribe of Bodleian Library MS Digby 102'.
103 Kerby-Fulton and Despres, *Iconography and the Professional Reader*, chapter 5, make the convincing case that the scribe was also the artist of this manuscript. For more on the illustrations, see Pearsall, 'Manuscript Illustration', and Scott, 'The Illustrations of *Piers Plowman*'.
104 See Pearsall, 'Introduction', in *Piers Plowman: A Facsimile*, p. xiii.
105 Alford, 'The Design', p. 34. This is not to say that the poem has not also been read as a radical document — only that there is a vibrant tradition of criticism attending to Langland's fundamental conservatism vis-à-vis social class. For some insightful remarks on the variety

class commitments as receptive to, and explicitly not hostile towards, contemporary social changes, but yet still fundamentally committed to reinscribing traditional class ideals.[106] Others yet have read Langland's class commitments more dialectically, showing how the poem reveals fissures in the feudal order and heightens class contradictions.[107] But such critics still concur that Langland is, at heart, a social conservative. Britton J. Harwood, in particular, usefully catalogues the various moments in *Piers* wherein Langland raises the class inequities inherent to feudalism without simultaneously lodging any overt objections or offering any vantage point of critique, noting how frequently Langland 'helps to perpetuate feudal relationships by referring them to the order of nature'.[108] To Harwood's comprehensive list, I would add that, in addition to nature, Langland also grounds feudalism within scriptural history. In Holy Church's discourse, for example, she contends that 'Dauid in hise dayes dubbed kny3tes' and that Christ himself 'kny3ted' the ten orders of angels (A.1.96, 103; see also B.1.98–106; C.1.101–05). Whether or not this is an intentional anachronism, it grounds the first estate in both the Old and New Testaments, thereby sanctifying contemporary class relations.

Numerous other moments point to a public imagined to be in the privileged position of effecting largesse — that is, the lay aristocracy. As Kate Crassons points out, in one of the major C text additions (passus 9), Langland added an extended rumination on poverty, twisting himself into knots over how to discriminate between the worthy and unworthy poor, and thus, late in his writing career, he was still very much exercised by the ethics of poverty.[109] In all three versions of the poem, Holy Church pivots from telling Will about the importance of Truth to addressing 'yow riche', admonishing them, 'haueþ ruþe on þe pouere; / Thou3 ye be my3ty to mote, beeþ meke in youre werkes' (B.1.175–76; see also A.1.149–50 and C.1.170–71) and to share generously with the poor. It is striking that Holy Church here breaks the fourth wall while speaking about caring for the poor, ceasing to harangue Will and turning to speak directly to the wealthy among the poem's readership, in a move that Ian Cornelius brilliantly describes as Holy Church 'pitch[ing] her tutelary voice over Wille's head and outside the poem'.[110]

Vocatives like these announce that those with financial resources are primary among the poem's public. Such moments, then, presume

---

of responses to Langland's take on social class, see Donaldson, *'Piers Plowman': The C-Text and Its Poet*, pp. 85–86.
106 Baldwin, 'The Historical Context', pp. 68–72.
107 Aers, *Chaucer, Langland, and the Creative Imagination*, chapter 1; Cole, 'Trifunctionality'; and Harwood, 'The Plot of *Piers Plowman*'.
108 Harwood, 'The Plot of *Piers Plowman*', p. 110.
109 Crassons, *Claims of Poverty*, pp. 73–82.
110 Cornelius, 'Langland Parrhesiastes', p. 115.

a readership in a position of wealth. These stern imperatives are then followed by numerous moments of anxiety about how one ought to treat the poor.[111] Stephen Barney usefully catalogues all such moments when a speaker directly harangues the poem's readership, counting twenty-two in the B text. One such address is aimed at beggars, one at 'lewed men', and one at all Christians, but the rest target the rich, lords, clerics, monastics, and friars — in other words, almost all such addresses are to the first or second estate.[112]

Four manuscripts are securely connected to early lay, aristocratic owners. Above, I discussed **BL ADD. 35157** as a London production, whose scribe, Preston, may have copied the ornate Litlyngton Missal. But this manuscript has even more patent evidence of its early ownership among the wealthy lay elite. The manuscript moved around a lot, as a series of names, from quite disparate parts of England, appear throughout its margins, in hands from the fifteenth and sixteenth centuries. Grindley carefully traces the earliest ownership, showing that, in the late fifteenth century, it was in the possession of the Surtees family of Durham.[113] Then, by the mid-sixteenth century, it was owned by the Ayscoughs, a gentry family from Cottam, Lincolnshire. Grindley also suggests that the 'thomas thyrnbeke, clarke' who signed fol. 124ᵛ was the scribe responsible for sixteenth-century additions to the text, making up for deficiencies by copying from Crowley's print edition, further hypothesizing that he may have been in the employ of the manuscript's sixteenth-century owners.[114]

Overleaf from Thyrnbeke's signature are memoranda, which contain a series of names. Most are now illegible, but I do make out the following: 'Item þat thomas conesoun has paye to Johannes lumley iiid ob / Jhon Robert machell' (fol. 125ᵛ, sec. xv/xvi). I have not identified the Thomas Conesoun named here. There are numerous references to John Lumleys and John and Robert Machells surviving in the archives.[115] The Lumleys and Machells who were prominent Westmorland landowners in the fifteenth and sixteenth centuries are the most likely candidates, if only

---

111 For a thorough bibliography of studies concerning Langland's treatment of poverty, see Crassons, *Claims of Poverty*, pp. 202–03 n. 6. As Crassons shows (chapter 1), Langland continued to wrestle with how to understand and respond to poverty all the way through the revisions in the C text.
112 Barney, *Penn Commentary*, p. 72.
113 Grindley, 'Life of a Book', pp. 156–57, 198–201.
114 Grindley, 'Life of a Book', pp. 173–74.
115 On John Lumley, see *Letters and Papers, Foreign and Domestic, Henry VIII, Volume 12, Part 1*, p. 349; *Calendar of State Papers*, pp. 1–2; Nicholson and Burn, *History and Antiquities*, vol. I, pp. 60–63. On John and Robert Machell, see *Calendar of Inquisitions Post Mortem: Henry VII: Volume II*, p. 518; *Descriptive Catalogue of the Ancient Deeds*, vol. VI, pp. 100–01; London, TNA C 1/1490/13; 1/1246/2–5; 78/6/38; STAC 2/25/236, 3/7/104, 3/7/64; Hyde and Pevsner, *Cumbria*, pp. 157, 303; Nicholson and Burn, *History and Antiquities*, vol. I, p. 346; and Stockdale, *Annales Caermoelenses*, pp. 512–15.

because of their proximity to one another. These Westmorland individuals may have been somehow affiliated with the manuscript sec. xv/xvi, though I do not know of any connection between them and the Surtees or Ayscough families, whom Grindley shows to have owned the manuscript earlier. Regardless, the manuscript had now passed to a new family.

BL Harley 6041 is another manuscript with ties to an aristocratic family: it was produced for the Hoos of Bedfordshire in the first quarter of the fifteenth century.[116] Kane identifies the series of arms sketched in the margins of the manuscript with Sir William Hoo, noting that most of them were drawn by the scribe.[117] This suggests that the manuscript was commissioned by the Hoo family. Michael Cornett also notes that the confessional formula that follows *Piers* reflects the penitential concerns of a landowner, further pointing to the armigerous Hoos.[118] But the manuscript did not remain in lay hands, later passing into the possession of William Holingborne, a monk in Canterbury: fol. 96^v records Holingborne's *ex libris*, in which he calls himself 'dane', (i.e., Don/Dom). Holingborne shows up several times in the records as a monk at, variously, Leeds Abbey and St Augustine's Abbey in Canterbury in the early sixteenth century, and he was the chaplain to the Abbot of St Augustine's at the time of the disendowment.[119] Since, as Kane notes, the Hoos had connections to Canterbury, it is likely that the book passed from them — its original commissioners — directly to Holingborne.[120]

As with **BL Harley 6041**, the final two manuscripts can be connected to armigerous owners because of heraldic devices inscribed along their borders. Above, I discussed the **Clopton MS** as a non-London production. Its heraldic devices show it was owned by Sir William Clopton, a gentry landowner in the south-west Midlands. Ryan Perry shows that Clopton was likely not the original owner, contending that the manuscript arose somewhere within the Beauchamp affinity in the south-west Midlands.[121] But it was soon in the possession of the Cloptons, regarding whom Turville-Petre remarks, 'Their traditional and orthodox piety, their

---

116 The hand is certainly of sec. xv$^{1/2}$, but, as Lyall, 'Materials', pp. 24–25, shows, watermarks allow us to narrow this dating down to sec. xv$^{1/4}$. The dialect of this manuscript has not been analysed in detail. On the theory that it would reflect local usage more than *Piers Plowman* would, I analysed the dialect of the confessional formula that follows *Piers*, as edited in Cornett, '*Piers Plowman*'. However, there were not enough distinguishing forms to allow for dialectal placement. I thank Michael Cornett for sharing initial, unpublished versions of this work with me.
117 Kane, ed., *Piers Plowman: The A Version*, p. 7 n. 1.
118 Cornett, '*Piers Plowman*'.
119 *Letters and Papers, Foreign and Domestic, Henry VIII, Volume 1*, p. 322; Hasted, 'The Abbey of St Augustine'; and Flaherty, 'A Help', p. 64.
120 Kane, ed., *Piers Plowman: The A Version*, p. 7 n. 1.
121 Perry, 'The Clopton Manuscript'.

wealth and social standing, and the range and character of their literary tastes, are all given fitting expression by Clopton's manuscript'.[122]

The final manuscript — **CAMBRIDGE, NEWNHAM COLLEGE MS 4** — has the most tendentious connection to aristocratic ownership: on four different leaves, always centred as a bas-de-page, someone has drawn an eagle, wings spread, standing on a patch of grass, with a capital -L on its chest. These accord with major textual divisions of the poem: the opening of the poem (fol. 1^r), and the three parts of the Vita (fols 35^r, 68^v, and 98^v). In a note appended to the front of the manuscript, W. W. Skeat refers to this as a 'crest'. Whatever its function, it could well signal the family who owned the manuscript. The consistent use of the letter -L inside the crest suggests that this is not a random drawing, but is meant to denote some surname. However, no scholar has yet succeeded in connecting this image to any particular owner.

A Lay, Non-Aristocratic Public and Audience

Langland's class commitments are, like much else in his poetry, notoriously resistant to easy definition. In some moments, he levels class divisions, reminding us, for example, that death marks the end of social class: 'For in a charnel at chirche cherles ben yuel to knowe, / Or a knyȝt from a knaue there — knowe this in þyn herte' (B.6.48–49). In Steven Justice's reading, some moments in the B text may have been provocative enough to inspire John Ball's ideas that all social divisions in this earthly life are unnatural and contrary to God's will.[123] Certainly, Langland's poem speaks to a broader audience than simply the clergy and the landed classes. If Hanna is correct in his assertion that Langland began his poetic endeavours by rewriting *Winner and Waster*, reorienting it away from overtly aristocratic discourse, then the very origin of *Piers Plowman* would lie within an attenuated impulse towards democratization.[124] Moreover, what are we to make of the fact that a ploughman is the ethical centre of the poem? The relationship between *Piers*'s ploughman and actual fourteenth-century ploughmen is quite complex, but it does seem clear that such figures were part of the peasant elite and, while they may have expropriated the surplus of their fellow peasants, they were identified squarely as members of that same peasant class.[125] The centrality of peasant Piers, then, points to a

---

122 Turville-Petre, 'The Relationship', p. 38.
123 Justice, *Writing and Rebellion*, chapter 3.
124 Hanna, *London Literature*, p. 278.
125 For concise summaries of this question, see Harwood, 'The Plot of *Piers Plowman*', pp. 101–02; and Dyer, '*Piers Plowman* and Plowmen'.

social vision that offers at least some room to resist conservative feudal ideologies that would deny any social capital to the *laboratores*.

But regardless of the class affiliations of ploughmen, the very figure of Piers also centres the identity of the laity, most notably when the priest reminds Piers of his non-sacerdotal status, attempting, as it were, to pull rank: '"Were þow a preest, Piers", quod he, "þow myȝtest preche where þow woldest"' (B.7.135). But Piers is not to be cowed: as a layman, Piers is the one who 'vnfoldeþ' the pardon (B.7.107); who then tears the pardon (at least, in A and B); who then redefines penance immediately following the pardon's destruction; who then shows up the priest for his arrogance; and who then brings the third vision to a close in mutual opposition to the priest — all of these things, coming in such quick succession, offer the lay Piers, at least for a moment, as an alternative to the traditional idea of pardons, penance and learning being solely mediated through the Church, an inversion Nicholas Watson provocatively terms 'the Piers hypothesis': 'Saving belief needs to be understood to move, not downward from priest to plowman, catechesis to understanding — the approach taken up to [B.5], by Reason and Holy Church — but upwards from an authentic source within the Christian community'.[126] Finally, we might locate such an elevation of the laity within the very final lines of the poem, when the unimpeachable figure of Conscience leaves Unity in search of Piers himself. Whatever one thinks of the ecclesiology inherent to such a departure, the final image is certainly one that underscores the indispensability of the laity for millenarian reform, for Conscience/the conscience — a gift from God common to all Christians — ends the text in pursuit of the poem's central lay figure.

We see the poem's centring of a non-aristocratic, lay public reflected in its audience — specifically, in six manuscripts. Above, I discussed **TCD 213** as a Durham or Northumberland production. Part of the evidence for this manuscript's connections to the far north is the constellation of names inscribed in its margins. Each of those inscriptions records merely a name and a village, which is not a way that those with titles would typically have styled themselves in this period — one that was becoming increasingly aware of social nomenclature. By the fifteenth century, a standard (though fluid and malleable) system of aristocratic titles had emerged, with the titles of earl and duke marking the nobility, while the gentry were graded in a hierarchy from knights, to esquires, to gentlemen, which formed the fuzzy outer margins of gentility.[127]

---

126 Watson, '*Piers Plowman*, Pastoral Theology, and Spiritual Perfectionism', p. 94.
127 On the growing importance of social designators in late medieval England, see Poos and Rust, 'Of *Piers*, Pollaxes, and Parliament'. On the developments of titles for the aristocracy, see Pugh, 'Magnates'; and Saul, *Knights and Esquires*, pp. 6–29.

Similarly lacking in titles are the owners of **BodL Laud misc. 656**. Someone jotted a draft of a bond from one John Cempe of the parish of Ticehurst, Kent (fol. 126^v, sec. xv/xvi). (Ticehurst is today in East Sussex.) The fact that Cempe does not get a title, nor is he said to be a priest, indicates that he may well have been a common parishioner of this diocese. On blank leaves in the same manuscript, from slightly earlier than Cempe, we find the names John Nasaby and Henry Nasond (fol. 131^v, sec. xv$^{2/2}$). Given the distinctiveness of the surname, this Nasaby was likely the same as the John Nasaby, notary and then Stationer of London in the 1450s–80s, discussed by C. Paul Christianson.[128] The script shows the manuscript as a product of the first half of the fifteenth century, but there is no clear evidence of where it was produced.[129] Wherever **BodL Laud misc. 656** was made, it was most likely in the hands of a lay commoner of Kent in the late fifteenth or early sixteenth century.

Lay Londoners owned the other four manuscripts in this category, two of which have connections to the John Thynne discussed above. The first, **BL Add. 10574**, was part of the BmBoCot series of manuscripts, almost certainly copied out in London and later purchased by Thynne. This same Thynne also signed fol. 92^r of **BodL Laud misc. 581**, a manuscript I discussed above as a London production. In the case of **Laud misc. 581**, Thynne was not the owner, but rather was associated with several men who passed this manuscript back and forth in the mid-sixteenth century. A Rauf Coppinger signed fol. 93^r, noting that he had borrowed the manuscript from one Mr Leigh, and had lent it to one Nicholas Brigham. Duggan and Hanna have noted that all these men's careers centred around London: Coppinger was a civil servant in the capital and Brigham worked for the Exchequer. Leigh was lord of Addington, Surrey, which lies in greater London.[130] Thynne, as discussed above, was a royal servant in London, and although his descendant would enter the titled nobility, Thynne himself soon entered the Mercers' Company.[131]

CUL Ff.5.35 stands out as one of only two copies of *Piers* to be entirely — both the Middle English and Latin — in textualis. (The other is **BL Harley 3954**, which I discussed above as an East Anglian production.) We cannot say anything definitive about where the manuscript was copied, for its dialectal evidence is inconclusive.[132] In the late fifteenth or

---

128 Christianson, *A Directory*, p. 138.
129 Hanna, *William Langland*, p. 41, reports a 'N. Oxfordshire language', though Madrinkian, 'Producing *Piers Plowman*', pp. 76–79, argues that the Oxfordshire forms are relict and that the scribe was likely from Gloucestershire.
130 Duggan and Hanna, 'Introduction', I.10.
131 Girouard, 'Thynne, Sir John'.
132 *eLALME* reports an Oxfordshire dialect (LP 6860, Grid 441 214), while Madrinkian, 'Producing *Piers Plowman*', pp. 81–82, argues that the Oxfordshire forms are relict and that the scribe was likely from the south-west Midlands.

early sixteenth century, it was in the hands of Thomas Jakes, a London lawyer connected to Thomas Roberts, a sixteenth-century book collector. Jakes, whose will dates to 1513, in addition to *Piers Plowman*, owned a number of law books as well as a healthy collection of Latin literature.[133]

Finally, **BODL BODLEY 814** was, like **BL ADD. 10574**, part of the London-produced BmBoCot series, and, like **BL ADD. 10574**, was later owned in London. **BODL BODLEY 814** has numerous names pointing to readers in the capital, many of which prove quite hard to decipher and represent rather conjectural transcriptions on my part: 'John thomas London lemmys *with* other proper namys werned the same daye of John thomas of lichefilde as aperithe by his accou*n*mpte for thre dayes' (fol. 93^r, sec. xvi^{med}); 'Jemye themghe' (fol. 93^r, sec. xv/xvi); 'This booke apartanithe aentes thomas hobsun' (fol. 93^r, sec. xv$^{2/2}$). Fol. 94^r has what looks to be a merchant's mark, though I have not been able to identify to whom this mark belonged; nor have I been able to identify any of these men, but there are several potential candidates. John Thomas is such an exceedingly common name that identifying him with confidence is quite hopeless. Two London Mercers by that name had their wills proved in 1506 and 1514.[134] A John Thomas of the Carpenters' Company shows up in their records in 1534–1535.[135] There are several Thomas Hobsons associated with greater London at the right time.[136] One was a landowner in Surrey, who also owned land in Marylebone. There were also Thomas Hobsons who were free of the city via the Carpenters' and Haberdashers' Companies. Either of these men could be the same as the Surrey landowner. The potential overlap of both John Thomas and Thomas Hobson within the Carpenters' Company is possible, but the Thomas Hobson I have identified was in the Company in 1490s, while the John Thomas was a member in the 1530s. Perhaps one was in the Company with the other's father or son, given the frequency with which sons were named after their fathers. These identifications remain overly speculative, and more research is needed into the ownership of this manuscript. But it remains exceedingly likely that **BODL BODLEY 814** remained in London for a good century after it was copied.

---

133 Connolly, *Sixteenth-Century Readers*, pp. 68–69.
134 London, TNA PROB 11/15/296, 11/17/607.
135 *Records of the Worshipful Company of Carpenters: Vol. III*, p. 4.
136 London, TNA E 327/488; *Descriptive Catalogue of the Ancient Deeds*, vol. I, p. 325; Noorthouck, 'Book 2, Ch. 15: Cheap Ward'; Lysons, 'Marylebone'; *Calendar of Wills*, pp. 499–502; *Records of the Worshipful Company of Carpenters: Vol. II*, pp. 45, 47, 51, 53, 60, 254; and *Abstract of Surrey Feet of Fines*, pp. 3–4.

A Clerical Public and Audience

There has been much disagreement about precisely what type of clergy the poem speaks to with the most urgency, or towards what sort of clerical role Langland's vision most closely hews, or even what sort of clerical role Will might have been imagined to fill. But, in short, every sort of role has been proposed, from the married man in minor orders, to the unbeneficed clergy, to the secular priesthood, to the friars and the monks.[137] Regardless of which clerical group one might decide the poem is most invested in, there is no doubt that whatever hope for social reform Langland's poem holds out, the chances of success hinge on the reform and the leadership of the clerical class writ large. Examples of Langland lamenting the failings of the clergy, urging their reform, and engaging with their ideals are so frequent throughout the poem, and hence so familiar to its students, that they need not detain us here.

But this putative public for *Piers* does not find comparatively much support in the manuscript record. I count five manuscripts with ties to the clergy. This paucity — particularly among the regular clergy — should not be surprising, given how little interest monastic houses had in vernacular texts. Extrapolating from the twenty-one volumes of the Corpus of British Medieval Library Catalogues that have been indexed, we can see that Middle English texts occupied an almost infinitesimally small place on the shelves of religious houses.[138] The twenty-one volumes in this corpus of catalogues include over 9000 works by over 3300 writers, copied into more than 40,000 manuscripts. Working through this index, I count references in library catalogues to a mere twenty-eight unique manuscript copies of Middle English literary and religious texts (none of *Piers Plowman*). Among these texts is found a copy of Lydgate's 'Dietary', as well as Chaucer's *Treatise on the Astrolabe* and *Boece*, *Dives and Pauper*,

---

137 On the married man in minor orders, see Donaldson, *'Piers Plowman': The C-Text and Its Poet*, chapter 7. On the secular priesthood, see Lawler, 'Secular Clergy'. On the friars, see Clopper, *Songes*. On the monastics, see Bloomfield, *'Piers Plowman'*. Schmidt, *Clerkly Maker*, argues for Langland as part of the general clerical class, writing largely for other clerics and creating a poem whose wordplay and rhetorical concerns suggest the clergy. Schmidt, however, does not define what sort of clerical status he imagines Langland to have inhabited. Wittig, '"Culture Wars"', likewise places Langland among the clerical classes, which he defines as those who pray and engage in intellectual labour for a living.

138 There are sixteen published volumes in the series, and a further five that are in press. All twenty-one have been included in an omnibus index, available at the University of Oxford Faculty of History website <https://www.history.ox.ac.uk/sites/default/files/history/documents/media/listofidentifications.pdf> [accessed 16 Aug. 2023]. In the tabulations that follow, I exclude printed books, as well as Middle English Bibles. I also exclude the volumes with catalogues from university libraries or other secular institutions, focusing only on the houses of regular religious. Some of the identifications are conjectural, but in all cases, I deferred to the editors' judgements.

The Owl and the Nightingale, and numerous devotional texts.[139] Twenty-eight manuscripts out of over 40,000 that have been indexed is a small proportion indeed. Certainly, many Middle English texts are hidden from sight within these catalogues, so I do not pretend that such a count is exhaustive. For example, in any given manuscript some Middle English texts may well have been copied after the main Latin text, when only the main Latin text received a title in the catalogue. In these cases, all trace of such Middle English texts would have vanished. At the same time, even taken impressionistically, the paucity of Middle English titles surviving from religious houses is telling.

This is not a total absence, of course, since the Augustinian canons in England took an interest in vernacular literary culture,[140] and we know, for example, of possibly six manuscripts of *The Prick of Conscience* that belonged to the regular clergy.[141] Several scholars have posited religious houses as a primary vector for the circulation of *Piers* manuscripts — with Kerby-Fulton even claiming that 'Benedictines are far and away the largest distinct group of identifiable early *Piers* owners' — but the case is almost entirely conjectural, since so few manuscripts bear actual evidence of transmission by the regular clergy.[142] Three manuscripts of

---

139 These twenty-eight manuscripts are: 2xChaucer's *Boece* (*St Augustine's Abbey,* ii, pp. 1010–11; and *Syon Abbey,* p. 451), Chaucer's *Treatise on the Astrolabe* (*Libraries of the Augustinian Canons,* p. 419), *Proverbs of Hending* (*Dover Priory,* p. 99), Lydgate's 'Dietary' (*Syon Abbey,* p. 39), Lydgate's *Life of St Alban and St Amphibal* (*English Benedictine Libraries,* p. 564), *A3enbite of Inwit* (*St Augustine's Abbey,* ii, pp. 1440–41), translation of Mechtild von Hackeborn (*Syon Abbey,* p. 252), *Owl and the Nightingale* (*Libraries of the Cistercians,* pp. 190–91), 5x*Speculum Christiani* (*Syon Abbey,* pp. 190–91, 208, 232–33, 236–37, 472–73), Walter Hilton, *Epistle on the Mixed Life* (*Syon Abbey,* pp. 469–70, 474–75), Hilton, *Scale of Perfection* (*Syon Abbey,* pp. 227, 252, 475), 2xRichard Rolle, English Psalter Commentary (Henry of Kirkestede, p. 447; *Syon Abbey,* p. 130), Rolle, *Form of Living* (*Syon Abbey,* pp. 257, 618), Rolle, *Meditation on the Passion* (*Syon Abbey,* p. 617), Nicholas Love, *Mirror of the Blessed Life of Jesus Christ* (*Syon Abbey,* p. 616), translation of Guillaume Deguileville, *Pilgrimage of the Life of Man* (*Syon Abbey,* p. 616), *Dives and Pauper* (*English Benedictine Libraries,* p. 569), and translation of Elizabeth of Töss, *Revelations* (*Syon Abbey,* p. 125).
140 Hanna, 'Augustinian Canons'; and Pouzet, 'Quelques aspects'.
141 Arundel Castle, Library of the Duke of Norfolk, MS of *The Prick of Conscience* (OFM); London, British Library MS Additional 24203 (O.Cist.); London, Lambeth Palace MS 260 (OP); London, Sion College, MS Arc.L.40.2/E.25 (OSB); Oxford, Bodleian Library MS Digby 99 (CRSA); Oxford, Bodleian Library MS Rawlinson poet. 138 (CRSA); Oxford, Bodleian Library MS Bodley 423 (CRSA). See Johnston, 'Copying and Reading *The Prick of Conscience*', pp. 779–800.
142 Kerby-Fulton, *Books under Suspicion,* p. 245. See also Fuller, 'The Craft of the "Z-Maker"', p. 33; Horobin, 'Harley 3954', pp. 77–82; and Madrinkian, 'Producing *Piers Plowman*', pp. 143–59. Middleton, 'Audience and Public', p. 109, remarks, 'This historical thematizing, and the poem's proximity in manuscript to legendary and historical narration, further associate *Piers* with monastic houses, in whose libraries and work this had long been a special strength'.

Piers, however, have likely connections to the regular clergy.[143] The first, **CUL Dd.1.17**, is an exceptionally large volume (with a page size measuring 440 × 300 mm), containing a compendium of Latin and Middle English historical, prophetic, and 'orientalist' texts (e.g., Geoffrey of Monmouth, Gildas, Guido delle Colonne, *Gesta Machometi*, *Piers Plowman*, and *Mandeville's Travels*). It is entirely in the hand of a single scribe, with frequent pen-flourished initials, and the book seems designed for reading on a lectern. As Kerby-Fulton shows, the manuscript must post-date 1382, and the script seems roughly from the late fourteenth or early fifteenth century.[144]

The scribe must have had access to an immense library, with copious holdings in Latin, suggesting production in and for a religious house. Doyle suggested the Austin Friars in York as a possible home for the manuscript, which was affirmed by Kerby-Fulton.[145] Hanna was initially a bit more circumspect, suggesting that this manuscript 'perhaps should be associated with York City. Certainly, the historical texts of the manuscript suggest origin among the regular clergy'. Later, in a more thorough examination, attending more closely to the scribal dialect and tracing the history of two sixteenth-century names in the manuscript, he suggests it may have been made at the Benedictine priory of Penwortham (Lancs.), from which it may have passed to Evesham Monastery, from which it could have passed to these sixteenth-century individuals.[146] Admittedly, this series of owners is speculative, but Hanna's narrative would account for how the manuscript ended up in lay hands after the Dissolution.

The other two manuscripts in the hands of the regular clergy are **BL Harley 6041** and **HM 143**. It is almost certain that neither was originally produced for these clerical owners. Harley was, as I discussed above, made for the Hoo family of Bedfordshire, but by the early sixteenth century was in the possession of William Holingborne, a Canterbury monk. Likewise, **HM 143**, as discussed above, was a London production, likely from sec. xiv/xv. On fol. 108ʳ, however, appears the name 'don Jhon redberry', from about a century later. So, this book had moved from

---

143 Hanna, *William Langland*, pp. 34–35, suggests two additional candidates for ownership by the regular clergy: HM 128 and TCD 212. I discuss my reasons for hesitating to accept HM 128's association with a religious house in the conclusion to this essay. The only potential connection between TCD 212 and a religious house is the supposition that it 'was owned by a person who perhaps had access to books from the library of Abergavenny Priory (OSB)': See Hanna, *William Langland*, p. 35.
144 Kerby-Fulton, *Books under Suspicion*, p. 112.
145 Doyle, 'Remarks on Surviving Manuscripts', p. 42; and Kerby-Fulton, *Books under Suspicion*, pp. 109–24.
146 Hanna, *William Langland*, p. 35; and Hanna, 'Cambridge University Library, MS DD.1.17', pp. 150–57.

London to the possession of this monk, whose identity has never been discovered.

Two further manuscripts were in the possession of clerics connected to secular cathedrals. **CUL ADD. 4325**, as I argued above, was likely the book of Thomas Lovell, a Doctor of Canon Law who held prebends at Bath and Wells. The second, **BODL RAWLINSON POET. 137**, as Horobin shows, was not only owned, but was also copied by, Thomas Tilot, a vicar to a canon at Chichester Cathedral, and subsequently rector of two parishes in the vicinity of Chichester. Horobin first identified Tilot as the copyist of both *Piers* and the copy of *The Prick of Conscience* in Oxford, University College MS 142, and my own analysis of both manuscripts affirms Horobin's identification of a single scribe across both.[147] Tilot may have copied these texts for himself, or he may have used them as an aid to preaching and pastoral care — or both.

***

Admittedly, many Middle English manuscripts are silent about their production and early circulation, and *Piers Plowman* is no exception to this. Of the forty-six manuscripts I listed at the opening of the essay, the foregoing has said nothing about sixteen, for which I find what I consider reliable evidence about neither production nor early provenance.[148] But to summarize: I identified eleven manuscripts as originating in rural locations, thirteen coming from London (with an additional one from Dublin), four belonging to the titled aristocracy, six belonging to the non-aristocratic laity, and five belonging to the clergy. Among the manuscripts I categorize as inconclusive, others might, on their own investigation, choose to be less circumspect, preferring to fit them into one category or another. Others yet might find my categorization of a given manuscript to lack circumspection and to overread the evidence. Such is the nature of this sort of endeavour.

The elephant in the room here is the **VERNON MS**, which many have assumed to be the product of a religious house for in-house reading.

---

147 Horobin, 'The Scribe of Rawlinson Poetry 137'. Interestingly, *eLALME*, unaware of this common scribe across both manuscripts, places their dialect within ten miles of one another, thereby offering testimony to the general reliability of dialectal localization. *eLALME* places Rawlinson in Sussex (LP 5690, Grid 500 107) and University College in Sussex (LP 5680, Grid 486 104).

148 Aberystwyth, National Library of Wales MS 733B; Cambridge, Corpus Christi College MS 293; Cambridge, Trinity College MS R.3.14; Cambridge, University Library MSS Dd.3.13, Ll.4.14; Liverpool, University Library MS F.4.8; BL Add. 34779; BL Harley 875; BL Harley 2376; London, Lincoln's Inn MS 150; BodL Digby 171; BodL Douce 323; Oxford, Oriel College MS 79; Oxford, Bodleian Library MS Rawlinson poet. 38 + London, British Library MS Lansdowne 398; San Marino, Huntington Library MS HM 128 and 137.

Derek Pearsall, for example, speculates that **VERNON** 'was produced in and could hardly have been produced anywhere other than in a well-equipped religious house'.[149] But such can be no more than a purely educated guess, based on the intuition that massive books, drawing on massive numbers of exemplars, would most likely be underwritten by a religious house. There is no codicological or palaeographical evidence within the manuscript itself to point to a religious house, and in fact, Wendy Scase makes (what strikes me as) a compelling case for the secular patronage of **VERNON**.[150] Thus, while I placed this as a rural, West Midlands production, I did not categorize this manuscript as belonging to either the laity or the clergy, but rather left its ownership undetermined.

HM 128 proves another ambiguous codex. Presumably gleaning its audience from its contents, Turville-Petre groups this manuscript among 'household anthologies'.[151] Hanna and David Lawton, on the other hand, suggest a religious house as its most likely production site. To make this claim, they argue that the scribe of this manuscript's copy of *The Siege of Jerusalem* worked up to a quarter-century later than the scribes of the manuscript's copy of *The Prick of Conscience* and *Piers Plowman*. Coupled with a consistent decorative scheme across the manuscript, Hanna and Lawton believe that this palaeographical evidence argues that the manuscript was most likely 'a corporate product and remained in situ', positing a religious house as best fitting this narrative.[152] But I am unconvinced: the scribe who appears to be copying his texts later could just as easily be a younger scribe working at the same time as a team of older colleagues. If this younger scribe learned to write from contemporaries, and the older scribes maintained a conservative script from their earlier training, then what presents as a discontinuity in copying could merely be scribes from a range of ages and periods of training, with the entire scribal team working simultaneously, thus giving us no reason to suspect the sorts of long-term projects presumably more common in a corporate setting. So my decision was to leave **HM 128** in the undefined category. And so it is with almost all manuscript analyses: any given scholar will develop a slightly varying set of categories and criteria for inclusion within those categories. It is, nevertheless, incumbent on scholars to adjudicate to the best of our abilities, exhibiting our evidence as fully as possible.

---

149 Pearsall, 'Introduction', in *Studies in the Vernon Manuscript*, p. x. See also Doyle, 'Codicology, Palaeography, and Provenance', pp. 14–18; Horobin, 'The Scribes of the Vernon Manuscript', pp. 27–28; and Hanna, *Pursuing History*, p. 231.
150 Scase, 'The Patronage of the Vernon Manuscript'.
151 Turville-Petre, *The Alliterative Revival*, p. 44.
152 Hanna and Lawton, 'Introduction', pp. xxi–xxii. See also Doyle, 'Remarks on Surviving Manuscripts', p. 40, who likewise believes HM 128 was a clerical production. More recently, Kittel, 'History of Contact', pp. 139–44, has presented what strikes me as a convincing refutation of this argument.

Other manuscripts certainly have provenance histories that are not recorded in their margins, flyleaves, etc., which thus will forever remain hidden. As I mentioned at the opening of this essay, we know from surviving wills that the earliest attested owners of *Piers Plowman* were clerics and civil servants, but none of the manuscripts mentioned in these early wills have survived.[153] And many of the manuscripts that do survive must have passed through numerous hands, with only a select number of those owners or readers feeling inspired to inscribe their names within the codex. So, a manuscript like **BODL LAUD 656**, discussed above, which bears the name of John Cempe, a layperson who gives the name of his parish, may well have come to this Cempe from his parish priest, with Cempe the only one ever to put his name in the manuscript. Or not.

Other manuscripts remind us that these various social categories of readership were quite porous. **TCD 213**, for example, bears the name of numerous villagers from the Northumberland coast, alongside the name of a comparatively wealthy Durham family and a reference to the performance of drama. This latter piece of evidence could point to the manuscript circulating among either clerics or civic authorities responsible for staging medieval cycle dramas. And **BL HARLEY 6041** was made for the Hoos, a landowning family, but within 75 years was in the hands of a Canterbury monk. Perhaps, however, the most interpenetration of these social groups happened in the parish, where the rector, or his curate, lived in regular contact with his parishioners. As Peter Coss reminds us, the worlds of the secular clergy and the rural landowners who commissioned numerous manuscripts were not so discrete as scholars often construe them to be: '[m]uch of the transmission of literature took place directly within secular society; we can say this even more emphatically if we understand by it both the laity and the secular clergy'.[154] All this is to say that manuscripts do not fall into neat and tidy categories; nor are the categories themselves neat and tidy. After all, social categories do not strictly respect — and never have respected — our scholarly taxonomies.

Much of what I have argued in the preceding analyses is ultimately a gloss upon Middleton's remarks, accompanied by a much more extensive consideration of the manuscript evidence than Middleton provided:

> [I]t can be fairly said that the poem attested by all three forms achieved a virtually nationwide distribution within a generation of

---

153 The earliest attested owner of a *Piers Plowman* manuscript was Walter Brugge, holder of numerous prebendaries, whose 1396 will mentions Langland's poem. Brooks, 'The "Piers Plowman" Manuscripts', pp. 151–53, furthers the argument of Oscar Cargill that TCD MS 212 itself was Brugge's manuscript. To the best of my knowledge, this is the only attempt to connect an early attested reader of *Piers* with a surviving manuscript. For a thorough study of Brugge's life, see Davies, 'The Life, Travels, and Library'.

154 Coss, 'Introduction', p. lxi.

their production. It is the purpose of this essay to demonstrate that *Piers Plowman* was received by a heterogenous and attentive readership, and that this was the kind of reception it actively and consciously sought by its choices of genre and form [...] In the mode of its construction, *Piers* is the first Middle English poetic fiction intentionally capable of a national resonance and reception. In this respect, as well as in the genesis of its form, it occupies a position comparable to that of Dante's poem in its vernacular literate culture.[155]

In closing, I would like to suggest that the diffuseness of *Piers Plowman*'s attested owners is, in fact, the very point. That is, the manuscript evidence encourages us to view Langland's audience as remarkably and consistently catholic: encompassing urban and rural dwellers, lay commoners, the aristocracy, secular clergy, and regular clergy. If we limit ourselves to a pre-determined slice of the literate population as owners and readers of Langland's poem — assuming, for example, that Langland wrote for a London audience, or an audience of secular clerics, or that *Piers Plowman* was a London-produced poem, or was produced in religious houses — we can certainly find evidence for that within the manuscript record. But if we pan out and look at the manuscript record as a whole, it reveals that Langland's audience was all these groups at once. The manuscript record, taken in its entirety, is the most robust source yielding information about Langland's readership in his lifetime and the first century after his poem began to circulate.

In late medieval England, those with the ability to read the vernacular and with the means to acquire a manuscript were numerous — certainly nothing like the majority of England's two million inhabitants, but certainly a not-insignificant portion of them.[156] Regular clerics, secular clerics, parish clerks, those who owned estates, those who administered estates, those who engaged in trade, those who owned smallholds, those who worked in cities and villages making wills or keeping records for guilds — all of these men, and some women, had reason to learn to read. Their worlds depended on them understanding the documents that regulated their economic lives. In the manuscript record of *Piers Plowman*, we find this whole panoply of the literate. Such is to be expected in a poem of such capacious imagination.

---

155 Middleton, 'Audience and Public', pp. 101, 118–19.
156 Truelove, 'Literacy'; Parkes, 'Literacy of the Laity'; and de Hamel, 'Books and Society'.

Works Cited

Archival Sources

London, Kew, The National Archives (TNA), C 78/6/38
———, C 1/1246/2–5
———, C 1/1490/13
———, E 327/488
———, PROB 11/15/296
———, PROB 11/17/607
———, STAC 2/25/236
———, STAC 3/7/64
———, STAC 3/7/104

Manuscripts

Aberystwyth, National Library of Wales, MS 733B
Arundel Castle, Library of the Duke of Norfolk, MS of *The Prick of Conscience*
Cambridge, Corpus Christi College, MS 293
Cambridge, Gonville and Caius College, MS 669/46
Cambridge, Newnham College, MS 4
Cambridge, Pembroke College, MS 312 C/6
Cambridge, Trinity College, MS B.15.17
———, MS R.3.2
———, MS R.3.14
Cambridge, University Library, MS Add. 4325
———, MS Dd.1.17
———, MS Dd.3.13
———, MS Ff.5.35
———, MS Gg.4.31
———, MS Ll.4.14
Dublin, Trinity College, MS 212
———, MS 213
John Holloway Collection, bifolium
Liverpool, University Library, MS F.4.8
London, British Library, MS Additional 10574
———, MS Additional 22283
———, MS Additional 24203
———, MS Additional 34779
———, MS Additional 35157

———, MS Additional 35287
———, MS Cotton Caligula A.xi
———, MS Cotton Vespasian B.xvi
———, MS Harley 875
———, MS Harley 2376
———, MS Harley 3943
———, MS Harley 3954
———, MS Harley 6041
———, MS Lansdowne 398
———, MS Royal 18 B.xvii
———, MS Sloane 2578
London, Lambeth Palace, MS 260
———, MS 491
London, Lincoln's Inn, MS 150
London, Sion College, MS Arc.L.40.2/E.25
London, Society of Antiquaries, MS 687
London, University of London, MS S.L.V.17
———, MS S.L.V.88
New Haven, Yale University, Beinecke Library, MS Takamiya Deposit 23
New York, J. P. Morgan Library, MS M.818
Oslo, Schøyen Collection, MS 1953
Oxford, Bodleian Library, MS Ashmole 1468
———, MS Bodley 423
———, MS Bodley 814
———, MS Digby 87
———, MS Digby 99
———, MS Digby 102
———, MS Digby 145
———, MS Digby 171
———, MS Douce 104
———, MS Douce 323
———, MS Eng. poet. a.1
———, MS James 2, part 1
———, MS Laud misc. 581
———, MS Laud misc. 656
———, MS Rawlinson poet. 38
———, MS Rawlinson poet. 137
———, MS Rawlinson poet. 138

———, MS Wood donat. 7
Oxford, Corpus Christi College, MS 201
Oxford, Oriel College, MS 79
Oxford, University College, MS 45
———, MS 142
Princeton, University Library, MS Taylor 10
San Marino, Huntington Library, MS HM 114
———, MS HM 128
———, MS HM 137
———, MS HM 143
Washington, DC, Folger Shakespeare Library, MS V.b. 236

Primary Sources

Abstract of Surrey Feet of Fines, 1509–1558, ed. by C. A. F. Meekings, Surrey Record Society, 19 (1946; repr. London: Dawson and Sons, 1968)

Baildon, W. Paley, ed., 'Escheator's Accounts: Various Years, 1513–30', *Calendar of the Manuscripts of the Dean and Chapter of Wells: Volume 2*, Historical Manuscripts Commission (London: HMSO, 1914)

Calendar of Inquisitions Post Mortem: Henry VII: Volume II (London: HMSO, 1915)

Calendar of State Papers Domestic: Edward VI, Mary and Elizabeth, 1547–80, ed. by Robert Lemon (London: HMSO, 1856)

Calendar of Wills Proved and Enrolled in the Court of Husting, London: Part 2, 1358–1688, ed. by R. R. Sharpe (London: J. Francis, 1890)

Christianson, C. Paul, *A Directory of London Stationers and Book Artisans, 1300–1500* (New York: Bibliographical Society of America, 1990)

A Descriptive Catalogue of the Ancient Deeds in the Public Record Office, 6 vols (London: HMSO, 1890–1915)

Dover Priory, ed. by William P. Stoneman, Corpus of British Medieval Library Catalogues, 5 (London: British Library, 1999)

English Benedictine Libraries: The Shorter Catalogues, ed. by R. Sharpe and others, Corpus of British Medieval Library Catalogues, 6 (London: British Library, 1996)

Fasti Ecclesiae Anglicanae, 1300–1541: Volume 8, Bath and Wells Diocese, ed. by B. Jones (London: Institute of Historical Research, 1964)

Henry of Kirkestede, *Catalogus de libris autenticis et apocrifis*, ed. by Richard H. Rouse and Mary A. Rouse, Corpus of British Medieval Library Catalogues, 11 (London: British Library, 2004)

Langland, William, *Piers Plowman*, trans. by A. V. C. Schmidt (Oxford: Oxford University Press, 1992)

——, *Piers Plowman Electronic Archive, I: Oxford, Corpus Christi College, MS 201 (F)*, ed. by Robert Adams, Hoyt N. Duggan, Eric Eliason, Ralph Hanna, John Price-Wilkin, and Thorlac Turville-Petre, 2nd edn (SEENET, 2014) <http://piers.chass.ncsu.edu/texts/F> [accessed 16 Aug. 2023]

——, *Piers Plowman Electronic Archive, II: Cambridge, Trinity College, MS B.15.17 (W)*, ed. by Thorlac Turville-Petre and Hoyt N. Duggan, 2nd edn (SEENET, 2014) <http://piers.chass.ncsu.edu/texts/W> [accessed 16 Aug. 2023]

——, *Piers Plowman: A Parallel-Text Edition of the A, B, C and Z Versions*, ed. by A. V. C. Schmidt, 2nd edn, 2 vols (Kalamazoo, MI: Medieval Institute Publications, 2011)

——, *Piers Plowman: The Z Version*, ed. by A. G. Rigg and Charlotte Brewer, Studies and Texts, 59 (Toronto: Pontifical Institute of Mediaeval Studies, 1983)

——, *The Vision of Piers Plowman: A Critical Edition of the B-text Based on Trinity College Cambridge MS B.15.17*, ed. by A. V. C. Schmidt, 2nd edn (London: Dent, 1995)

Letters and Papers, Foreign and Domestic, Henry VIII, Volume 1, 1509–1514, ed. by J. S. Brewer (London: HMSO, 1920)

Letters and Papers, Foreign and Domestic, Henry VIII, Volume 12, Part 1, January–May 1537, ed. by James Gairdner (London: HMSO, 1890)

The Libraries of the Augustinian Canons, ed. by Teresa Webber and A. G. Watson, Corpus of British Medieval Library Catalogues, 6 (London: British Library, 1998)

The Libraries of the Cistercians, Gilbertines and Premonstratensians, ed. by David N. Bell, Corpus of British Medieval Library Catalogues, 3 (London: British Library, 1992)

Records of the Worshipful Company of Carpenters: Vol. II: Warden's Account Book, 1438–1516, ed. by Bower Marsh (Oxford: Carpenters' Company, 1914)

Records of the Worshipful Company of Carpenters: Vol. III: Court Book, 1533–1573, ed. by Bower Marsh (Oxford: Carpenters' Company, 1915)

St Augustine's Abbey, Canterbury, ed. by Bruce Barker-Benfield, Corpus of British Medieval Library Catalogues, 13, 3 vols (London: British Library, 2008)

Syon Abbey, with the Libraries of the Carthusians, ed. by Vincent Gillespie and A. I. Doyle, Corpus of British Medieval Library Catalogues, 9 (London: British Library, 2001)

Secondary Sources

Adams, Robert, *Langland and the Rokele Family: The Gentry Background to 'Piers Plowman'* (Dublin: Four Courts, 2013)

Adams, Robert, and Thorlac Turville-Petre, 'The London Book-Trade and the Lost History of *Piers Plowman*', *Review of English Studies*, 65.269 (2013), 219–35

Aers, David, *Chaucer, Langland and the Creative Imagination* (London: Routledge & Kegan Paul, 1980)

——, *'Piers Plowman' and Christian Allegory* (New York: St Martin's, 1975)

Alexander, J. J. G., *Medieval Illuminators and Their Methods of Work* (New Haven: Yale University Press, 1992)

Alford, John A., 'The Design of the Poem', in *A Companion to 'Piers Plowman'*, ed. by John A. Alford (Berkeley, CA: University of California Press, 1988), pp. 29–65

Baldwin, Anna P., 'The Historical Context', in *A Companion to 'Piers Plowman'*, ed. by John A. Alford (Berkeley, CA: University of California Press, 1988), pp. 67–86

Barney, Stephen A., *The Penn Commentary on 'Piers Plowman': Vol. 5* (Philadelphia: University of Pennsylvania Press, 2006)

Barron, Caroline, 'William Langland: A London Poet', in *Chaucer's England: Literature in Historical Context*, ed. by Barbara Hanawalt, Medieval Cultures, 4 (Minneapolis: University of Minnesota Press, 1989), pp. 91–109

Bart, Patricia R., 'Intellect, Influence, and Evidence: The Elusive Allure of the Ht Scribe', in *Yee? Baw for Bokes: Essays on Medieval Manuscripts and Poetics in Honor of Hoyt N. Duggan*, ed. by Michael Calabrese and Stephen H. A. Shepherd (Los Angeles: Marymount Institute, 2013), pp. 219–39

Beadle, Richard, 'Middle English Texts and Their Transmission, 1350–1500: Some Geographical Criteria', in *Speaking in Our Tongues: Proceedings of a Colloquium on Medieval Dialectology and Related Disciplines*, ed. by Margaret Laing and Keith Williamson (Cambridge: Brewer, 1994), pp. 69–91

——, 'Prolegomena to a Literary Geography of Later Medieval Norfolk', in *Regionalism in Late Medieval Manuscripts and Texts: Essays Celebrating the Publication of 'A Linguistic Atlas of Late Mediaeval English'*, ed. by Felicity Riddy (Cambridge: Brewer, 1991), pp. 89–108

Benskin, Michael, and others, eds, *An Electronic Version of A Linguistic Atlas of Late Mediaeval English* (Edinburgh: © 2013– The Authors and The University of Edinburgh) http://www.lel.ed.ac.uk/ihd/elalme/elalme.html [accessed 16 Aug. 2023] (cited as *eLALME*)

Benson, C. David, *Public 'Piers Plowman': Modern Scholarship and Late Medieval English Culture* (University Park, PA: Pennsylvania State University Press, 2004)

Benson, C. David, and Lynne Blanchfield, *The Manuscripts of 'Piers Plowman': The B-Version* (Woodbridge: Brewer, 1997)

Black, W. H., *A Descriptive, Analytical, and Critical Catalogue of the Manuscripts Bequeathed unto the University of Oxford by Elias Ashmole* (Oxford: Oxford University Press, 1845)

Bloomfield, Morton W., *'Piers Plowman' as a Fourteenth-Century Apocalypse* (Brunswick, NJ: Rutgers University Press, 1962)

Bowers, John M., 'Two Professional Readers of Chaucer and Langland: Scribe D and the HM 114 Scribe', *Studies in the Age of Chaucer*, 26 (2004), 113–46

Brooks, E. St John, 'The *Piers Plowman* Manuscripts in Trinity College Dublin', *The Library*, 5th ser., 6 (1951), 144–51

Burrow, J. A., 'The Audience of *Piers Plowman*', *Anglia*, 75 (1957), 373–84 (repr. in J. A. Burrow, *Essays on Medieval Literature* (Oxford: Clarendon Press, 1984), pp. 102–16)

Carillo-Linares, María José, and Keith Williamson, 'The Linguistic Character of Manuscripts Attributed to the Beryn Scribe: A Comparative Study', in *The Multilingual Origins of Standard English*, ed. by Laura Wright, Topics in English Linguistics, 107 (Berlin: de Gruyter, 2020), pp. 87–139

Christianson, C. Paul, 'Evidence for the Study of London's Late Medieval Manuscript-Book Trade', in *Book Production and Publishing in Britain, 1375–1475*, ed. by Jeremy Griffiths and Derek Pearsall (Cambridge: Cambridge University Press, 1989), pp. 87–108

——, 'The Rise of London's Book-Trade', in *Cambridge History of the Book in Britain: Volume III: 1400–1557*, ed. by Lotte Hellinga and J. B. Trapp (Cambridge: Cambridge University Press, 1999), pp. 128–47

Clopper, Lawrence M., 'The Engaged Spectator: Langland and Chaucer on Civic Spectacle and the *Theatrum*', *Studies in the Age of Chaucer*, 22 (2000), 115–39

——, *Songes of Rechelesnesse: Langland and the Franciscans* (Ann Arbor, MI: University of Michigan Press, 1997)

Cole, Andrew, 'Trifunctionality and the Tree of Charity: Literacy and Social Practice in *Piers Plowman*', *ELH*, 62 (1995), 1–27

Connolly, Margaret, *Sixteenth-Century Readers, Fifteenth-Century Books: Continuities of Reading in the English Reformation*, Cambridge Studies in Palaeography and Codicology (Cambridge: Cambridge University Press, 2019)

Cornelius, Ian, 'Langland Parrhesiastes', in *Medieval Literary Voices: Embodiment, Materiality and Performance*, ed. by Louise D'Arcens and Sif Ríkharðsdóttir (Manchester: Manchester University Press, 2022), pp. 111–29

Cornett, Michael E., 'The *Piers Plowman* Form of Confession in British Library, MS Harley 6041', (unpublished edn)

Coss, Peter, 'Introduction to 1996 Edition', in *Thomas Wright's 'Political Songs of England: From the Reign of John to That of Edward II'* (Cambridge: Cambridge University Press, 1996), pp. xi–lxvii

Crassons, Kate, *The Claims of Poverty: Literature, Culture, and Ideology in Late Medieval England* (Notre Dame, IN: University of Notre Dame Press, 2010)

Davies, Sarah Rees, 'The Life, Travels, and Library of an Early Reader of *Piers Plowman*', *Yearbook of Langland Studies*, 13 (1999), 49–64

Davis, Brian, 'The Rationale for a Copy of a Text: Constructing the Exemplar for British Library Additional MS. 10574', *Yearbook of Langland Studies*, 11 (1997), 141–56

Dennison, Lynda, and Nigel Morgan, 'The Decoration of Wycliffite Bibles', in *The Wycliffite Bible: Origin, History and Interpretation*, ed. by Elizabeth Solopova (Leiden: Brill, 2017), pp. 266–345

Donaldson, E. Talbot, *'Piers Plowman': The C-Text and Its Poet* (New Haven: Yale University Press, 1949)

Donovan, Claire, *The de Brailes Hours: Shaping the Book of Hours in Thirteenth-Century Oxford* (London: British Library, 1991)

Doyle, A. I., 'Codicology, Palaeography, and Provenance', in *The Making of the Vernon Manuscript: The Production and Contexts of Oxford, Bodleian Library, MS Eng. poet. a. 1*, ed. by Wendy Scase, Texts and Transitions, 6 (Turnhout: Brepols, 2013), pp. 3–25

——, 'Penwork Flourishing of Initials in England from *c.* 1380', in *Tributes to Kathleen L. Scott: English Medieval Manuscripts: Readers, Makers and Illuminators*, ed. by Marlene Villalobos Hennessy (Turnhout: Brepols, 2009), pp. 65–72

——, 'Remarks on Surviving Manuscripts of *Piers Plowman*', in *Medieval English Religious and Ethical Literature: Essays in Honour of George H. Russell*, ed. by Gregory Kratzmann and James Simpson (Cambridge: Brewer, 1986), pp. 35–48

——, 'Ushaw College, Durham, MS 50: Fragments of *The Prick of Conscience*, by the Same Scribe as Oxford, Corpus Christi College, MS 201, of the B Text of *Piers Plowman*', in *The English Medieval Book: Studies in Memory of Jeremy Griffiths*, ed. by A. S. G. Edwards, Vincent Gillespie, and Ralph Hanna (London: British Library, 2000), pp. 43–49

Doyle, A. I., and M. B. Parkes, 'The Production of Copies of the *Canterbury Tales* and the *Confessio Amantis* in the Early Fifteenth Century', in *Medieval Scribes, Manuscripts and Libraries: Essays Presented to N. R. Ker*, ed. by M. B. Parkes and A. G. Watson (London: Scolar, 1978), pp. 163–210

Duggan, Hoyt, and Ralph Hanna, 'Introduction', *'Piers Plowman' Electronic Archive*, IV: Oxford, Bodleian Library MS Laud misc. 581 (S. C. 987) (L)', 2nd edn (SEENET, 2014) <http://piers.chass.ncsu.edu/texts/L> [accessed 16 Aug. 2023]

Duggan, Hoyt, and Thorlac Turville-Petre, 'Introduction', *The Wars of Alexander*, ed. by Hoyt Duggan and Thorlac Turville-Petre, EETS, s.s. 10 (Oxford: Oxford University Press, 1989), pp. ix–lviii

Dyer, Christopher, '*Piers Plowman* and Plowmen: A Historical Perspective', *Yearbook of Langland Studies*, 8 (1994), 155–76

——, 'Were Late Medieval Villages "Self-Contained"?' in *The Self-Contained Village? The Social History of Rural Communities, 1250–1900*, ed. by Christopher Dyer, Explorations in Local and Regional History, 2 (Hartfield: University of Hertfordshire Press, 2007), pp. 6–27

Edwards, A. S. G., 'The Selling of *Piers Plowman* Manuscripts in the Twentieth Century', *Yearbook of Langland Studies*, 27 (2013), 103–11

Eliason, Eric, Hoyt N. Duggan, and Thorlac Turville-Petre, 'Introduction', *'Piers Plowman' Electronic Archive, V: London, British Library, MS Additional 35287 (M)*, 2nd edn (SEENET, 2014) <http://piers.chass.ncsu.edu/texts/M> [accessed 16 Aug. 2023]

Eyler, Joshua, and C. David Benson, 'The Manuscripts of *Piers Plowman*', *Literature Compass*, 2.1 (2005)

Fisher, John H., '*Piers Plowman* and the Chancery Tradition', in *Medieval English Studies Presented to George Kane*, ed. by Edward Donald Kennedy, Ronald Waldron, and Joseph S. Wittig (Woodbridge: Boydell, 1988), pp. 267–78

Flaherty, W. E., 'A Help toward a Kentish Monasticon', *Archaeologia Cantiana*, 2 (1859), 49–64

Frank, Jr., Robert Worth, *'Piers Plowman' and the Scheme of Salvation* (New Haven: Yale University Press, 1957; repr. n.p.: Archon Books, 1969)

Friedman, John B., *Northern English Books, Owners, and Makers in the Late Middle Ages* (Syracuse, NY: Syracuse University Press, 1995)

Fuller, Karrie, 'The Craft of the "Z-Maker": Reading the Z Text's Unique Lines in Context', *Yearbook of Langland Studies*, 27 (2013), 15–43

——, 'Langland in the Early Modern Household: *Piers Plowman* in Oxford, Bodleian Library MS Digby 145, and Its Scribe-Annotator Dialogues', in *New Directions in Medieval Manuscript Studies and Reading Practices: Essays in Honor of Derek Pearsall*, ed. by Kathryn Kerby-Fulton, John J. Thompson and Sarah Baechle (Notre Dame, IN: University of Notre Dame Press, 2014), pp. 324–41

Galloway, Andrew, 'Non-Literary Commentary and Its Literary Profits: The Road to Accounting-Ville', *Yearbook of Langland Studies*, 25 (2011), 9–23

——, 'Uncharacterizable Entities: The Poetics of Middle English Scribal Culture and the Definitive *Piers Plowman*', *Studies in Bibliography*, 52 (1999), 59–87

Gee, Stacey, 'The Printers, Stationers and Bookbinders of York before 1557', *Transactions of the Cambridge Bibliographical Society*, 12.1 (2000), 27–54

Gillespie, Alexandra, and Daniel Wakelin, 'Introduction', in *The Production of Books in England, 1350–1500*, ed. by Alexandra Gillespie and Daniel Wakelin (Cambridge: Cambridge University Press, 2011), pp. 1–11

Girouard, Mark, 'Thynne, Sir John (1512/13–1580), Estate Manager and Builder of Longleat', *Oxford Dictionary of National Biography*, 23 Sept. 2004 https://doi.org/10.1093/ref:odnb/27421 [accessed 18 Feb. 2021]

Grindley, Carl James, 'The A-Version Ancestor of BmBoCot', *Yearbook of Langland Studies*, 24 (2010), 63–88

——, 'The Life of a Book: British Library Additional 35157 in Historical Context' (unpublished doctoral dissertation, University of Glasgow, 1996)

de Hamel, Christopher, 'Books and Society', in *The Cambridge History of the Book in Britain: Volume II: 1100–1400*, ed. by Nigel Morgan and Rodney M. Thomson (Cambridge: Cambridge University Press, 2008), pp. 3–21

Hanna, Ralph, 'Augustinian Canons and Middle English Literature', in *The English Medieval Book: Studies in Memory of Jeremy Griffiths*, ed. by A. S. G. Edwards, Vincent Gillespie, and Ralph Hanna (London: British Library, 2000), pp. 27–42

——, 'Cambridge University Library, MS DD.1.17: Some Historical Notes', *Transactions of the Cambridge Bibliographical Society*, 16.2 (2017), 141–60

——, *London Literature, 1300–1380* (Cambridge: Cambridge University Press, 2005)

——, *Pursuing History: Middle English Manuscripts and Their Texts*, Figurae: Reading Medieval Culture (Stanford, CA: Stanford University Press, 1996)

——, 'The Scribe of Huntington HM 114', *Studies in Bibliography*, 42 (1989), 120–33

——, *William Langland*, Authors of the Middle Ages, 3 (Aldershot: Variorum, 1993)

Hanna, Ralph, and David Lawton, 'Introduction', *The Siege of Jerusalem*, ed. by Ralph Hanna and David Lawton, EETS, 320 (Oxford: Oxford University Press, 2003), pp. xiii–xcix

Harwood, Britton J., 'The Plot of *Piers Plowman* and the Contradictions of Feudalism', in *Speaking Two Languages: Traditional Disciplines and Contemporary Theory in Medieval Studies*, ed. by Allen J. Frantzen, SUNY Series in Medieval Studies (Albany, NY: State University of New York Press, 1991), pp. 91–114

Hasted, Edward, 'The Abbey of St Augustine: Abbots', in *The History and Topographical Survey of the County of Kent: Volume 12* (Canterbury: n.p., 1801), pp. 177–225

Horobin, Simon, 'Adam Pinkhurst and the Copying of British Library, MS Additional 35287 of the B Version of *Piers Plowman*', *Yearbook of Langland Studies*, 23 (2009), 61–83

——, 'Adam Pinkhurst, Geoffrey Chaucer, and the Hengwrt Manuscript of the *Canterbury Tales*', *Chaucer Review*, 44.4 (2010), 351–67

——, 'Harley 3954 and the Audience of *Piers Plowman*', in *Medieval Texts in Context*, ed. by Graham D. Caie and Denis Renevey, Context and Genre in English Literature (London: Routledge, 2008), pp. 68–84

——, '"In London and opeland": The Dialect and Circulation of the C Version of *Piers Plowman*', *Medium Ævum*, 74 (2005), 248–69

——, 'John Cok and His Copy of *Piers Plowman*', *Yearbook of Langland Studies*, 27 (2013), 45–59

——, 'Manuscripts and Readers of *Piers Plowman*', in *The Cambridge Companion to 'Piers Plowman'*, ed. by Andrew Cole and Andrew Galloway (Cambridge: Cambridge University Press, 2014), pp. 179–97

——, 'The Scribe of Bodleian Library MS Digby 102 and the Circulation of the C Text of *Piers Plowman*', *Yearbook of Langland Studies*, 24 (2010), 89–112

——, 'The Scribe of Rawlinson Poetry 137 and the Copying and Circulation of *Piers Plowman*', *Yearbook of Langland Studies*, 19 (2005), 3–26

——, 'The Scribes of the Vernon Manuscript', in *The Making of the Vernon Manuscript: The Production and Contexts of Oxford, Bodleian Library, MS Eng. poet. a. 1*, ed. by Wendy Scase, Texts and Transitions, 6 (Turnhout: Brepols, 2013), pp. 27–47

Horobin, Simon, and Daniel W. Mosser, 'Scribe D's SW Midlands Roots: A Reconsideration', *Neuphilologische Mitteilungen*, 106.3 (2005), 289–305

Horobin, Simon, and Linne R. Mooney, 'A *Piers Plowman* Manuscript by the Hengwrt/Ellesmere Scribe and Its Implications for London Standard English', *Studies in the Age of Chaucer*, 26 (2004), 65–112

Hovland, Stephanie R., 'Apprenticeship in Later Medieval London (*c.* 1300–*c.* 1530)' (unpublished doctoral dissertation, Royal Holloway, University of London, 2006)

Hudson, Anne, 'Epilogue: The Legacy of *Piers Plowman*', in *A Companion to 'Piers Plowman'*, ed. by John A. Alford (Berkeley: University of California Press, 1988), pp. 251–66

Hyde, Matthew, and Nikolaus Pevsner, *Cumbria: Cumberland, Westmorland and Furness* (1967; repr. New Haven: Yale University Press, 2010)

James, Montague Rhodes, *The Western Manuscripts in the Library of Trinity College, Cambridge: A Descriptive Catalogue*, 4 vols (Cambridge: Cambridge University Press, 1900–1904)

James-Maddocks, Holly, 'The Peripatetic Activity of Thomas Tresswell, London Stationer (*fl. c.* 1440–1470)', in *Manuscripts in the Making: Art & Science*, ed. by Stella Panayotova and Paola Ricciardi, 2 vols (London: Harvey Miller, 2018), I, pp. 109–23

Johnston, Michael, 'The Clerical Career of William Rokele', *Yearbook of Langland Studies*, 33 (2019), 112–25

——, 'Copying and Reading *The Prick of Conscience* in Late Medieval England', *Speculum*, 95.3 (2020), 742–801

——, 'The Household and Literary Production in England, 1350–1500', in *The Elite Household in England, 1100–1550*, ed. by C. M. Woolgar (Donington: Shaun Tyas, 2018), pp. 93–109

——, *The Middle English Book: Scribes and Readers, 1350–1500* (Oxford: Oxford University Press, 2023)

Justice, Steven, *Writing and Rebellion: England in 1381*, The New Historicism, 27 (Berkeley: University of California Press, 1994)

Kane, George, 'Introduction', *Piers Plowman: The A Version. Will's Visions of Piers Plowman, Do-well, Do-better and Dobest*, rev. edn (London: Athlone, 1988), pp. 1–172

——, 'The "Z Version" of *Piers Plowman*', *Speculum*, 60 (1985), 910–30

Kane, George, and E. Talbot Donaldson, 'Introduction', *Piers Plowman: The B Version. Will's Visions of Piers Plowman, Do-well, Do-better and Dobest*, rev. edn (London: Athlone, 1988), pp. 1–220

Kaufmann, Martin, 'Decoration and Illustration', in *The European Book in the Twelfth Century*, ed. by Erik Kwakkel and Rodney Thomson (Cambridge: Cambridge University Press, 2018), pp. 43–67

Keen, Maurice, *English Society in the Later Middle Ages, 1348–1500*, The Penguin Social History of Britain (London: Penguin Books, 1990)

Ker, N. R., *Medieval Manuscripts in British Libraries*, 4 vols (Oxford: Clarendon Press, 1969–1992)

Kerby-Fulton, Kathryn, *Books under Suspicion: Censorship and Tolerance of Revelatory Writing in Late Medieval England* (Notre Dame: University of Notre Dame Press, 2006)

——, *The Clerical Proletariat and the Resurgence of Medieval English Poetry* (Philadelphia: University of Pennsylvania Press, 2021)

——, 'Confronting the Scribe-Poet Binary: The Z Text, Writing Office Redaction, and the Oxford Reading Circles', in *New Directions in Medieval Manuscript Studies and Reading Practices: Essays in Honor of Derek Pearsall*, ed. by Kathryn Kerby-Fulton, John J. Thompson and Sarah Baechle (Notre Dame, IN: University of Notre Dame Press, 2014), pp. 489–515

——, 'Langland and the Bibliographic Ego', in *Written Work: Langland, Labor and Authorship*, ed. by Steven Justice and Kathryn Kerby-Fulton (Philadelphia: University of Pennsylvania Press, 1997), pp. 67–143

——, 'Professional Readers of Langland at Home and Abroad: New Directions in the Political and Bureaucratic Codicology of *Piers Plowman*', in *New Directions in Later Medieval Manuscript Studies: Essays from the 1998 Harvard Conference*, ed. by Derek Pearsall (Woodbridge: York Medieval, 2000), pp. 103–29

——, 'The Women Readers in Langland's Earliest Audience: Some Codicological Evidence', in *Learning and Literacy in Medieval England and Abroad*, ed. by Sarah Rees Jones, Utrecht Studies in Medieval Literacy, 3 (Turnhout: Brepols, 2003), pp. 121–34

Kerby-Fulton, Kathryn, and Denise L. Despres, *Iconography and the Professional Reader: The Politics of Book Production in the Douce 'Piers Plowman'*, Medieval Cultures, 15 (Minneapolis: University of Minnesota Press, 1999)

Kerby-Fulton, Kathryn, Maidie Hilmo, and Linda Olson, *Opening up Middle English Manuscripts: Literary and Visual Approaches* (Ithaca, NY: Cornell University Press, 2012)

Kerby-Fulton, Kathryn, and Steven Justice, 'Langlandian Reading Circles and the Civil Service in London and Dublin, 1380–1427', *New Medieval Literatures*, 1 (1997), 59–83

Kittel, Thomas, 'A History of Contact between *Piers Plowman* and *The Prick of Conscience*' (unpublished doctoral dissertation, University of Oxford, 2020)

Knapp, Ethan, 'Towards a Material Allegory: Allegory and Urban Space in Hoccleve, Langland, and Gower', *Exemplaria*, 27.1–2 (2015), 93–109

Lawler, Traugott, 'The Secular Clergy in *Piers Plowman*', *Yearbook of Langland Studies*, 16 (2002), 85–113

Lewis, Robert E., and Angus McIntosh, *A Descriptive Guide to the Manuscripts of The 'Prick of Conscience'*, Medium Ævum Monographs, n.s. 12 (Oxford: Society for the Study of Mediæval Languages and Literature, 1982)

A Linguistic Atlas of Late Mediaeval English, ed. by Angus McIntosh, M. L. Samuels, and Michael Benskin, 4 vols (Aberdeen: Aberdeen University Press, 1986)

Lyall, R. J., 'Materials: The Paper Revolution', in *Book Production and Publishing in Britain, 1375–1475*, ed. by Jeremy Griffiths and Derek Pearsall (Cambridge: Cambridge University Press), pp. 11–29

Lysons, Daniel, 'Marylebone', in *The Environs of London: Volume 3, County of Middlesex* (London: T. Jun. and W. Davies, 1795), pp. 242–79

Madrinkian, Michael, 'Producing *Piers Plowman* to 1475: Author, Scribe and Reader' (unpublished doctoral dissertation, University of Oxford, 2016)

Manly, John M., and Edith Rickert, eds, *The Text of 'The Canterbury Tales': Studies on the Basis of All Known Manuscripts*, 8 vols (Chicago: University of Chicago Press, 1940)

Manuscripts of the West Midlands: A Catalogue of Vernacular Manuscript Books of the English West Midlands, c. 1300–c. 1475 <https://www.dhi.ac.uk/mwm/> [accessed 16 Aug. 2023]

Michael, M. A., 'Oxford, Cambridge and London: Towards a Theory for "Grouping" Gothic Manuscripts', *Burlington Magazine*, 130.1019 (1988), 107–15

Middleton, Anne, 'The Audience and Public of *Piers Plowman*', in *Middle English Alliterative Poetry and Its Literary Background*, ed. by David A. Lawton (Woodbridge: Boydell and Brewer, 1982), pp. 101–23

Mooney, Linne R., 'Chaucer's Scribe', *Speculum*, 81.1 (2006), 97–138

——, 'Locating Scribal Activity in Late Medieval London', in *Design and Distribution of Late Medieval Manuscripts in England*, ed. by Margaret Connolly and Linne R. Mooney (Woodbridge: York Medieval, 2008), pp. 183–204

Mooney, Linne R., and Estelle Stubbs, *Scribes and the City: London Guildhall Clerks and the Dissemination of Middle English Literature, 1375–1425* (Woodbridge: York Medieval, 2013)

Nicholson, Joseph, and Richard Burn, *The History and Antiquities of the Counties of Westmorland and Cumberland*, 2 volumes (London: W. Strahan, 1777)

Noorthouck, John, 'Book 2, Ch. 15: Cheap Ward', in Noorthouck, *A New History of London Including Westminster and Southwark* (London: R. Baldwin, 1773), pp. 587–93

O'Neill, Rosemary, 'Counting Sheep in the C Text of *Piers Plowman*', *Yearbook of Langland Studies*, 29 (2015), 89–116

Parkes, Malcolm B., 'The Literacy of the Laity', in Malcolm B. Parkes, *Scribes, Scripts and Readers: Studies in the Communication, Dissemination and Presentation of Medieval Texts* (London: Hambledon, 1991), pp. 275–97

——, 'The Provision of Books', in *History of the University of Oxford: Volume II: Late Medieval Oxford*, ed. by J. I. Catto and T. A. R. Evans (Oxford: Oxford University Press, 1992), pp. 407–83

Pates, Stella, '*Piers Plowman* Trinity College: Dublin 212 — The Annals Revisited', *Notes and Queries*, 59 (2009), 336–40

Pearsall, Derek, 'Manuscript Illustration of Late Middle English Literary Texts, with Special Reference to the Illustrations of *Piers Plowman* Bodleian Library MS Douce 104', in *Suche Werkis to Werche: Essays on 'Piers Plowman' in Honor of David C. Fowler*, ed. by Míċeál F. Vaughan (East Lansing: Colleagues, 1993), pp. 191–210

——, 'Langland's London', in *Written Work: Langland, Labor and Authorship*, ed. by Steven Justice and Kathryn Kerby-Fulton (Philadelphia: University of Pennsylvania Press, 1997), pp. 185–207

——, 'Introduction', in *Piers Plowman: A Facsimile of Bodleian Library, Oxford, MS Douce 104* (Cambridge: Brewer, 1992), pp. ix–xxv

——, 'Introduction', in *Studies in the Vernon Manuscript*, ed. by Derek Pearsall (Cambridge: Brewer, 1990), pp. ix–xi

Pearson, David, *English Bookbinding Styles, 1450–1800: A Handbook* (New Castle, DE: Oak Knoll, 2014)

Perry, Ryan, 'The Clopton Manuscript and the Beauchamp Affinity: Patronage and Reception Issues in a West Midlands Reading Community', in *Essays in Manuscript Geography: Vernacular Manuscripts of the English West Midlands from the Conquest to the Sixteenth Century*, ed. by Wendy Scase (Turnhout: Brepols, 2007), pp. 131–59

Phillips, Noëlle, 'Compilational Reading: Richard Osbarn and Huntington Library MS HM 114', *Yearbook of Langland Studies*, 28 (2014), 64–104

Pigg, Daniel F., 'Life on the Manor and in Rural Space: Answering the Challenges of Social Decay in William Langland's *Piers Plowman*', in *Rural Space in the Middle Ages and Early Modern Age: The Spatial Turn in Premodern Studies*, ed. by Albrecht Classen (Berlin: de Gruyter, 2012), pp. 351–66

Pollard, Graham, 'The University and the Book Trade in Mediaeval Oxford', in *Beiträge zum Berufsbewusstsein des mittelalterlichen Menschen*, ed. by Paul Wilpert (Berlin: de Gruyter, 1964), pp. 336–44

Poos, L. R., *A Rural Society after the Black Death: Essex 1350–1525*, Cambridge Studies in Population, Economy and Society in Past Time, 18 (Cambridge: Cambridge University Press, 1991)

Poos, L. R., and Martha Dana Rust, 'Of *Piers*, Polltaxes and Parliament: Articulating Status and Occupation in Late Medieval England', *Fragments*, 5 (2016), 96–127

Pouzet, Jean-Pascal, 'Quelques aspects de l'influence des chanoines augustins sur la production et la transmission littéraire vernaculaire en Angleterre (XIIIe–XVe siècles)', *Comptes rendus des séances de l'Académie des Inscriptions et Belles-Lettres*, 148 (2004), 169–213

Prescott, Andrew, 'Administrative Records and the Scribal Achievement of Medieval England', *English Manuscript Studies, 1100–1700*, 17 (2012), 173–99

Pugh, T. B., 'The Magnates, Knights, and Gentry', in *Fifteenth Century England 1399–1509: Studies in Politics and Society*, ed. by S. B. Chrimes, C. D. Ross, and R. A. Griffiths (Manchester: Manchester University Press, 1972), pp. 86–128

Quinn, J., 'Earlier Owners of the Vernon Manuscript', *Bodleian Library Record*, 4 (1952–1953), 133–137

Rentz, Ellen, 'Half-acre Bylaws: Harvest Sharing in Piers Plowman', *Yearbook of Langland Studies*, 25 (2011), 95–115

Rhodes, William, 'Medieval Political Ecology: Labour and Agency on the Half Acre', *Yearbook of Langland Studies*, 28 (2014), 105–36

Roberts, Jane, 'On Giving Scribe B a Name and a Clutch of London Manuscripts from *c*. 1400', *Medium Ævum*, 80.2 (2007), 247–70

Robinson, P. R., 'The Vernon Manuscript as a "Coucher Book"', in *Studies in the Vernon Manuscript*, ed. by Derek Pearsall (Cambridge: Brewer, 1990), pp. 15–28

Russell, Josiah Cox, *British Medieval Population* (Alburquerque: University of New Mexico Press, 1948)

Samuels, M. L., 'Dialect and Grammar', in *A Companion to 'Piers Plowman'*, ed. by John Alford (Berkeley: University of California Press, 1989), pp. 201–21

——, 'Langland's Dialect', *Medium Ævum*, 54 (1985), 232–47

Sandler, Lucy Freeman, *A Survey of Manuscripts Illuminated in the British Isles, vol. 5: Gothic Manuscripts, 1285–1385*, ed. by J. J. G. Alexander, 2 vols (London: Harvey Miller, 1986)

Saul, Nigel, *Knights and Esquires: The Gloucestershire Gentry in the Fourteenth Century* (Oxford: Clarendon Press, 1981)

Scase, Wendy, 'The Artists of the Vernon Initials', in *The Making of the Vernon Manuscript: The Production and Contexts of Oxford, Bodleian Library, MS Eng. poet. a. 1*, ed. by Wendy Scase, Texts and Transitions, 6 (Turnhout: Brepols, 2013), pp. 207–26

——, 'The Patronage of the Vernon Manuscript', in *The Making of the Vernon Manuscript: The Production and Contexts of Oxford, Bodleian Library, MS Eng. poet. a. 1*, ed. by Wendy Scase, Texts and Transitions, 6 (Turnhout: Brepols, 2013), pp. 269–93

Schmidt, A. V. C., *The Clerkly Maker: Langland's Poetic Art*, Piers Plowman Studies, 4 (Cambridge: Brewer, 1987)

Scott, Kathleen, 'The Illustrations of *Piers Plowman* in Bodleian Library MS. Douce 104', *Yearbook of Langland Studies*, 4 (1990), 1–86

——, *A Survey of Manuscripts Illuminated in the British Isles, vol. 6: Later Gothic Manuscripts, 1390–1490*, 2 vols (London: Harvey Miller, 1996)

———, 'Lydgate's "Lives of St Edmund and Fremund": A Newly-Located Manuscript in Arundel Castle', *Viator*, 13 (1982), 335–66

Scott-Fleming, Sonia, *The Analysis of Pen Flourishing in Thirteenth-Century Manuscripts*, Litterae Textuales: A Series on Manuscripts and Their Texts, ed. by J. P. Gumbert, M. J. M. de Haan, and A. Gruys (Leiden: Brill, 1989)

Simpson, James, '"After Craftes Conseil clotheth yow and fede": Langland and London City Politics', in *England in the Fourteenth Century: Proceedings of the 1991 Harlaxton Symposium*, ed. by N. Rogers, Harlaxton Medieval Studies, 3 (Stamford: Watkins, 1993), pp. 109–27

Smith, Jeremy J., 'Mapping the Language of the Vernon Manuscript', in *The Making of the Vernon Manuscript: The Production and Contexts of Oxford, Bodleian Library, MS Eng. poet. a. 1*, ed. by Wendy Scase, Texts and Transitions, 6 (Turnhout: Brepols, 2013), pp. 49–70

———, 'Studies in the Language of Some Manuscripts of Gower's *Confessio amantis*', 2 vols (unpublished doctoral dissertation, University of Glasgow, 1985)

Sobecki, Sebastian, 'Communities of Practice: Thomas Hoccleve, London Clerks, and Literary Production', *Journal of the Early Book Society*, 24 (2021), 51–106

———, 'The Handwriting of Fifteenth-Century Privy Seal and Council Clerks', *Review of English Studies*, 72.304 (2020), 253–79

———, *Last Words: The Public Self and the Social Author in Late Medieval England*, Oxford Textual Perspectives (Oxford: Oxford University Press, 2019)

Stenroos, Merja, and Kjetil V. Thengs, 'The Geography of Middle English Documentary Texts', in *Records of Real People: Linguistic Variation in Middle English Local Documents*, ed. by Merja Stenroos and Kjetil V. Thengs, Advances in Historical Sociolinguistics, 11 (Amsterdam: John Benjamins, 2020), pp. 69–92

Stockdale, James, *Annales Caermoelenses, or Annals of Cartmel* (Ulverston: William Kitchin, 1872)

Taylor, Sean, 'The F Scribe and the R Manuscript of *Piers Plowman B*', *English Studies*, 77 (1996), 530–48

Thomson, Rodney M., *The Bury Bible* (Woodbridge: Boydell and Brewer, 2008)

Truelove, Alison, 'Literacy', in *Gentry Culture in Late-Medieval England*, ed. by Raluca Radulescu and Alison Truelove (Manchester: Manchester University Press, 2005), pp. 84–99

Turville-Petre, Thorlac, *The Alliterative Revival* (Cambridge: Brewer, 1977)

———, 'Putting it Right: The Corrections of Huntington Library MS. HM 128 and BL Additional MS. 35287', *Yearbook of Langland Studies*, 16 (2002), 41–65

———, 'The Relationship of the Vernon and Clopton Manuscripts', in *Studies in the Vernon Manuscript*, ed. by Derek Pearsall (Cambridge: Brewer, 1990), pp. 29–44

———, 'Sir Adrian Fortescue and His Copy of *Piers Plowman*', *Yearbook of Langland Studies*, 14 (2000), 29–48

Uhart, Marie-Claire, 'The Early Reception of *Piers Plowman*' (unpublished doctoral dissertation, University of Leicester, 1986)

Warner, Lawrence, *Chaucer's Scribes: London Textual Production, 1384–1432* (Cambridge: Cambridge University Press, 2018)

———, *The Myth of 'Piers Plowman': Constructing a Medieval Literary Archive* (Cambridge: Cambridge University Press, 2014)

———, 'An Overlooked *Piers Plowman* Excerpt and the Oral Circulation of Non-Reformist Prophecy, c. 1520–55', *Yearbook of Langland Studies*, 21 (2007), 119–43

Watson, Nicholas, '*Piers Plowman*, Pastoral Theology, and Spiritual Perfectionism: Hawkyn's Cloak and Patience's Pater Noster', *Yearbook of Langland Studies*, 21 (2007), 83–118

Whittle, Jane, 'Population Mobility in Rural Norfolk among Landholders and Others *c.* 1440–*c.* 1600', in *The Self-Contained Village? The Social History of Rural Communities, 1250–1900*, ed. by Christopher Dyer, Explorations in Local and Regional History, 2 (Hartfield: University of Hertfordshire Press, 2007), pp. 28–45

Willetts, Pamela J., *Catalogue of Manuscripts in the Society of Antiquaries in London* (Woodbridge: Brewer, 2000)

Wittig, Joseph S., '"Culture Wars" and the Persona in *Piers Plowman*', *Yearbook of Langland Studies*, 15 (2001), 167–95

Wood, Robert A., 'A Fourteenth-Century London Owner of *Piers Plowman*', *Medium Ævum*, 53 (1984), 83–90

Wood, Sarah, *'Piers Plowman' and Its Manuscript Tradition*, York Manuscript and Early Print Studies 5 (Woodbridge: Boydell and Brewer, 2022)

———, 'Two Annotated *Piers Plowman* Manuscripts from London and the Early Reception of the B and C Versions', *Chaucer Review*, 52.3 (2017), 274–97

THOMAS CABLE AND
NORIKO INOUE

Langland's Rhythm and the Clock in the Brain

▼ **ABSTRACT** The traditional methods of philology and historical linguistics have served well to reveal the metrical patterns of older poetry. In particular, we have gained a fuller understanding of Middle English alliterative metre, including that of *Piers Plowman*, during the past forty years. Investigators have been careful to avoid subjective impressions of rhythm, using instead objective categories such as parts of speech. However, this discussion of the sound of the poetry cannot be complete without consideration of the perceiving consciousness. We show how the many experiments of phonetics labs establishing norms of perception, prediction, and entrainment fit with our subjective impressions.

▼ **KEYWORDS** metre, rhythm, beat, eurhythmy, entrainment, *Piers Plowman*, *Gawain*-poet, embodiment of rhythm, pre-caesural beat, internal clock

In a major study of the alliterative tradition, Judith Jefferson and Ad Putter introduce their chapter 4, 'Sentence Stress and Beat in Alliterative Metre', with a conundrum that we will invoke for our own introduction: 'A fundamental problem that bedevils the study of alliterative metre concerns

Thomas Cable (tcable@utexas.edu) is Jane Weinert Blumberg Chair Emeritus in English at the University of Texas at Austin.

Noriko Inoue (n-inoue@kansai-u.ac.jp) is Professor in the Faculty of Foreign Language Studies at Kansai University in Osaka, Japan.

the number of beats in the alliterative long line. In over a century of modern scholarship, views on the subject have varied considerably'.[1] Among the scholars named who have worked on this problem are Karl Luick, Marie Borroff, Joan Turville-Petre, and '[m]ore recently', Hoyt Duggan and Thomas Cable. Most of the critique by Jefferson and Putter in chapter 4 focuses on the last two scholars, Duggan and Cable.

We are persuaded that their criticisms are right. There is 'an underlying assumption' that Jefferson and Putter find 'seriously flawed', the assumption that morphological class is an adequate determination of patterns of stress. ('Open-class' words such as nouns and adjectives are stressed. 'Closed-class' words such as prepositions and articles are unstressed.) We agree that '[t]he crude dichotomy between "stressed" and "unstressed" words misses the point that some "unstressed words" are more "unstressed" than others'.[2] Furthermore, we agree with their assertion, again with reference to Duggan and Cable, that 'lexical category is, in our view, an unreliable indicator of "sentence stress" (or "accent"), i.e., the stress given to words in connected speech'.[3]

We might note in passing that Duggan and Cable, who worked independently in the early 1980s without knowledge of the other, were using the crude tools at hand to hack through a largely unmapped field.[4] Between the two investigators, some 12,000 lines were copied (at first on index cards, then directly into a computer) and every syllable metrically notated. These were taken in various proportions from *Cleanness*, the *Wars of Alexander*, *Sir Gawain and the Green Knight*, the *Parliament of the Three Ages*, *Morte Arthure*, *Piers Plowman*, *Alexander A*, and other poems. Since then, brilliant refinements have been made by a number of scholars, including, of course, Putter, Jefferson, and their coauthor Myra Stokes.[5] However, we would like to move on to the more interesting matter of sentence accent and its relationship to the rhythmical beat. Jefferson and Putter have done an admirable job of bringing two scholarly groups into contact: medievalists from departments of English and phonologists from departments of linguistics. A primary goal of this essay is to argue for bringing more specialists into contact with English metre, especially cognitive scientists and music theorists.

---

1 Putter, Jefferson, and Stokes, *Studies in the Metre*, p. 145. Putter, Jefferson, and Stokes's preface allocates the division of labour in the individual chapters among the three authors.
2 Putter, Jefferson, and Stokes, *Studies in the Metre*, p. 149 n. 22.
3 Putter, Jefferson, and Stokes, *Studies in the Metre*, p. 147.
4 Duggan, 'Shape of the Alliterative Long Line', Duggan, 'Shape of the B-Verse', Cable, 'Unperceived Strictness', and Cable, *English Alliterative Tradition*.
5 See also Yakovlev, 'Development of Alliterative Metre'; Weiskott, *English Alliterative Verse* and Weiskott, *Meter and Modernity*; Cornelius, *Reconstructing Alliterative Verse*; and Russom, *Evolution of Verse Structure*.

With the aim in mind of widening our scope of inquiry, we will not revisit the detailed debate over the number of beats in an a-verse.[6] The evidence and arguments have become increasingly subtle and sophisticated over the years. As Ian Cornelius put it, his argument is dense, 'but that density reflects the complexity of the Middle English alliterative a-verse'.[7] Indeed, his excellent analysis requires several readings. We have to acknowledge some of the same difficulty in rereading our own analyses of the subject.

In this essay we will go in the opposite direction. We will step back and ask, 'What is the point of all these morphological lists?' 'What does *rhythm* mean, and where is the rhythm of the poem?' We will try to show that the spacings between beats that we hear are not just a modern predilection. Rather they seem to be grounded in human anatomy and physiology. They match fairly directly with experiments showing entrainment to external stimuli at an optimum perceptual periodicity of about 600 milliseconds. As far as we can determine, there is no corresponding natural match to the most extreme intervals allowed by Jefferson and Putter on the basis of alliteration, or to the shorter intervals of many 'extended' (or 'crowded') a-verses as read by Nicolay Yakovlev, Eric Weiskott, and Cornelius. At the same time, all of these scholars are sensitive readers of poetry, and we assume that they find their own readings more natural than the ones we have proposed.

We acknowledge that rhythmical correspondence between experiments in the phonetics lab and a way of reading a line of fourteenth-century poetry does not decide the contentious issues, especially how many beats are in a line of verse and where they are located. Rather, it points the way toward further investigations. In the lab, the stimuli for entrainment have been beeps, musical passages, and short sentences of ordinary speech in familiar modern languages, which may or may not be periodic. Poetry of any kind has almost never been tested.[8]

Metre and Rhythm

In all this, it is important to emphasize the distinction between metre and rhythm. The terms seem both familiar and uncertain because of their variant usages, going back to Bede in eighth-century England and much further in classical commentary. However, the definitions that we presume to offer will make it instantly clear whether a topic under discussion belongs to one or the other.

---

6 For the most recent summary and critique, see Inoue, 'Eurhythmic Dips'.
7 Cornelius, *Reconstructing Alliterative Verse*, p. 115.
8 An exception is Shattuck-Hufnagel and Turk, 'Durational Evidence'.

Metre will always refer to the prescribed patterns of syllables in a line of verse: their number, their linguistic prominence, and where appropriate their length and quality (for example, whether reduced or full). *Rhythm* will always refer to the instantiation of these syllabic patterns in the body — the body of the composer, the performer, the listener, or the silent reader — through 'the clock in the brain'.[9] By this definition, nearly all prosodic studies of Middle English alliterative verse during the past two centuries, including our own, have dealt with metre. Few that we know of deal seriously with rhythm. As should be clear from our previous remarks, Jefferson and Putter's critique points us in the right direction.

The usual procedure is to start with metre and aim for rhythm afterwards if at all. Metre is more accessible and more tangible to analyse, though it is fair to say that rhythm is more accessible and more tangible intuitively. The study of metre — metrics — requires the whole panoply of linguistic categories: the parts of speech and their presumed stress, syllable count, phrasal structure, syllable quantity, syllable quality, and where relevant the grouping of syllables into metrical feet. Not all of these categories are obvious in their details for fourteenth-century English verse. Some require a separate study: for example, syllable count if some syllables are possibly silent, as is famously the question for the reduction and loss of final *-e*.

Rhythm, by contrast — the beat — as noted, is more intuitive but also more difficult to analyse. The difficulty is partly because different people have different abilities in perceiving the beat, and partly because the beat is not intrinsically in the language but in the body. This point may seem to verge on the phenomenological, or the mystical, in contrast with assumptions in the analysis of metre. As Jessica A. Grahn and J. Devin McAuley put it:

> Rhythm is fundamental to auditory communication and arguably all social interaction [...] An important element in the perception of most rhythms is the sense of a periodic pulse or "beat" [...] When people listen to music, for example, it is evident that they are sensitive to the beat by the way they readily clap, tap their feet, or generally move their body in time with the rhythm.[10]

In contrast with clapping hands and tapping feet, metrical analysis of Middle English verse typically uses the familiar methods of historical

---

9 This concept is a central one in cognitive science studies of the past two decades when the focus is on the phonetics of speech and motor timing, especially with the help of MRI technology: for example, Allman and others, 'Properties of the Internal Clock', and Teki, Grube, and Griffiths, 'Unified Model'.
10 Grahn and McAuley, 'Neural Bases', p. 1894. See also Large and Palmer, 'Perceiving Temporal Regularity', p. 2, and Grahn and Brett, 'Rhythm and Beat Perception', p. 803.

linguistics: scanning thousands of lines and collating them to reveal patterns of non-occurrence, co-occurrence, and contrasting occurrence in various positions. Exhausted and satisfied by the metrical discoveries that these methods lead to, metrists seldom get to the hand clapping and foot tapping of rhythm. In the past, the coauthors of this essay have used the discovery procedures of historical scansion and all its tools with gusto, and we, like nearly all other metrists, have fallen short in not engaging the principles of rhythm in an explicit way. Borroff and Turville-Petre have gone some distance in this direction. Noriko Inoue and Stokes have come close in their assumptions, evidence, and conclusions regarding beats before the caesura and in other positions.[11] However, the workings of 'the internal clock' and the way its beats align with the beats of alliterative poetry can be made more explicit, drawing on research in cognitive science of the past two decades.

By centring the present study on rhythm and the brain, we are mainly focusing on a way of reading fourteenth-century alliterative poetry. For the moment, we will glance at metre only to state two generalizations, then turn to rhythm in some detail before returning to the specifics behind the metrical generalizations at the end. This back-and-forth has an element of circularity.

The generalizations are easy to state and at this point in the ongoing study of Middle English alliterative verse, fairly obvious: (1) the first half-line is generally longer and looser than the second half-line; and (2) the second half-line is not only shorter and tighter, but it also requires a set of metrical patterns than can be considered a signature for concluding the long line.

Eurhythmy: The Placing and Spacing of Beats

Speculations on eurhythmy in Modern English are suggestive of the choices before us. Bruce Hayes writes: 'Phrasal stress rules typically conspire to achieve a particular rhythmic target. In general terms, the rules tend to create output configurations in which stresses are spaced not too closely and not too far apart. A grid having these properties is said to be **eurhythmic;** one can also speak of **degrees** of eurhythmy' (boldface in original).[12] Hayes continues to describe the original conception of eurhythmy developed by Mark Liberman and Alan Prince within metrical phonology as the avoidance of *stress clash*.[13] However, he refers to reasons

---

11 Borroff, 'Sir Gawain and the Green Knight'; Turville-Petre, 'Metre of *Sir Gawain and the Green Knight*'; and Inoue and Stokes, 'Caesura and the Rhythmic Shape'.
12 Hayes, *Metrical Stress Theory*, p. 372.
13 Liberman and Prince, 'On Stress'.

why this conception is inadequate and says: 'What seems to work better is a kind of gradient principle: adjacent stresses are strongly avoided; stresses that are close but not adjacent are less strictly avoided; and at a certain distance (perhaps four syllables) the spacing becomes fully acceptable. Beyond the ideal distance we find that stresses are too far apart, so that rhythmic phonology tends to interpolate stresses to fill the gap'.[14]

The following line from *Piers Plowman* can be considered eurhythmic for these reasons:[15]

    x x / x x /   / x   x / x
    For a cat of a court   cam whan hym liked.

(B.Prol.149)

The x's and /'s in the notation are familiar ways of representing phonological accent. Other standard notations include columns of x's for relative stress, as in 'metrical phonology' since the 1970s. In attributing scansions to individual scholars, we will try to use their own notation. To show our assignment of 'beats' and 'offbeats', we will borrow a system from Derek Attridge: 'B' represents a 'beat'; 'o' an unstressed 'offbeat'; 'O' a stressed offbeat; '(o)' an implied offbeat, sometimes called a 'metrical pause'; and slight changes in the notation indicate other patterns.[16] When phonological accent and rhythmical beats coincide, the two systems will be exactly equivalent:

    x x / x x /   / x   x / x
    For a cat of a court   cam whan hym liked.
    o o B o o B   B o   o B o

In contrast with this eurhythmic verse, the following verse from *Sir Gawain and the Green Knight* can be considered 'dysrhythmic' (both phonologically and metrically) if read in the following unbalanced way in accord with the alliteration, as Jefferson and Putter would do:

---

14 Hayes, *Metrical Stress Theory*, p. 372.
15 The current coauthors are not textual editors, and we depend on the division of labour between editors and prosodists. We recognize the need for a stable text. Some of the verses we have used for illustration may eventually need to be replaced by other verses if there is a textual problem.
16 Attridge, *Rhythms of English Poetry*.

```
x / x / x x x x x      x x   /   / x
A hoge haþel for þe nonez   and of hyghe eldee.
```
                                              (*Gawain* 844)

From a cursory glance and a normal reading of the Middle English, one's impression might be that the prescribed scansion is lopsided and front-heavy, both visually and aurally, with a sag of seven unstressed syllables in the middle. By our theory, notation showing beats for this reading would be inaccurate and misleading; therefore, we will not use B and o.

A reading that would approach the *Sir Gawain and the Green Knight* line in terms of eurhythmy would require a simple shift of the presumed rhythmical beat from *hoge* at the beginning of the a-verse to the non-alliterating word *nonez* at the end. The first syllable of *hoge* receives a degree of linguistic stress but not a metrical beat — no tapping of a finger. Here, because the verse is eurhythmical, it is appropriate to use the notation of beats and offbeats:[17]

```
o O o B o o   o B o      o  o B (o) B o
A hoge haþel for þe nonez   and of hyghe eldee.
```

We have, then, two readings: one without a beat before the caesura, the other with a beat; one that is not eurhythmic, the other that is. It is also important to note that one reading has strict conformity between the alliteration and the beat (the non-eurhythmic one); the other reading has a disjunction between alliteration and beat (the eurhythmic one). We imagine that Jefferson and Putter would reject our non-eurhythmic characterization of the reading that adheres to alliteration (a rejection perhaps more intellectual than intuitive). This essay will try to show that judgements of rhythm are deeply embodied and are not simply the result of variable personal preference.

Studies by Inoue and by Inoue and Stokes have provided evidence that theories that reject the second reading, with beats spaced as they are despite alliteration, fall into complications and inconsistencies. Much of the present essay is complementary to these earlier arguments. In addition to rejecting theories that seem to us faulty, we will argue that the theory

---

17 The 'O' on *hoge* is equivalent to Borroff's 'minor chief syllable'. See Borroff, '*Sir Gawain and the Green Knight*', p. 193.

proposed here has positive support from a range of linguistic studies, including the lengthening of syllables at a phrasal break.

Hayes's impression of the ideal spacing in Modern English (four unstressed syllables between stressed syllables) can be compared with Inoue's empirically derived 'Spacing Rule' for Middle English verse: 'The long dip between the two a-verse stresses or what Joan Turville-Petre calls the "standard" rhythm seems, in the crowded a-verse, to serve as a *rhythmic marker* to signal on which words metrical stress falls'.[18] Both Turville-Petre and Inoue posit a standard rhythm, two unstressed syllables, which is shorter than Hayes's ideal of four unstressed syllables. In fact, Inoue and Stokes present evidence that four unstressed syllables in the b-verse are unmetrical and that four unstressed syllables in the a-verse are grammatically constrained.[19] The explanation for different conceptions of eurhythmy is the obvious difference between the casual speech that Hayes analyses and the tighter, more formal, periodic framework of poetry.

Phonological Accents and Rhythmical Beats

As noted at the beginning, one of the main debates in Middle English alliterative metrics during the past century has been whether the long line invariably has four metrical stresses (which we call 'beats'), or whether a significant minority of lines contain five. More precisely, the question almost always lodges in the first half-line (the a-verse): whether the a-verse always has two beats, or occasionally three (or even four). An example would be the extended or crowded verse *Piers Plowman* B.Prol.16a, as read and scanned two ways:

```
    x   / x  /  x  x   / x
With depe diches and derke    and dredfulle of siʒte

    x   x x /  x x    / x
With depe diches and derke    and dredfulle of siʒte.
                                        (B.Prol.16)
```

In previous studies Inoue has argued for the second reading, using familiar methods of co-occurrence and non-occurrence of diagnostic

---

18 Inoue, 'New Theory', p. 110, referring to Turville-Petre, 'Metre of *Sir Gawain and the Green Knight*'.
19 See also Inoue, '"Extra-Long" Dip'.

patterns. These methods will be supplemented below by summaries of studies of the clock in the brain.

We acknowledge that accent has a crucial place in English verse but not to the extent of a one-to-one correspondence of ordinary linguistic accent and rhythmical beat. Rather, there are certain places where the accent establishes the beat and certain places where it would contradict the beat. We propose that the establishment of the beat happens early on in any passage, and its perception in the body involves specific anatomical structures that we will simply note, without going into detail, as having been identified in multiple experiments.[20] Once the periodicity of the beat is established, the phrases of language that are matched with it do not have to have a beat on every accented syllable. The reverse is also true: a beat can occur on an unaccented syllable in Middle English alliterative verse, as it can in Middle and Modern English iambic pentameter. Both of these contexts involve subtle questions that open onto large implications for the typology of metres.

On these matters more has been done in music than in poetry, and we will be drawing on ideas in music research, such as this from Edward W. Large and Caroline Palmer:

> Beats are perceived pulses that mark equally spaced (subjectively isochronous) points in time, either in the form of sounded events or hypothetical (unsounded) time points. Beat perception is established by the presence of musical events; however, once a sense of beat has been established, it may continue in the mind of the listener even if the event train temporarily comes into conflict with the pulse series, or after the event train ceases (Cooper & Meyer, 1960). This point is an important motivator for our theoretical approach; once established, beat perception must be able to continue in the presence of stimulus conflict or in the absence of stimulus input.[21]

For one of the main questions before us, the disjunction between alliteration and beat, it is interesting that the problematic pattern generally does not occur at the beginning of the poem until the opening lines establish the regular pattern. Thus, in *Patience* it is not until verse 12a *Sunderlupes, for hit dissert*, that the beat occurs on the non-alliterating third syllable of *Sunderlupes*. In *Cleanness* the first disjunction happens at 23a *Kryst kydde hit Hymself*, with beats on *kydde* and *-self*. In *Sir Gawain and the Green Knight* it is at 21a *Bolde bredden þerinne*, with beats on *bred-* and *-in-*. And in *Piers Plowman* B.Prol.11a *Thanne gan [me] to meten*, the beats are on

---

20 Especially the basal ganglia and the supplementary motor areas of the cerebrum, although other structures of the brain interact. See Teki and others, 'Distinct Neural Substrates'. See also the references above, n. 10.
21 Large and Palmer, 'Perceiving Temporal Regularity', p. 3.

gan and *met-*. In all these instances, the poet showcases to the listener the major rhythmic sets he is going to use in his poem. Once he does this, he becomes more playful with his metre.

On a larger scale, the sonata form of classical music provides an analogy. Its musical structure consists of three main sections: an exposition, a development, and a recapitulation. The exposition presents the primary thematic material for the movement, which is developed in the next phase.

Within Middle English alliterative metrics, various theories focus on one or another phonological or grammatical category. Putter and Jefferson focus on alliteration and on several rules of rhythm in ordinary speech. In contrast, Inoue argues in her dissertation and in a series of articles, including coauthored articles with Stokes, for rhythmical considerations over considerations of alliteration. Several of those arguments trace the complications and inconsistencies into which a theory devolves if it adheres to the pattern of alliteration, in this case the theory of Putter and Jefferson, but also elsewhere in detail, Duggan's theory. Note that Inoue's scansion of *Sir Gawain and the Green Knight* 844a subordinates the first stressed word, *hoge*, an adjective that happens to alliterate, to the following noun, which also alliterates:

o O o B o o o B o
A hoge haþel for þe nonez.

Now consider the reading by Inoue of the following verse, which at first sight may seem to show an inconsistency in the reading just illustrated:

o B o o o B o O
So bisied him his ȝonge blod.

(*Gawain* 89a)

A critic might say: 'Aha! You subordinated the adjective to the noun in *hoge haþel* but the noun to the adjective in *ȝonge blod* in order to fit your theory of rhythm. You are inconsistent in reading adjective plus noun combinations.' Our response is, 'That's exactly the point. The rhythmic beat in different parts of the line may fall on different categories of syllables, regardless of their grammatical classification.' There has been progress in the ongoing discussion over the past thirty-five years (and before that in Borroff's work) in making a distinction between phrasal accent and rhythmical beat. We share many (but not all) of the assumptions of W. K.

Wimsatt, who wrote: 'It is not quite as if we had ironclad linguistic rules of stress, so that if we try to write a meter which does not quite illustrate these rules we might as well write scientific prose and call it meter'.[22]

Our approach does not invoke changes of meaning (or semantic emphasis or grammatical category or alliteration). Our point of reference is the clock in the brain. Once the beat is established, we can predict subsequent beats approximately every 600 milliseconds, regardless of the overlay of language on the internal ticking. The ticking is persistent. The language stretches and shrinks to fit the ticking. Our argument is that there has been a fundamental confusion of cause and effect. The language does not *cause* the ticking (though at the outset it is crucial in identifying it). The language is *shaped by* the ticking. This is our main thesis, as the rest of this essay tries to demonstrate through examples from *Piers Plowman* and *Sir Gawain and the Green Knight* with reference to the relevant cerebral structures for timing.

This approach builds on traditional ways of doing historical phonology and metrics. A method used throughout Inoue's studies is the detailed examination of closely related syntactic and lexical doublets, specifically those differing in syllable count, for example: *on molde / upon molde, to* + infinitive / *for to* + infinitive, *lufly/luflyche* for adverbs and adjectives. By tracing the occurrence and non-occurrence of each item in the pair and asking, 'Why this choice?', inferences about deliberate strategies for metrical structure can be drawn. To these arguments we will add insights from phonology and phonetics on the marking of phrasal units approximately the size of those that occur in Middle English alliterative verse.

Another feature of the theory of Inoue and Stokes can be seen in their divergence from Putter and Jefferson. Both theories limit the number of beats in the a-verse to two; however, as we saw above in *Sir Gawain and the Green Knight* 844a, there are verses in which Inoue and Stokes allow a beat on a non-alliterating syllable at the expense of an alliterating one. Putter and Jefferson assign a-verse beats invariably to alliterating syllables:

x / x / x x x x x
A hoge haþel for þe nonez.

In scansions adhering strictly to beats only on alliterating syllables in the a-verse, *Gawain* 844a has a third dip of five offbeats. In Putter and Jefferson's terminology, a dip of four or more syllables is an 'extra-long dip', and it figures significantly in their theory as a kind of compensation

---

22 Wimsatt, 'Rule and the Norm', p. 785.

when the rest of the a-verse lacks a 'long dip' (two or more unstressed syllables). By our view, dips that are apparently extra-long are rhythmically problematic, and our usual procedure is to break them up with a beat in the middle, or reduce the number of syllables by elision. We are not aiming for strict isochrony but for patterns that can be perceived as slight extensions of the standard two-syllable dip and can be accommodated without disruption of the rhythm. In this we are close to Borroff's approach, even if some of our specific readings diverge. She remarks on 'the operation of the tendency toward isochrony' and concludes her perceptive discussion with an impression we endorse: 'Thus, though the temporal intervals among the chief syllables remain unequal [...] an effect of rhythmical regularity is produced'.[23]

Dips that could possibly be considered extra-long are not very numerous in Middle English verse by any reading. Our fullest compilation is from the poems of the *Gawain*-poet, although extensive samplings indicate that *Piers Plowman* is similar. By our reading, extra-long dips of four, five, or six syllables are rare, between six and seven per cent of the standard a-verses (those with only two possible beat positions) in three poems by the *Gawain*-poet: *Sir Gawain and the Green Knight*, *Cleanness*, and *Patience*. Many of the ones in *Gawain*, in particular, can be reinterpreted as having two long dips (of two or three syllables apiece) instead of one extra-long dip. Although the poets did occasionally write an a-verse with a four-syllable dip, a dip of four syllables is the maximum length. The majority of a-verses with a regular interval rhythm could absorb the occasional instances of a four-syllable dip, and we are able to maintain the perceptually isochronous tapping of fingers, two to the verse, four to the long line, as described earlier in this section by Large and Palmer for tapping the beat in music on 'perceived pulses that mark equally spaced (subjectively isochronous) points in time'. By this way of thinking about it, the idea of compensation by an extra-long dip seems to move in the opposite direction from what is required for perceiving, maintaining, and predicting a regular beat.

To be specific, in *Sir Gawain and the Green Knight*, if one assumes the invariable coincidence between alliteration and beat, a five- or six-syllable dip occurs in thirty-five a-verses (1.73 per cent: thirty-five out of 2025 lines excluding bob-and-wheels). Out of thirty-five, ten instances have an extra-long initial dip, and the other twenty-five have an extra-long medial dip. In all thirty-five instances, a dip of five or six syllables can always be reduced to a dip of two, three, or four syllables by various ways. Typically, an extra-long dip involves a verb + simple adverb combination such as *kneled down* and *boȝez forth*. The following a-verses, for instance, would

---

23 Borroff, '*Sir Gawain and the Green Knight*', p. 192. On perceptual isochrony, see also Lehiste, 'Isochrony Reconsidered'.

be regarded by Putter and Jefferson as having an extra-long dip of five unstressed syllables:

/ x x x x x /
Kneled doun bifore þe kyng

(*Gawain* 368a)

/ x x   x   x x   /
Boȝez forth, quen he watz boun.

(*Gawain* 1311a)

However, we treat a verb + simple adverb as forming one sense unit (like an adjective + noun combination), in which the simple adverb can take a beat.[24]

O o B   o o o B
Kneled doun bifore þe kyng

O o B   o   o o   B
Boȝez forth, quen he watz boun.

Therefore, these two verses and other similar a-verses can be reinterpreted as having two dips of the standard two or three unstressed syllables at the initial and the medial positions.

Similar problems occur in *Piers Plowman* if one assumes the invariable coincidence of alliteration and metrical stress; for example:

/ x x x x /
Wenten forth in hire wey.

(B.Prol.48a)

And the solution is the same. We shift the first metrical stress from the verb to the non-alliterating adverb, and eurhythmy is maintained:

---

24 See Inoue, 'A-Verse of the Alliterative Long Line', pp. 100–03.

```
    O  o  B  o  o   B
Wenten forþ in hire wey.
```

Thus, apparent instances of the a-verses that Putter and Jefferson scan with an extra-long dip can often be reinterpreted as having two long dips of two or three unstressed syllables.

After eliminating such apparent instances, in *Gawain* just around one hundred instances of a four-syllable dip with or without another long dip occur in the a-verses, whether these a-verses include two, three, or even four possible beat positions, accounting for around five per cent of 2025 lines. In other words, roughly ninety-five per cent of the a-verses in *Gawain* have the standard rhythm, consisting of dips of two (or three) unstressed syllables.[25]

For Middle English alliterative metre, we agree with Putter and Jefferson that not all open-class words receive a beat, especially in crowded verses. Inoue shows the obverse to be true, that closed-class words can receive a beat.[26] This controlled flexibility — this double escape from rigidity — is essential to the craft of the past seven centuries of poetry in the English language. The clearest and most succinct statement of the effect of metre that we know was made by Wimsatt in his commentary on the generative prosody of Morris Halle and Samuel Jay Keyser. The following four sentences by Wimsatt could serve as the guiding principle for any investigation of English metre. It captures the Modern English iambic pentameter eloquently. Less obviously it captures Middle English alliterative metre in ways that need to be made more precise with regards to rhythm in the terms we have been discussing:

> For it is a fairly prevalent view, and I think a correct one, that the metrical pattern is not quite a mere result of linguistic arrangements, a mere inert epiphenomenon. The meter establishes a certain expectancy; it exerts a certain kind of coercion and performs a certain kind of self-assistance. It has assimilative powers. A quiet 'promotion' of certain weaker syllables (as Arnold Stein has put it) and a partial 'suppression' (or demotion) of certain stronger ones would appear

---

[25] Putter and Jefferson explicitly set crowded a-verses aside. If their a-verse rules are to be applied to the crowded a-verse with three or more possible beat positions, substantially more a-verses would have a medial or final dip that would be extra-long and, sometimes, heavy, because the resulting extra-long dip would contain a word with linguistic or phrasal stress, which is a candidate for a beat, as in *Gawain* 844a *A hoge haþel for þe nonez*, discussed above.

[26] Inoue, 'A-Verse of the Alliterative Long Line', pp. 58–68. See also Cornelius, *Reconstructing Alliterative Verse*, pp. 9–13.

to take place in much of our reading — and according to plausible enough norms.[27]

Our only quarrel with this is their use of 'promotion' and 'suppression'. We assume that the 'strength' of each word (the 'accent') must be determined individually within the context of the sentence.

Here we will make some simple assertions of metrical typology, which we have argued at length elsewhere. Old English metre is basically a syllabic metre, in which each position is filled by a syllable or syllable-equivalent, with the allowed variation of one string of unstressed syllables in each half-line. (The very use of 'unstressed syllables' implies that 'stressed syllables' figure into it. Elements of accentual metre and of quantitative metre are part of the amalgam of Old English metre.) Middle English alliterative metre is basically a strong-stress metre with four eurhythmically spaced beats usually on accented syllables in each line, two to the half-line. The iambic pentameter of Middle English and Modern English is basically an alternating metre, in which stressed syllables are important but not determinative, a crucial fact in providing the aesthetic quality of tension and avoiding doggerel. Competent iambic pentameter is replete with beats that have little linguistic stress and offbeats that have considerable stress. The craft is in their placement.

The implications of this differentiation between Old and Middle English alliterative metre are of an order the coauthors are only now beginning to appreciate. They contrast with Weiskott's 'durable alliterative tradition' and with assertions and philological methods of our own earlier selves.[28]

Wimsatt's statement of a 'quiet "promotion" of certain weaker syllables [...] and a partial "suppression" (or demotion) of certain stronger ones' (with iambic pentameter especially in mind) puts the dynamics of the Middle English alliterative line in an interesting light. To this point, we have seen a handful of lines from *Sir Gawain and the Green Knight* and *Piers Plowman* that we would read with an offbeat on certain stronger syllables and which amount to four to eight per cent of the a-verses in the *Gawain* poet.[29]

In summary, in Middle English alliterative verse it is rhythmically natural to make adjustments when normal phonology is in tension with the metrical template. Implicit in all this is our assumption that in well-formed lines of stichic metres, there is a fixed and invariable number of beats per line. (There is, of course, prescribed variation of beats in specific and recurring places, such as the alexandrine that concludes the Spenserian

---

[27] Wimsatt, 'Rule and the Norm', p. 785.
[28] Weiskott, *English Alliterative Verse*, and Weiskott, '*Piers Plowman*'.
[29] See Inoue, 'A-Verse of the Alliterative Long Line', pp. 250–51.

stanza, or the 4–3–4–3 alternation of the ballad stanza.) The segmentation of discourse into units of variable beat-count is a feature of prose, not verse. This is the universal that seems reasonable as a working hypothesis.[30]

We turn now to recent research that by our understanding shows a grounding of the production and perception of rhythm in the anatomy and physiology of the human body.

The Internal Clock

An obvious charge that might be levelled against our statements of eurhythmy, balance, dysrhythmy, awkwardness of spacing, pleasantness of spacing, and so on, going back to Inoue's dissertation, is that these are impressions of the modern reader. One could plausibly claim that the expectations of the fourteenth-century reader, author, or hearer might have been different. We do not have a treatise from the period discussing patterns that were pleasing or displeasing. We do not even have a treatise stating the basic rules of metre and rhythm from which divergent interpretations might be made (hence the activity of prosodists of the past two centuries). How can we presume to impose our preferred readings on fourteenth-century verse?

A compelling answer is that the anatomy and physiology of the human body have clearly not evolved to something different since the fourteenth century. The scale of evolution is unimaginably vaster. If William Langland, Geoffrey Chaucer, or any of their scribes were to appear for an MRI scan at a lab in modern-day London, we can assume that the range of results showing entrainment to spaced beats would be about the same as what the lab usually sees.[31] That's not to say the results would be the same for everyone, because there are variations even now. For example, those with musical training may identify the beat more readily, although as Grahn and James B. Rowe note, 'whether musically trained or not, beat perception occurs spontaneously in most people without great effort'.[32]

What do we know about perceiving a beat? First, it is crucial to understand that the perception of time by humans can be divided into two large categories: whether the interval recurs regularly, in which case we say it is rhythmic and use the terms *beat* and *entrainment* (the internal synchronization to a stimulus), or whether it is an isolated interval that is not a part of a recurring rhythm. The analogy for the first is often

---

30 For the predominance of traditions of lines of verse with a fixed number of 'strong' or 'ictus' positions, see Gasparov, *History of European Versification*.
31 For groundbreaking work in the application of cognitive science to Middle English poetics, see Myklebust, 'Misreading English Meter'.
32 Grahn and Rowe, 'Feeling the Beat', p. 7547.

a metronome, for the second a stopwatch or an hourglass.[33] These are referred to as 'beat-based' and 'duration-based' perceptions, respectively.[34] The mind can process both, though it is usually more accurate in perceiving and predicting rhythmic beats after entrainment occurs.

How long are beat intervals? It turns out that a normal reading tempo and our understanding of human perception in evolutionary terms are interestingly in sync. As Grahn and McAuley summarize experiments using audible beeps (not poetry): 'Beat sensitivity is thought to be maximal around 600 m[illi]s[econds].'[35] It takes only an Apple watch to record a walk along a road at about one hundred steps per minute. If the person walking can recite a poem without danger of being struck by a car, the pace of the walk will fit well with the tempo of the poem. Whether the text is a sonnet by Shakespeare or lines from the Prologue of *Piers Plowman*, each footstep will tend to strike the pavement on a beat. (Although this may seem counterintuitive for the two metres, we will explain below.) There will also usually be two or three footsteps at the end of each line, lest the lines be run together and rushed, without a natural pause. The tempo can be said to be *andante* 'at a walking pace'. At one hundred steps per minute, which is a normal average for the coauthors of this essay, the footfalls and the metrical beats will occur every 600 milliseconds within the line (with two or three extra steps at line's end), the period of maximal sensitivity.[36] Whether there are steps between the two half-lines of Middle English alliterative verse at the caesura is a question we haven't yet answered.

We also have not answered the prior question of whether all this information about the timing of steps has anything to do with the perception of beats in a line of verse. The cautious statement to make at this point in the progress of research (our understanding of the progress of research) is that there is a correlation in the structures of the brain that enable the perception and production of audible beats and those that enable bodily movement, such as finger-tapping, foot-tapping, or walking.

---

33 McAuley and Jones, 'Modeling Effects', p. 1102.
34 See, for example, Teki, Grube, and Griffiths, 'Unified Model'.
35 Grahn and McAuley, 'Neural Bases', p. 1900. Cf. London, *Hearing in Time*, p. 31: 'a range of pulse perception from 200 to 1800 m[illi]s[econds], with a pronounced peak of *maximal pulse salience* around 600 m[illi]s[econds] (100 B[eats]P[er]M[inute])' (emphasis in original). See also Patel, *Music, Language, and the Brain*, p. 100, for 500–700 m[illi]s[econds].
36 Recent walks of two to three miles by one of the authors have these values for steps per minute: 105, 99, 104, 105, 102, 99, 106, 100. See also Borroff, '*Sir Gawain and the Green Knight*', p. 271 n. 3: 'My own recitation of the four lines quoted above from *Gawain* averages roughly about 100 chief syllables [beats] per minute; at an average pace of below 85, the lines seem to drag and at an average pace of over 115, they seem hurried'.

Four Beats, the Elastic Phrase, and the Durational Marking of Boundaries

Let us now return to the two generalizations with which this essay began and see how in the light of subsequent discussion they pose problems and also suggest solutions: (1) the first half-line is generally longer and looser than the second half-line; and (2) the second half-line is not only shorter and tighter, but it also requires a set of metrical patterns that can be considered a signature for concluding the long line. Now we have a problem with simple arithmetic. If the timing of the four beats is constant throughout a line of alliterative verse, but the second half-line has fewer syllables than the first half-line, how do the two half-lines match up their syllables with the beats? Dani Byrd and Elliot Saltzman introduce a suggestive concept into the study of conversational speech, 'the elastic phrase'. Their theory happens to be close to the ideas proposed by Inoue and Stokes of prominence and slowing at a syntactic or intonational boundary, especially the caesura (and by extension the end of the line). Byrd and Saltzman write:

> This modulation of the 'clock-rate' that controls the temporal unfolding of an utterance near junctures is such that the clock slows increasingly as the boundary is approached and speeds up again as the boundary recedes. Viewing phrase boundaries as warping the temporal fabric of an utterance represents a promising confluence of the field of prosody and of speech dynamics.[37]

Their focus is on the temporal constraints in the articulation of phonetic segments (vowels, consonants, etc.), but as they indicate, there is a confluence with the higher abstraction of prosody, which is our focus. They are not alone in seeing a hierarchical structure to the topics we are investigating, patterns nested within patterns at different levels.

They are also not alone in investigating the slowing and prominence at boundaries. It has been a flourishing topic in phonetic research of the present century. In her exhaustive survey of this topic, Janet Fletcher presents a succinct summary: 'There is little controversy these days that preboundary lengthening can be interpreted as a major perceptual cue to levels of linguistic structure in many languages along with other juncture-marking phenomena including intonational features'.[38]

Similarly, Inoue and Stokes have in mind preboundary lengthening as a perceptual cue in Middle English alliterative verse: 'It is indeed plainly critical to a proper appreciation of the alliterative line that one should know where the caesura falls. The phrasal or syntactic boundary it

---

37 Byrd and Saltzman, 'Elastic Phrase', p. 149.
38 Fletcher, 'Prosody of Speech', p. 542.

coincides with is often quite a minor one. But in most cases the second alliterative beat of the a-verse falls indisputably on the word after which the caesura falls and thus serves to announce it'.[39]

If the elastic phrase can be seen to stretch over fewer syllables in the b-verse and also to lengthen a syllable before the caesura so that it receives the prominence of a beat, it would seem that the opposite would be true of the beginning and middle of the a-verse, especially the crowded a-verses. Our conclusion is that the expected result of a faster pronunciation of syllables in a-verse patterns does not have a clear parallel in experiments in Modern English because the normal speech (of any period) does not replicate the patterns of metred poetry, including the unique conditions of Middle English metre.

To hold in mind what to expect in the b-verse, our own studies over the years have argued for a pattern somewhat like this:

```
o   o   B   o   o   o   B         o   o   B (o) B o
And he granted and hym gafe       with a goud wylle.
```
(Sir Gawain and the Green Knight 1861)

The four beats of the two half-lines are approximately, or perceptually, isochronous, though the first verse has eight syllables and the second only five. There is a temporal interval, an implied offbeat, between the two beats of the b-verse. This pattern was arrived at through considerations quite different from the ones elaborated here, but the results are compatible, and mutually supportive.[40]

It is as though the elastic phrase is stretched thin in the first part of the a-verse but then loosened for prolongation in the syllable before the caesura and in the b-verse. One might perceive a speeding up of the unstressed syllables in the beginning and middle of the a-verse, yet, as we have acknowledged, modern experimental evidence does not support this idea. Why? Our conclusion is that the metre of Middle English alliterative verse is designed to be periodic, but the normal speech of Modern English is not.[41] If there is no periodicity, no external timekeeper, in ordinary conversation, then the length of a phrase might well increase linearly with

---

39 Inoue and Stokes, 'Caesura and the Rhythmic Shape', p. 2.
40 See Cable, 'Clashing Stress', pp. 19–20.
41 There have been many studies in response to the idea of English as a stress-timed language. See, for example, Dauer, 'Stress-Timing and Syllable-Timing Reanalyzed', and Lehiste, 'Isochrony Reconsidered'.

extra syllables. On this point, which is controversial, we are persuaded by Alice Turk and Stefanie Shattuck-Hufnagel.[42]

After all, crowding syllables into an interval exerts a cost. A useful comparison is with the iambic pentameter of Modern English, which, like Middle English alliterative metre and all other metres in English that we know, is designed to be periodic. The usual periodicity is an even alternation between single-syllable beats and single-syllable offbeats, although double offbeats occur frequently, especially in the 'inverted first foot' or 'trochaic substitution' at the beginning of the line:

```
B  o  o  B   o b o   B  o  B
Now is the winter of our discontent.
```

In a chapter entitled 'Lines with Extra Syllables', in *Shakespeare's Metrical Art*, George T. Wright illustrates many places in the iambic pentameter where an extra syllable causes a double offbeat (our terminology taken from Attridge, though analyses using feet or some other system would show the same result): 'feminine endings', 'epic caesuras', 'double onsets', and so on:[43]

```
o o  B  o B   o   B   o b   o  B   o
Not a word, a word, we stand upon our manners.
```
(Winter's Tale 4.4.164)

It is interesting that throughout this chapter, Wright comments on the slightly disruptive effect of the double offbeats in production and perception:

> In all cases, the line with such an extra syllable changes the procedures a little, ruffles the current, modifies the pattern.

and

> Shakespeare not only pursues elision and syncopation as far as he can, but he evidently means us to slur phrases, drop (or almost drop)

---

42 Turk and Shattuck-Hufnagel, *Speech Timing*, pp. 145 and 255.
43 Wright, *Shakespeare's Metrical Art*, p. 170.

unstressed final syllables of words or phrases, or say several syllables so quickly that they sound like fewer than they are.[44]

In noting Wright's impressions of slurring, ruffling, hurrying, eliding, and so on, we do not intend to suggest that Middle English alliterative verse is even more rushed than Shakespeare's expanded lines. The point is that iambic pentameter has a disyllabic base — one offbeat, one beat, repeated five times — and expansion to a double offbeat requires accommodation. If the base of Middle English alliterative verse is a double offbeat (the standard rhythm proposed by Turville-Petre), then expansion to three or four offbeats requires a similar accommodation.

There is no need to require a rhetorical or semantic reason for the expansion (though rhetoric and semantics often fit). It is simply part of the music of a line with four beats and a varying number of offbeats (though with specifications for certain patterns in certain parts of the line). Prosodic analysis through clusters of examples and tables of statistics, which both coauthors have used, can have a deadening and misleading effect. We recommend reading long passages aloud and tapping the fingers, perhaps beginning with the Harley lyrics, then on to *Sir Gawain and the Green Knight*, and finally to *Piers Plowman*. A kind of verbal music should lodge in the mind, and the occurrence of the next beat should be easy to predict. Grahn describes 'the internal generation of the beat'.[45] In fact, the relevant timing structures of the brain are most active when the external stimulus is weak and the beat comes from within the body.

Our conclusion is that Middle English alliterative verse has a periodicity, as do all other metres in English, but it is unlike any other metre in its specifics. There is a feature of Old English metre that is similar but more highly constrained. In modern iambic pentameter, two unstressed syllables can easily be accommodated, but when there are three, there is the possibility of the middle syllable rising to prominence, often producing a dipodic movement.

The Anatomy of the Internal Clock

Langland's brain and ours have the same structures for perceiving time and for perceiving rhythm, and nothing we can do will remove us from these bodily instantiations. The rhythm of metrical poetry is obviously different from the rhythm of ordinary speech. Is it possible that in certain modes of speech, namely metrical poetry, a timekeeper external to the phonology

---

44 Wright, *Shakespeare's Metrical Art*, pp. 160 and 172.
45 Grahn, 'Role of the Basal Ganglia', p. 35.

and phonetics of English causes the language to *adapt* to a certain rhythm in a particular context?

First it is necessary to acknowledge that our vivid metaphors of 'the external timekeeper', 'the internal clock', 'the clock in the brain', and so on, may oversimplify the situation by suggesting that there is a single structure in the brain that we might visualize as a small bedside clock, an Apple watch ticking away, or even a miniature orchestral conductor! Turk and Shattuck-Hufnagel survey and summarize a vast amount of research on the subject and conclude:

> it isn't the case that a single neural structure behaves as a neural 'clock' exclusively dedicated to timing, and nothing else ... [T]he basal ganglia, thalamus, cerebellum, and cortical structures are all involved in timing behavior, making it difficult to assign a timing role exclusively to one single structure ... [R]esearchers such as Merchant, Harrington, and Meck (2013) have suggested that these structures thus appear to be part of an interconnected, distributed timing network, in which different structures within the network can compensate for each other.[46]

It is beyond our scope and ability to sort out the physiology of these structures in the brain, a complex topic of recent and ongoing research, making full use of MRI technology. However, we can sketch hypotheses that future collaborative investigation might confirm or refute. One hypothesis worth testing is that both the long line of *Piers Plowman* and certain Harley lyrics depend on beat entrainment: they have different metres but similar rhythms.[47] We can call the *Piers Plowman* long-line metre accentual and the metre of the Harley lyrics by a choice of equivalent names: strict stress-metre, iambic-anapestic, logaoedic, dolnik, mixed metre, loose iambic.[48] A convenient mnemonic representation of this mixed metre could be 'o B o o B', which also happens to be a representation of the most common b-verse pattern in *Piers Plowman* up to the final schwa; furthermore, it contains the standard rhythm of the double offbeat. We are excited at the prospect of synthesizing traditional philology from the 1960s and 1970s (Borroff and Turville-Petre, especially) with extensions of traditional philology from the 1980s to the present and with cognitive science, hopefully to confirm the hypothesis that fourteenth-century alliterative poetry was entrained to a periodic, embodied beat.

---

46 Turk and Shattuck-Hufnagel, *Speech Timing*, p. 244. Cf. McAuley and others, 'Detecting Changes in Timing', p. 571: 'Part of the lack of consensus may also stem from the assumption that there is only a single timing mechanism. It seems more plausible to us that timing engages multiple mechanisms, which in some cases have redundant functions'.
47 See Cable, 'Foreign Influence'.
48 See Hanson, 'Resolution in Modern Meters', and Tarlinskaja, *Strict Stress-Meter*.

It is beyond the scope of the present essay to analyse the 'morphological metre' proposed by Yakovlev and applied and developed by Weiskott and Cornelius. The obvious point of comparison with our own theory would be the extent of match and mismatch between the structures of language by a particular reading and the structures of anatomy and the workings of physiology. The issue that especially crystallizes a comparison of readings was invoked at the beginning of this essay: the choice between two- and three-beat a-verses.

We have tried to show a high degree of conformity (about ninety-five per cent) between a way of reading and the intervals of the timekeeper in the brain. If an a-verse is read with three beats instead of two, we assume there will be fewer intervals of standard rhythm; there will definitely be more short intervals. (We have not worked through the statistics.) The task for readers of a-verses with three beats is first to say whether the rhythm of fourteenth-century alliterative poetry, unlike prose, is periodic; if so, then to show wherein the periodicity lies.

As for the intersection with cognitive science, Grahn and Brett summarized the situation in 2007: 'A role for the basal ganglia and SMAs [supplementary motor areas] in beat induction is consistent with their involvement in motor prediction (the spontaneous response to hearing a beat is often to move at the time when the next beat is predicted)'.[49] Melissa J. Allman and her coauthors see an understanding of the internal clock as a key to understanding consciousness itself: 'The quest for the internal clock (translating objective time into subjective time) and its neurological basis [...] is perhaps the elusive key to understanding consciousness in the mind and brain'.[50]

Understanding Middle English Alliterative Metre since the 1980s

For the more limited concerns of the specialist in Middle English alliterative metrics, a discouraging fact is that the various features of the metre are so technical and difficult that the non-specialist, whether a medievalist, a compiler of anthologies, or a writer of poetics handbooks, usually backs away from the details in search of a generalization. Unfortunately, the generalizations that have always been invoked for this subject do not simplify the metre but distort it, making it something other than what it is.

A clear example is the description in the editions of Norton anthologies over the years in the section of the introduction entitled 'Old and Middle English Prosody'. For Middle English alliterative verse, the only

---

49 Grahn and Brett, 'Rhythm and Perception', pp. 902–03.
50 Allman and others, 'Properties of the Internal Clock', p. 760.

rules given are for alliteration and the caesura (which in the example from *Piers Plowman* in modernized English happens to be misplaced, between a preposition and its object). For the rhythmic structure of the verse, the Norton account says only 'four principal stresses' to the line, adding, 'There is no rule determining the number of unstressed syllables'.[51] This description appears in most of the previous editions of the Norton, and it is completely misleading.

But we can mislead ourselves in the other direction, seeing the elegance of metrical rules as an end in itself. The coauthors of the present essay may have to plead guilty to this temptation in the past. But what is the point of these metrical schemes? What kind of psychological reality do these rules have? What is the point of casting language as poetry? Surely it is something different from the kind of intellectualization attendant on creating acrostics or palindromes. Surely it is to feel the rhythm, the beat, to clap the hands and snap the fingers — to become attuned to and yield to the clock in the brain. In these terms the need for collaboration among neighbouring scholarly fields is clear.

---

51 *Norton Anthology*, ed. by Abrams and others, p. 24.

Works Cited

Primary Sources

Langland, William, *Piers Plowman: A Parallel-Text Edition of the A, B, C and Z Versions*, ed. by A. V. C. Schmidt, 2 vols, 2nd edn (Kalamazoo: Medieval Institute, 2011)

Sir Gawain and the Green Knight, ed. by J. R. R. Tolkien and E. V. Gordon, 2nd edn, rev. by Norman Davis (Oxford: Clarendon Press, 1967)

Secondary Sources

Allman, Melissa J., Sundeep Teki, Timothy D. Griffiths, and Warren H. Meck, 'Properties of the Internal Clock: First- and Second-Order Principles of Subjective Time', *Annual Review of Psychology*, 65 (2014), 743–71

Attridge, Derek, *The Rhythms of English Poetry* (London: Longman, 1982)

Borroff, Marie, *'Sir Gawain and the Green Knight': A Stylistic and Metrical Study* (New Haven: Yale University Press, 1962)

Byrd, Dani, and Elliot Saltzman, 'The Elastic Phrase: Modeling the Dynamics of Boundary-Adjacent Lengthening', *Journal of Phonetics*, 31 (2003), 149–80

Cable, Thomas, 'Clashing Stress in the Metres of Old, Middle, and Renaissance English', in *English Historical Metrics*, ed. by C. B. McCully and J. J. Anderson (Cambridge: Cambridge University Press, 1996), pp. 7–29

——, *The English Alliterative Tradition* (Philadelphia: University of Pennsylvania Press, 1991)

——, 'Foreign Influence, Native Continuation, and Metrical Typology in Alliterative Lyrics', in *Approaches to the Metres of Alliterative Verse*, ed. by Judith Jefferson and Ad Putter (Leeds: School of English, 2009), pp. 219–34

——, 'The Unperceived Strictness of Strong-Stress Meter', paper presented at Modern Language Association meeting, Chicago, December 1985

Cornelius, Ian, *Reconstructing Alliterative Verse: The Pursuit of a Medieval Meter* (Cambridge: Cambridge University Press, 2017)

Dauer, R. M., 'Stress-Timing and Syllable-Timing Reanalyzed', *Journal of Phonetics*, 11 (1983), 51–62

Duggan, Hoyt N., 'The Shape of the Alliterative Long Line', paper presented at Modern Language Association meeting, Chicago, December 1985

——, 'The Shape of the B-Verse in Middle English Alliterative Poetry', *Speculum*, 61 (1986), 564–92

Fletcher, Janet, 'The Prosody of Speech: Timing and Rhythm', in *The Handbook of Phonetic Sciences*, ed. by William J. Hardcastle and others, 2nd edn (Malden, MA: Blackwell, 2010), pp. 523–602

Gasparov, M. L., and G. S. Smith, and Marina Tarlinskaja, trans., *A History of European Versification,* ed. by G. S. Smith with L. Holford-Strevens (Oxford: Clarendon Press, 1996)

Grahn, Jessica A., 'The Role of the Basal Ganglia in Beat Perception: Neuroimaging and Neuropsychological Investigations', *Annals of the New York Academy of Sciences,* 1169 (2009), 35–45

Grahn, Jessica A., and Matthew Brett, 'Rhythm and Beat Perception in Motor Areas of the Brain', *Journal of Cognitive Neuroscience,* 19 (2007), 893–906

Grahn, Jessica A., and J. Devin McAuley, 'Neural Bases of Individual Differences in Beat Perception', *NeuroImage,* 47 (2009), 1894–1903

Grahn, Jessica A., and James B. Rowe, 'Feeling the Beat: Premotor and Striatal Interactions in Musicians and Nonmusicians during Beat Perception', *Journal of Neuroscience,* 29 (2009), 7540–48

Hanson, Kristin, 'Resolution in Modern Meters' (unpublished doctoral dissertation, Stanford University, 1991)

Hayes, Bruce, *Metrical Stress Theory: Principles and Case Studies* (Chicago: University of Chicago Press, 1995)

Inoue, Noriko, 'The A-Verse of the Alliterative Long Line and the Metre of *Sir Gawain and the Green Knight*' (unpublished doctoral thesis, University of Bristol, 2002)

——, 'Eurhythmic Dips in Middle English Alliterative Verse', *Filologia Germanica,* 15 (2023)

——, 'The "Extra-Long" Dip in the Poems of the *Gawain* Poet', *Chaucer Review,* 58.2 (2023), 232–58

——, 'A New Theory of Alliterative A-Verses', *Yearbook of Langland Studies,* 18 (2004), 107–32

Inoue, Noriko, and Myra Stokes, 'The Caesura and the Rhythmic Shape of the A-Verse in the Poems of the Alliterative Revival', *Leeds Studies in English,* 40 (2009), 1–26

Large, Edward W., and Caroline Palmer, 'Perceiving Temporal Regularity in Music', *Cognitive Science,* 26 (2002), 1–37

Lehiste, Ilse, 'Isochrony Reconsidered', *Journal of Phonetics,* 5 (1977), 253–63

Liberman, Mark, and Alan Prince, 'On Stress and Linguistic Rhythm', *Linguistic Inquiry,* 8 (1977), 249–336

London, Justin, *Hearing in Time: Psychological Aspects of Musical Meter* (Oxford: Oxford University Press, 2004)

McAuley, J. Devin, Deborah Fraser, Kellie Janke, and Nathaniel S. Miller, 'Detecting Changes in Timing: Evidence for Two Modes of Listening', in *Proceedings of the 9th International Conference on Music Perception and Cognition* (Bologna: Bologna University Press, 2006), pp. 566–73

McAuley, J. Devin, and Mari Reiss Jones, 'Modeling Effects of Rhythmic Context on Perceived Duration: Comparison of Interval and Entrainment Approaches to Short-Interval Timing', *Journal of Experimental Timing,* 29 (2003), 1102–125

Myklebust, Nicholas, 'Misreading English Meter' (unpublished doctoral dissertation, University of Texas at Austin, 2012)

The Norton Anthology of English Literature, ed. by M. H. Abrams and others, 9th edn (New York: Norton, 2013)

Patel, Aniruddh D., *Music, Language, and the Brain* (Oxford: Oxford University Press, 2007)

Putter, Ad, Judith Jefferson, and Myra Stokes, *Studies in the Metre of Alliterative Verse* (Oxford: Society for the Study of Medieval Language and Literature, 2007)

Russom, Geoffrey, *The Evolution of Verse Structure in Old and Middle English Poetry: From the Earliest Alliterative Poetry to Iambic Pentameter* (Cambridge: Cambridge University Press, 2017)

Shattuck-Hufnagel, Stefanie, and Alice Turk, 'Durational Evidence for Word-Based vs. Prominence-Based Constituent Structure in Limerick Speech', in *Proceedings of the 17th International Congress of Phonetic Sciences* (Hong Kong: City University of Hong Kong, 2011), pp. 1806–09

Tarlinskaja, Marina, *Strict Stress-Meter in English Prosody: Compared with German and Russian* (Calgary: University of Calgary Press, 1993)

Teki, Sundeep, Manon Grube, and Timothy D. Griffiths, 'A Unified Model of Time Perception Accounts for Duration-Based and Beat-Based Timing Mechanisms', *Frontiers in Integrative Neuroscience*, 5 (2012), 1–7

Teki, Sundeep, Manon Grube, Sukhbinder Kumar, and Timothy D. Griffiths, 'Distinct Neural Substrates of Duration-Based and Beat-Based Auditory Timing', *Journal of Neuroscience*, 31 (2011), 3805–12

Turk, Alice, and Stefanie Shattuck-Hufnagel, *Speech Timing: Implications for Theories of Phonology, Phonetics, and Speech Motor Control* (Oxford: Oxford University Press, 2020)

Turville-Petre, Joan, 'The Metre of *Sir Gawain and the Green Knight*', *English Studies*, 57 (1976), 310–29

Weiskott, Eric, *English Alliterative Verse: Poetic Tradition and Literary History* (Cambridge: Cambridge University Press, 2016)

——, *Meter and Modernity in English Verse, 1350–1650* (Philadelphia: University of Pennsylvania Press, 2021)

——, '*Piers Plowman* and the Durable Alliterative Tradition', *Yearbook of Langland Studies*, 30 (2016), 123–73

Wimsatt, W. K., 'The Rule and the Norm: Halle and Keyser on Chaucer's Meter', *College English*, 31 (1970), 774–88

Wright, George T., *Shakespeare's Metrical Art* (Berkeley: University of California Press, 1988)

Yakovlev, Nicolay, 'The Development of Alliterative Metre from Old to Middle English' (unpublished doctoral thesis, University of Oxford, 2008)

PATRICK OUTHWAITE

The Commercialization of *lechecraft* in *Piers Plowman**

▼ **ABSTRACT** Different attitudes towards payment distinguish effective from ineffective healers in *Piers Plowman*. When *leches* approach healing with a charitable spirit, they typically succeed in curing their patients, whereas those that are overly concerned with making a profit invariably fail. *Piers Plowman* and associated texts, such as *Mum and the Sothsegger*, praise the virtues of those healers who resist professionalization and commercialization, performing *lechecraft* as one part of a greater charitable role. These tensions between commerce and charity are not merely literary issues but also reflect contemporary concerns surrounding efforts at regulating medicine and surgery in late medieval English cities. This article contends that texts of the *Piers Plowman* tradition add to an existing body of medical satire and serve as valuable sources in the social history of medicine, voicing concerns surrounding the commercialization of *lechecraft* in Langland's London.

---

* I wish to thank Michael Van Dussen, Stephen Yeager, the editors of *YLS*, and the two anonymous readers for their comments and insights. I am especially grateful to Katharine Breen for her patience and generosity in helping me to refine this essay. Finally, I thank the members of the IPPS *Piers Plowman* Reading Group.

Patrick Outhwaite is Assistant Professor of English Literature at the University of Groningen.

▼ **KEYWORDS** *Piers Plowman*, medicine, surgery, *lechecraft, Mum and the Sothsegger*, charity, commerce, London

In the sixth passus of the B text of *Piers Plowman*, Hunger declares: 'Ther are mo lieres than leches — Lord hem amende!' (B.6.272).[1] This exclamation is one of several criticisms that Hunger makes about the avaricious and exploitative nature of physicians. Physic, as described by Hunger, dresses extravagantly and rather than healing his vulnerable patients, seeks only to make a profit. Piers the Plowman is thankful for this warning: 'By Seint Poul [...] thise arn profitable wordes! / For this is a lovely lesson: Lord it thee foryelde!' (B.6.274–75). This 'lovely lesson' foreshadows subsequent episodes in which healers act against the interests of their patients.

Hunger's criticism of Physic is particularly topical because there were repeated attempts by craft guilds and companies, urban magistrates and, at one point, the crown to regulate healing in late medieval London.[2] In the late fourteenth century, the London companies of surgeons (founded c. 1368) and barbers (founded before 1308) frequently complained to the mayor and aldermen that unauthorized practitioners were treating patients.[3] Although the two companies were distinct, the surgeons and barbers introduced similar measures to control treatment and distinguish legitimate members from unsanctioned practitioners.[4] For instance, in 1369 the Fellowship of Surgeons obtained a court ordinance to examine all surgeons of the city and inspect their instruments. Similarly, in 1376 the Company of Barbers established that two masters be appointed yearly to inspect and regulate the craft. These measures were compounded in 1387 when further ordinances were made to ensure that all barbers made payments to the company each year, or else they would be charged with penalties or prohibited from practising within the city.[5] Nevertheless, the impetus for reform did not simply come from the companies themselves, but also urban magistrates and the crown.[6] The measures of London were replicated in urban centres across the country, such as Beverley, Norwich, and York. In York, the guild of barbers and surgeons fined practitioners

---

1 All quotations of the B text are from Langland, *Vision of Piers Plowman*, ed. by Schmidt.
2 For more, see Colson and Ralley, 'Medical Practice, Urban Politics'.
3 *Annals of the Barber-Surgeons of London*, ed. by Young, see especially pp. 35–40.
4 Since surgeons had more prestige than barbers, they were keen not to be treated analogously. Bullough, 'Training of the Nonuniversity-Educated Medical Practitioners'.
5 *Annals of the Barber-Surgeons of London*, ed. by Young, pp. 30–36.
6 Rawcliffe, 'A Crisis of Confidence?'.

for various offences, for example attending meetings without their gowns, speaking 'indecent words' or otherwise bringing scandal to the guild.[7]

Still, London was a special case, with an elite fellowship of surgeons and an even larger guild of barbers that had closer dealings with the citizenry than other cities.[8] The guild of surgeons of London exerted a relatively small influence in relation to the barbers, as the guild had roughly a dozen or so senior members throughout the fourteenth and early fifteenth centuries, and their patients typically came from the aristocracy and gentry. Barbers, on the other hand, were employed to treat large swathes of the population. Therefore, there was a clear distinction between the small body of elite master surgeons and the more common practitioners who were not comparable with what Michael McVaugh terms 'rational surgeons'.[9]

Of course, barbers and surgeons were not the only medical practitioners in late medieval London.[10] Physicians had a long history associated with their profession that gave them a standing above that of other healers.[11] They were trained at university medical faculties where they received theoretical and deontological training, which was fundamental in distinguishing their approach from the manual work of surgeons.[12] Further, while surgeons and barbers were limited to operating in the city of their guilds or companies, physicians had fewer restrictions.[13] Nevertheless, in England there was not a strong university medical faculty to produce physicians, as Oxford and Cambridge had limited facilities in comparison to continental institutions like Paris.[14] Throughout the entirety of the fourteenth century, Oxford had only three medical fellows (New College had two and Magdalen one), and it is estimated that the university produced a physician approximately once every five years.[15] Between 1300 and 1500,

---

7 *Guild Book of the Barbers and Surgeons of York*, ed. by Wragg, pp. 210–14.
8 Colson and Ralley, 'Medical Practice, Urban Politics'.
9 McVaugh, *Rational Surgery*, pp. 50–54; Jones, 'John of Arderne and the Mediterranean Tradition of Scholastic Surgery'.
10 This is not to give the impression that the duties of the surgeon and barber were the same. The barbers' guild recognized a difference in approach between those who practised barbery, including phlebotomy and dentistry, and those who practised surgery.
11 Bullough, 'Training of the Nonuniversity-Educated Medical Practitioners', p. 458.
12 Kudlien, 'Medicine as a "Liberal Art"'.
13 For instance, the fellowship of surgeons required surgeons from outside of London to pass a competency test and pay an entry fee before allowing them to practise within the city. See Theilmann, 'Regulation of Public Health', p. 207; Colson and Ralley, 'Medical Practice, Urban Politics', p. 1102.
14 See O'Boyle, *Art of Medicine*, especially pp. 116–27.
15 Vern L. Bullough states that by the second half of the fifteenth century, Cambridge granted fifty bachelors of medicine each year; see Bullough, 'Medieval Medical School at Cambridge', p. 164. Bullough has come under scrutiny for this claim, however, as the number seems too

ninety-four people are known to have obtained the degree of MB at Oxford and only fifty-nine at Cambridge.[16]

Throughout the period, university-trained physicians constituted a small body of elite practitioners who typically were employed by the households of aristocratic and noble patrons. Yet there were too few physicians to accommodate the wealthiest cross-section of society, let alone to keep up with the demands of an expansive urban marketplace. As a result of the minimal output of physicians from English universities, a patient was far more likely to encounter a barber than a physician in fourteenth-century London.[17] Further, the relatively conservative syllabus of English medical faculties, which focused on theory, was ill suited to the demands of the majority of patients. Most common men and women sought quick, cheap, and effective cures as opposed to protracted treatments that focused on lifestyle and regimens of health.[18] Many throughout England employed the services of those deemed unqualified to practice medicine, termed 'irregulars' by the college of physicians.[19]

Despite these clear divisions between surgeons, barbers, and physicians, Langland uses the term *leche* to denote all practitioners indiscriminately.[20] In *Piers Plowman*, *lechecraft* is a term that subsumes the distinctions between medicine and surgery. Physicians were tarred with the same brush as barbers and surgeons of being too focused on commercialization. As a result, we see a flattening of the different roles in an urban marketplace of healing where all types of *leches* compete for patients. This commercial attitude contrasts with the charitable mission of other healers, typically members of religious orders. Some friars, for example, practised medicine and surgery, yet they were not permitted to make a profit from their services, only to accept donations for their orders.[21] Nevertheless,

---

high when compared with the size of the Cambridge medical faculty; see Talbot, *Medicine in Medieval England*, p. 68.

16 Getz, 'Medical Education in England'; Rawcliffe, *Medicine and Society*, pp. 108–09.
17 For estimates as to the numbers of surgeons and barbers in England, see Butler, 'Portrait of a Surgeon', p. 246. Bryon Grigsby claims that there were twelve surgeons and nine physicians working in London in the 1420s in his 'Social Position of the Surgeon', p. 72.
18 Rawcliffe *Urban Bodies*, p. 293; Getz, *Medicine in the English Middle Ages*, pp. xxii–xxiv.
19 Pelling, *Medical Conflicts*, pp. 4, 10.
20 *MED*, s.v. 'leche'. At various points in *Piers Plowman*, Langland refers to 'Phisik' and 'surgien', yet their roles are not distinct. Friar Flatterer is even referred to as a 'phisicien and surgien', suggesting that he could perform both medicine and surgery. Of course, he proves in the end to be ineffective in both (see B.20.357–62). The reference to physicians and surgeons suggests that the author was aware of a distinction between the professional categories, but chose not to separate their duties in the text.
21 See Montford, *Health, Sickness, Medicine and the Friars*, pp. 90–93, 95–102. For instance, in the fourteenth century, the black friars of Edinburgh were licensed to practise surgery and medicine with the aim of adding emoluments to the income of their priory; see Moir Bryce, *Black Friars of Edinburgh*, pp. 26–27. This is not necessarily to say that all friars

contemporary anxieties surrounding medicine as a commercial practice bleed into Langland's antifraternal satire on ineffective spiritual healers. In *Piers Plowman*, friars always seek to charge for their services, which reflects a general lack of distinction between secular and religious healers in the text. Whether friars, graduates of medical faculties, or members of incorporated craft guilds and companies, those who perform *lechecraft* represent a commercial culture that has a reputation for exploitation and corruption.

Placed in direct contrast to these corrupt healers is Christ the Divine Physician, *Christus medicus*. Raymond St-Jacques has shown that the *Christus medicus* tradition pervades *Piers Plowman* — from Holy Church's speech in the first passus (especially B.1.204–07; C.1.199–204) to Conscience's call for a 'leche' in the Barn of Unity in the final passus (B.20.304–05; C.22.304–05). Christ is intended to be an exemplar for earthly practitioners to follow, and he is positioned in direct contrast to those who repeatedly fail to fulfil their duties to an acceptable standard.[22] Rosanne Gasse and Rebecca Krug have suggested that Christ-like healers, such as Piers the Plowman himself, are successful in their healing because they treat the soul as well as the body and recognize that bodily and spiritual health are connected. Those healers who neglect the soul and focus entirely on the body, by contrast, are typically presented as fraudsters.[23] Similarly, Julie Orlemanski has convincingly argued that Langland pushes the figural mutability of body and soul while simultaneously resisting it. At various points throughout the text, healers treat the body and soul as one, and in fact on several occasions the body becomes a metaphor for the soul. Yet at other points the soul is entirely neglected, as avaricious healers lack the required spiritual understanding to recognize the ways in which the flesh can stand in the way of spiritual health.[24]

---

treated patients without any form of personal payment. Eryk de Vedica, a Dutch friar of the Greyfriars of London, for instance, found himself in trouble in 1477 when he received 20s. from a patient who suffered 'soo grete a disease in her lymmes that a grete part of the fflessh of her legges was rotyn awey'. The patient's husband claimed that Eryk had not cured his wife's ailment but had still taken a payment. There is no indication that he had asked for the money, but rather that it was a donation given after five weeks of treatment. Nevertheless, the court ruled against Eryk because the patient's husband had not authorized the payment. See *Additional Material for the History of the Grey Friars*, ed. by Kingsford, pp. 147–49.

22 St-Jacques, 'Langland's *Christus medicus* Image'.
23 Furthermore, as Rosanne Gasse has stated, medicine in *Piers Plowman* should not simply be read as a 'metaphor for something else'. Interpretations of the medical passages that merely take spiritual and metaphysical implications into account miss out on a key aspect of Langland's commentary on the practice of medicine and its earthly practitioners. See Gasse, 'Practice of Medicine in *Piers Plowman*', as well as Krug, '*Piers Plowman* and the Secrets of Health'.
24 Orlemanski, 'Langland's Poetics of Animation', pp. 161–63.

On the surface, the medical and surgical treatments offered by Piers and other faithful healers do not fundamentally differ from those condemned by Hunger in passus 6 of the B text. In *Piers Plowman*, the Samaritan salves and wraps wounds (B.17.66–78; C.19.67–82), which is the same treatment used by the fraudulent Friar Flatterer in the Barn of Unity (B.20.363–80; C.22.362–79). In *Mum and the Sothsegger* — a text often associated with *Piers Plowman* due to similarities in structure, allegory, and theme[25] — *sothseggers* reject the complexity of *phisic* and its practitioners, instead using salves and bandages to heal the allegorical wounds of society, as well as the literal wounds inflicted by those who do not appreciate their honesty. While the Samaritan and *sothseggers* may have considered the soul as well as the body, their treatments do not explicitly cater to the spiritual any more than those of false healers. Both good and bad healers perform wound repair, yet the effectiveness of these treatments differs wildly depending on the intentions of the healer. In the words of Orlemanski, the 'language of medicine' is presented as both 'a similitude for spiritual care and as a dangerously materialist craft'.[26]

I argue that the difference between effective and ineffective practitioners in *Piers Plowman* lies in their attitudes towards payment. Payment does not automatically equal fraud in the text, and to suggest so would be to oversimplify the matter, yet healers are criticized when they seek an unjust price for their services.[27] Inherent in Langland's depiction of medical practitioners is what Mike Rodman Jones has termed an 'imaginative preoccupation' with London. At various points within the text, Langland appears to be suspicious of the commercial malpractice associated with specific urban trades. London tradesmen who pursue a commercial self-interest instead of serving the common good are depicted as agents of moral disruption.[28] This is not to suggest that Langland is entirely opposed to a merchant economy. David Aers and Robert Epstein have illustrated that Langland seems to endorse the just price in a market that is not manipulated.[29] Further, D. Vance Smith has asserted that *Piers Plowman* (especially the B text) is unexpectedly tolerant of some merchants and

---

25 For more on the relationship between *Mum and the Sothsegger* and *Piers Plowman*, see *Piers Plowman Tradition*, ed. by Barr, pp. 22–30.
26 Orlemanski, 'Langland's Poetics of Animation', p. 177.
27 John Alford, for instance, claims that healers are criticized in the text when they demand *pre manibus* payments before they provide healing; see Alford, 'Medicine in the Middle Ages', p. 393.
28 Rodman Jones, *Radical Pastoral*, pp. 14–16.
29 See Epstein, 'Summoning Hunger', p. 64; Aers, 'Justice and Wage-Labor after the Black Death', p. 179. Odd Langholm's analysis of confessional manuals shows that the criteria for a 'just price' depended on the situation and a notion of a common price determined by an aggregate of transactions; see Langholm, *Merchant in the Confessional*, pp. 245–47.

even sees their commercial activities as part of an economy of salvation.[30] What these scholars establish is that Langland does not necessarily praise or condemn a merchant economy, rather problems in *Piers Plowman* arise when an unfair price is demanded for goods or services.[31]

Still, *leches* were not merchants and thus physicians, barbers, surgeons, and members of religious orders had to tread a fine line between commerce and charity when they performed *lechecraft*. As Holy Church explains in passus 2 of the B text, he who claims Meed as his wife will lose 'a lappe of *Caritatis*' (B.2.35).[32] The issue of payment was always thorny for medieval practitioners. On the one hand, one of their most respected authorities, Galen, was often cited as stating that certain forms of medicine and surgery should be performed charitably and not for monetary gain.[33] Indeed, surgeons performed charitable acts. For example, Thomas Morstede (d. 1450), the master surgeon to Henry V, bestowed a munificent legacy of £100 to the poor of London.[34] Similarly, in the 1440s the royal physician John Somerset personally funded the establishment of an almshouse for the elderly and disabled sick poor in Brentford.[35] Such charitable works challenged popular stereotypes perpetuated in texts of medical satire about the greed of elite surgeons and physicians, and ensured that healing was not out of reach of all of those living in poverty.[36] On the other hand, craft guilds and companies sought to professionalize healing. Perhaps the key impetus for professionalization was to increase the credibility of barbers and surgeons in London by excluding unsanctioned competitors.[37] Navigating this path between a craft and Galen's notion of charity caused numerous conflicts in the regulation of *lechecraft*, as authorities reached different conclusions on the question of payment.[38] Medicine and surgery were constantly strained by a charitable desire

---

30 Smith, *Arts of Possession*, pp. 111–13.
31 Galloway, 'Economy of Need', pp. 313–15. Arvind Thomas notes a distinction in the text between payment given in advance of labour and the just wage for labour already completed in reference to 'mede' and 'mercede'; see Thomas, *Piers Plowman and the Reinvention of Church Law*, pp. 63–65.
32 For more on the charity of Holy Church and medicine, see Salisbury, *Narrating Medicine*, pp. 53–54.
33 See, for instance, *Quod optimus medicus* in *Claudii Galeni Oergameni scripta minora*, ed. by Marquardt, von Müller, and Helmreich, vol. II, pp. 3–4.
34 Beck, *Cutting Edge*, p. 95.
35 Rawcliffe, *Urban Bodies*, p. 302.
36 For more on medical satire, see Orlemanski, *Symptomatic Subjects*, pp. 79–112; Mann, *Chaucer and Medieval Estates Satire*, pp. 90–99.
37 The English surgeon John of Arderne expressed a typical sentiment in his *Treatises of Fistula in Ano* when he advised that a surgeon should always be conscious that a patient would be able to pay his fee before taking on a case. See John of Arderne, *Treatises of Fistula in Ano*, pp. 5–6.
38 Kudlien, 'Medicine as a "Liberal Art"'.

to heal and a need to turn healing into a profitable profession. Unlike merchants, who were expected to make some profit, Langland deems *leches* who are involved in the mercantile economy to be unethical, exploiting the vulnerable who require charitable healing.

Of course, the assertion that healers have to be somewhat charitable is not unexpected from a Christian allegory and from an author who criticizes a great many professions and aspects of commercial, mercantile culture.[39] Nonetheless, I contend that *Piers Plowman*, and associated texts such as *Mum and the Sothsegger*, reject professional *leches* and display a preference for what we might term 'amateur' healers — that is, those who adopt the role of a healer as one of a host of charitable duties. As a consequence, *sothseggers*, the Samaritan, and Piers are depicted as the ideal healers who cater to both the body and soul. It is no coincidence that these successful healers do not compete in an urban marketplace for patients. They do not pursue *lechecraft* as a profession and are thus not preoccupied with profit. Through this critique of professional *leches*, Langland and the *Mum*-poet not only criticize the formalized, profit-based culture of healing emerging in late fourteenth-century English cities, but also weigh in on contemporary medical debates surrounding patient scepticism towards certain treatments, the bedside manner of professional healers, the efficacy of medical charms, and even the ways in which physicians should dress. *Piers Plowman* and *Mum and the Sothsegger* hence prove to be valuable sources in the social history of medicine in Langland's London.

Phisic and Wound Treatment in *Mum and the Sothsegger*

Mum and the Sothsegger is an ideal text with which to begin, as it presents a clear overview of professional healing in late medieval English cities. Written during the first decade of Henry IV's reign (1399–1413), the incomplete poem's central thesis is that keeping mum and manipulating facts can benefit the individual, but truth telling is the only way to serve the common good. The *Mum*-poet identifies the ideal healer as the truth-telling *sothsegger* who performs wound treatment throughout the text. Yet before we encounter this charitable, truthful *leche*, the poet criticizes what he sees as the overly confusing nature of learned medicine. In a discussion of the seven sciences that a clerk studies at Oxford and Cambridge, *phisic* is described as the only science to defy both Mum and the Sothsegger —

---

[39] For instance, P. M. Kean has demonstrated that law is a common good and thus while minstrels and merchants should be paid, lawyers must not be, as truth is deemed to be for love and not for hire; see Kean, 'Love, Law, and Lewte in *Piers Plowman*'.

that is, to defy both those who withhold or manipulate the facts and those who tell the truth:

> Phisic diffied al the bothe sides,
> Bothe Mum and me and the Soethsiggre;
> He was accumbrid of oure cumpaignye, by Crist that me bought,
> And as fayn of oure voiding as foul of his make.
>
> $(334-37)^{40}$

Unlike many contemporary medical satires that criticize some practitioners while maintaining the truth of medicine as a discipline, the *Mum*-poet seems to condemn medicine wholesale.[41] Far from being a legitimate science with certain bad practitioners who damage its reputation, *phisic* is a science that baffles and maddens all. Physicians have no intention of curing patients and are as glad of their *voiding* as a bird of attracting his mate. Here *voiding* denotes Mum and the *sothsegger* leaving, but there is a pun on the emptying of the stomach or bowels of a patient.[42] Physicians do not wish to be investigated by Mum or the *sothsegger*, and they also wish to void their patients on a regular basis as part of a purgative act of medicine that was consistent with dietic treatments associated with the humours.[43] Above all, the more people who are ill, the greater the opportunities for business and repeat business.

This exploitative attitude demonstrates that those who study *phisic* are embedded in the active life of commerce, where accumulating wealth is the only motivating factor for their practice. At first, the commercial focus of *phisic* would seem to align with Mum, who is likewise commonly associated with personal gain at the expense of the kingdom, but in fact *phisic* is of little help to any patient. No matter how much money a patient may have, old age and death cannot be delayed forever, and thus according to the medieval tradition of the *ars moriendi*, *phisic* is little use to anybody. By contrast, true healers are able to grant a form of eternal life in salvation.

Not all those who perform *lechecraft* in *Mum and the Sothsegger* are condemned; *sothseggers* perform wound treatments on themselves and others throughout the text. Nevertheless, there is a distinction between the scholastic medicine of *phisic* and the surgery of *sothseggers*. Wound treatment was part of the duties of barbers and surgeons, who typically did not study in a university setting. Barbers learnt their trade through an apprenticeship in which they shadowed a master barber. Surgeons were

---

40 All quotations are from *Richard the Redeless and Mum and the Sothsegger*, ed. by Dean.
41 Mann, *Chaucer and Medieval Estates Satire*, p. 95; Orlemanski, *Symptomatic Subjects*, pp. 79–112.
42 *MED*, s.v. 'voidinge'.
43 Orlemanski, *Symptomatic Subjects*, pp. 14–15.

trained in a similar manner. They sometimes attended university, but this was not universally the case. The English surgeon John of Arderne, for instance, attended grammar school and that was the extent of his formal education.[44] Nowhere in *Mum and the Sothsegger* are *sothseggers* explicitly labelled barbers or surgeons, but they certainly take on wound care responsibilities and thus somewhat align themselves with those practitioners who were not trained at a university.[45] While one might object that the *sothsegger's* wound treatment is entirely figurative and refers directly to his amelioration of the body politic rather than any physical body, in fact, the *sothsegger's* actions are repeatedly framed in a surgical framework that equates wounds with the truth in a semantically ambiguous relationship. Often it is unclear whether the *sothsegger* is treating a literal body or the body of society, which is indeed the aim of the *Mum*-poet.[46] Alongside commenting on statecraft and the nature of the truth, the allegorical representations of the poem provide direct comments on the contemporary commercialization of *lechecraft*.

Throughout the text, *sothseggers* perform acts of literal wound treatment that the poet explicitly distinguishes from the avaricious practices of *leches*. Above all, *sothseggers* are humble, Christ-like figures who are able to heal themselves. The narrator searches for a *sothsegger* and finds him practising an ideal form of healing in an urban, mercantile setting, a *shoppe*:

> And as I lokid the loigges along by the streetz,
> I sawe a sothesigger, in sothe as me thought,
> Sitte in a shoppe and salwyn his woundes.
> *Beati qui persecucionem paciuntur propter iusticiam. Euaungelium.*
>
> [Matt. 5. 10] (845–48a)

By salving himself in the *shoppe*, a location in which craftsmen carried out their trades, this *sothsegger* serves as a charitable exemplar to those around him. Upon discovering the *sothsegger*, the narrator realizes that perhaps Mum has the merrier life, as the *sothsegger* has been dealt these wounds by those who have been told the truth. Of course, just because angry people may harm a *sothsegger*, it does not mean that a *sothsegger* should shy away from the truth. On the contrary, as Matthew 5.10 explains, those who suffer are blessed. The suffering, Christ-like *sothsegger* is successful

---

44 Jones, 'John of Arderne and the Mediterranean Tradition of Scholastic Surgery'. For more on John of Arderne's dates and the details of his life, see p. 294. See also Bullough, 'Training of the Nonuniversity-Educated Medical Practitioners'; Wallis, 'Pre-modern Surgery', p. 50.

45 This is not to suggest that wound treatment was the only role of the barber or surgeon. Surgery was used to treat a broad range of conditions, from leprosy to cataracts. See Wallis, 'Pre-modern Surgery'.

46 Eve Salisbury makes the same point in relation to Langland and Gower, *Narrating Medicine*, pp. 51–52, 60–64, 73–74.

in his self-treatment, echoing Luke 4.23 where Christ says to those who doubt him, 'Medice cura teipsum [Physician, cure yourself]'.[47] Indeed, the *sothsegger* is a Christ-like practitioner who endures wounds for the sake of truth and is able to heal himself.

Although the *sothsegger* sustains injuries, he ultimately proves that the truth may be sore at first but will lead to better health.[48] The narrator spends some time weighing up the benefits of telling the truth or obscuring it from the monarch. He concludes that for all the soreness that *sothe* creates, greater problems arise when the truth is withheld or lies are told to those in power. In a description of the harms created by Mum in the parliament, which is depicted as a body, the narrator uses the figurative language of wound treatment:[49]

> When knightz for the comune been come for that deede,
> And semblid forto shewe the sores of the royaulme
> And spare no speche though thay spille shuld,
> But berste oute alle the boicches and blaynes of the hert
> And lete the rancune renne oute arusshe al at oones,
> Leste the fals felon festre withynne;
> For as I herde have, thay helen wel the rather
> Whanne th'anger and th'attre is al oute yrenne,
> For better were to breste oute there bote might falle
> Thenne rise agayne regalie and the royaulme trouble.
> The voiding of this vertue doeth venym forto growe
> And sores to be salvelees in many sundry places
>
> (1119–30)

It is the duty of parliament to tell the monarch the truth about his problems so that he can fix them before they fester into 'boicches' (boils, buboes, growths, or tumours) and 'blaynes' (pox or sores). Telling the truth would cause some distress, yet it would result in a healthier kingdom — but those who keep mum are unwilling to speak:

> Thay wollen not parle of thoo poyntz for peril that might falle,
> But hiden alle the hevynes and halten echone
> And maken Mum thaire messaigier thaire mote to determyne,

---

47 *Biblia sacra vulgata*, ed. by Weber and Gryson. All biblical quotations refer to this edition.
48 This attitude is also typical of depictions of harsh penance that will later be explored in relation to Friar Flatterer in the final passus of the B and C texts of *Piers Plowman*.
49 The poet hints at the organological model of secular rule in which the government was depicted as a living body — with the crown as the head and parliament as members — most famously depicted in the twelfth century in John of Salisbury's *Policraticus*. See Kantorowicz, *The King's Two Bodies*, pp. 194–206.

> And bringen home a bagge ful of boicches un-ycurid,
> That nedis most by nature ennoye thaym thereafter.
>
> (1136–40)

Those who do not tell the truth develop signs of ill health and continue to lie in order to benefit themselves monetarily. If those who cause this misrule were to tell the truth, they would no longer be able to manipulate the situation for their own gain, and so they are willing to endure *boicches* and *blaynes*.

In contrast to those who keep mum or lie to the monarch, a *sothsegger* tells the truth no matter how insensitive it might at first seem. This process is likened to exposing and treating wounds because it is only by investigating wounds that a *leche* can judge the extent of the patient's illness or injury. Following the narrator's dream in which he meets the wise beekeeper, he comes across a bag of books that had been hidden by Mum. He then compares opening up the bag of neglected books to probing wounds:

> Thenne softe I the soores to serche thaym withynne,
> And seurely to salve thaym, and with a newe salve
> That the Sothesigger hath sought many yeres
> And mighte not mete therewith for Mum and his ferys
> That bare aweye the bagges and many a boxe eeke.
> Now forto conseille the king unknytte I a bagge
> Where many a pryve poyse is preyntid withynne
> Yn bokes unbredid in balade-wise made,
> Of vice and of vertue fulle to the margyn,
> That was not y-openyd this other half wintre.
>
> (1340–47)

The role of the surgeon is to examine wounds and root out illness, which here is akin to opening the bag and finding a book, containing vices and virtues, that has not been opened in a long time. It is significant that this book contains receipts, records of goods bequeathed to bishops as well as visitation records because these accounts expose the truth about clerical corruption, abuses, and hypocrisy. Exploring the book and a sinful wound have similar consequences for the patient, who requires truth or confession, however unpleasant, to change their ways and purge their sins. While the book would undoubtedly bring to light some embarrassing clerical abuses, exposing them is vital for reform.

The narrator continues that, much like the neglected book, some surgeons do not visit their patients for as long as seven years, thus leaving them vulnerable and in a state of illness:

> For pouraile of thaire parroishens, and present to be among thaym
> Forto salve thaire shepe whenne thay sike were.
> But how shuld a surgean serve wel his hyre
> That cometh not in sevene yere to se the sore oones,
> That thay shal not se oon shyne how soutelly thay wirchen.
> *Ve pastoribus*!
>
> *[Jeremiah 23. 1] (1380–85a)*

Surgeons do not visit their poor patients, who are likened to a priest's poor parishioners, because the practitioners lack a charitable spirit. Priests and surgeons alike spend more time with the rich in the hope of making a profit and thus neglect their duties to the humble sheep. In the words of Jeremiah 23. 1: 'Woe to the shepherds that destroy and tear the sheep of my pasture'. The only surgeon-shepherd who cares for his sheep charitably, with no regard for their wealth or status, is the *sothsegger*, who rushes to their aid with his wound treatments. Even when the treatments disadvantage the *sothsegger* or put him in harm's way, he selflessly performs them for the health of the kingdom.

Through *Mum and the Sothsegger*, then, we are able to form an image of a successful healer. Far from the university-trained elite physician, the humble *sothsegger* is not a professional healer. As part of his duties, which include exposing truths and advising monarchs, the *sothsegger* performs literal as well as allegorical wound treatments. The *sothsegger* does not claim to make his treatments mild, fully acknowledging the pain involved in exposing and exploring wounds. Crucially, the *sothsegger* does not charge for his services or present himself as part of a marketplace of healers. While he salves his wounds in his *shoppe*, he serves as a charitable exemplar for all other healers to follow.

The Commercial *Lechecraft* of Liar and Friar Flatterer

Liar from *Piers Plowman* is an obvious counterpoint to the *sothsegger* healer. While the *sothsegger* humbly performs his duties of wound treatment for the common good, Liar is immersed in the urban marketplace, drifting from one healing role to the next in order to exploit as many sufferers as possible for personal gain. In the second passus of the B and C texts, Liar along with False, Guile, and Favel looks to bribe officials in London for the marriage of Meed and False to go ahead. Conscience finds out about the plans of False and Liar and intends to have them hanged. To avoid his punishment, Liar seeks refuge in the religious and mercantile world of London after Holy Church exposes his hypocrisy. Liar stays among pardoners, physicians, and then finally apothecaries when he is rejected elsewhere:

> Lightliche lyere leep awey thenne,
> Lurkynge thorugh lanes, tolugged of manye.
> He was nowher welcome for his manye tales,
> Overal yhouted and yhote trusse,
> Til pardoners hadde pite, and pulled hym into house.
> They wesshen hym and wiped hym and wounden hym in cloutes,
> And senten hym on Sondayes with seles to chirches,
> And gaf pardoun for pens poundemele aboute.
>   Thanne lourede leches, and lettres thei sente
> That he sholde wonye with hem watres to loke.
> Spycers speken to hym to spien hire ware,
> For he kouthe on hir craft and knew manye gommes.
>
> *(B.2.216–27)*

Liar's journey presents a précis of fourteenth-century concerns relating to urban occupations and the supposed hypocrisy of friars, pardoners, physicians, and apothecaries. First, Liar stays with pardoners who provide him with a bishop's seal, which gives him authority to preach and collect money for indulgences.[50] His skills are useful because he is required to lie in order to sell his false pardons. Next, he joins the physicians who glowered because Liar works with the pardoners rather than them. These physicians invite Liar to stay with them so that he can lie about urine specimens and increase their profits. The final profession at which Liar tries his hand is pharmacy. Liar has experience and knowledge of making 'gommes', and so the apothecaries acquire his services, as clearly his former experience and lying could be an asset in exploiting patients.

The proximity of these medical and religious references is intriguing, suggesting not only a parallel in regulating these occupations and roles, but also a comparable scepticism. After all, they are all part of the same market of spiritual and physical healing. While pardoners and friars chiefly seek to heal the soul, *cura animarum*, physicians and apothecaries seek to heal the body, *cura corporum*. Yet instead of working cooperatively to ensure total health — friars and pardoners hearing confessions and offering pardons, and physicians prescribing the medicines that apothecaries make — they are presented in direct competition for Liar's services. Each community uses lies in their sales patter to convince customers that theirs is the most effective treatment for various maladies and there is no concern for the joint processes of spiritual and physical health.

---

50 The relation between *Piers Plowman* and the development of legal and legislative culture has been examined by Stephen Yeager and Emily Steiner. Steiner explains that Langland and the texts of the *Piers Plowman* tradition 'used documentary culture both to challenge orthodox notions of textual authority and to construct an oppositional rhetoric'. See Steiner, *Documentary Culture*, p. 194; Yeager, *From Lawmen to Plowmen*, p. 162.

The licence that is given to Liar to inspect urine should be met with particular scepticism. Liar does not possess the necessary training or skill to accurately diagnose patients through uroscopy, and in fact uroscopy itself was not always recognized as a legitimate practice. Authorities were concerned throughout the high and later Middle Ages that practitioners inspected urine and made diagnoses without any formal training in uroscopy. One of the earliest restrictions on friars who practised medicine was a specific ban on inspecting urine, first mentioned at the Provincial Chapter at Palencia (1249) and repeated at the General Chapter held at Metz (1251).[51] Scepticism of uroscopy was widely expressed in Middle English medical satire.[52] For instance, in *The Simonie*, a long-line alliterative poem that is a possible source for *Piers Plowman*,[53] the author accuses a physician of simply swirling a vial of urine to convince a patient that he is more ill than he actually is:

> And yit ther is another craft that toucheth the clergie,
> That ben thise false fisiciens that helpen men to die;
> He wole wagge his urine in a vessel of glaz,
> And swereth that he is sekere than evere yit he was,
>   And sein,
> 'Dame, for faute of helpe, thin housebonde is neih slain'.
> [...]
> Anon he wole biginne to blere the wives eighe;
> He wole aske half a pound to bien spicerie.
> The viii. shillinges sholen up to the win and the ale,
> And bringe rotes and rindes bret ful a male
>   Off noht;
> Hit shal be dere on a lek, whan hit is al i-wrouht.
>
> He wole preisen hit i-nohw, and sweren, as he were wod,
> For the king of the lond the drink is riche and god;
> And geve the gode man drinke a god quantite,
> And make him worse than he was — evele mote he the,
>   That clerk,
> That so geteth the silver, and can noht don his werk![54]

After requesting silver for ingredients and giving the patient a tonic that will in fact make him more ill, the physician runs off with the money. The

---

51 Montford, *Health, Sickness, Medicine and the Friars*, pp. 115–17.
52 See in particular Mann, *Chaucer and Medieval Estates Satire*, pp. 91–99, and Getz, *Medicine in the English Middle Ages*, pp. 45–53.
53 Galloway, *Penn Commentary*, p. 282.
54 *The Simonie* in *Medieval English Political Writings*, ed. by Dean, ll. 211–34.

physician knows that he cannot heal the patient and would be forced to return the payment if he did not flee.

These stanzas are followed in the B version of *The Simonie* with a further stanza on the physician's tactics of exploiting his patient:

> He maket hym merie þe ferst, as mery as he can,
> And loke þat he fare wel his hors and his man.
> A-morwe he taket þe uryne and schaket aen þe sonne.
> 'Dame', he seis, 'drede þe not. Þe maister is wonne',
>   And li[ket].
> But þus he fereð a-wey þe silver and þe wif be skikket.[55]

This physician holds the urine up to the sun and claims that the man will eventually return to health, but not before he has plundered all his silver. The science of uroscopy is central to the physician's deception, as his diagnosis amounts to little more than swishing a urine vial and demanding payment in exchange for expensive ingredients. It is this initial diagnosis from the urine flask that gives the physician the appearance of authority because his patient is too willing to trust this spurious display of science.

The depiction of the trickster physician was not merely a literary stereotype in medical satires. Although the caricature in *The Simonie* is exaggerated for effect, those who studied uroscopy were aware of its reputation. Henry Danyel's *Liber uricrisiarum* or 'Þe Boke of Demyng of Vryn', written in the late 1370s, was the product of a charitable impulse to disseminate medical learning, yet he displays an acute awareness of the dangers of writing a text of uroscopy in the vulgar tongue — namely, that it might lead unskilled practitioners to try their hand, unsuccessfully.[56] Danyel explains:

> Forsoþe he þat biholdeþ wel and parfitely þis boke made in wlgare, i. in comune tonge, he shal mowe be a parfite domesman in this crafte and wiþoute doute he schal gete gode & richez and helthe of his soule; neuerþeles if he mysvse noȝt a pompouse lif or bostful, ful of wordes, ful of fables & ful of lesingez, as leches þat bene now ar wonte to done.[57]

Those who read Danyel's work faithfully and carefully can become better diagnosticians, provided that they do not live a pompous or boastful life, as was supposedly typical for *leches* in his day (or at least this was the perception of sceptical patients). Danyel includes this warning because he knows that some may think of uroscopy as a false science, namely because

---

55 *The Simonie* in *Medieval English Political Writings*, ed. by Dean, note to l. 211.
56 Star, 'Introduction: Reading Henry Daniel', p. 4.
57 Daniel, *Liber uricrisiarum*, ed. by Harvey, Tavormina, and Star, p. 37, ll. 64–69.

it is difficult to make diagnoses from urine and hard for the uninitiated to comprehend how it works. Patients are asked to trust that practitioners can distinguish between different shades, transparencies, and consistencies of urine, but to the untrained eye the distinctions can appear relatively arbitrary. Leches like Danyel were mindful that uroscopy should be used sparingly and only by those who had mastered it. Those who lied about their skill could gain a profit, but not without endangering patients.

One *leche* who represents those 'ful of words', 'fables', and 'lesingez' is Friar Flatterer from *Piers Plowman*. In Bodleian Library, MS Douce 104, a copy of the C text, Friar Flatterer features in a miniature inspecting a flask of urine.[58] This image of the friar physician was based on a long tradition of representing uroscopy in medieval manuscripts. A figure inspecting a vial of urine was one of the ways in which to pictorially represent physicians, even in manuscripts that had no intention of besmirching uroscopy or medicine more broadly.[59] In *Piers Plowman*, the symbol of the urine vial is incorporated into the medical satire. For instance, in passus 15 of the C text, a gluttonous friar is described by the narrator as a 'iurdan', a urine flask or chamber pot: 'Y schal iangle to this iurdan with his iuyste wombe / And apose hym what penaunce is and purgatorie on erthe / And why a lyueth nat as a lereth!' (C.15.91–93; cf. B.13.84–85).[60] The narrator possibly uses 'iurdan' to pun on the name of the Dominican master William Jordan, who is used as a symbol to represent the hypocrisy of all friars in their supposed commercial activities of charging for enjoined penances.[61] By referring to the friar as a urine flask, Langland is not simply equating Jordan with a receptacle for human waste, but also connecting the medical roles of certain friars with the exploitation of penitents who seek out friars for confession. After all, for one sceptical of uroscopy and its practitioners, paying for a diagnosis is as foolish as buying a false indulgence or pardon.

Adding to the antifraternal satire of medicine, in the final passus of the B and C texts, Friar Flatterer fails to function as a skilled *leche* in treating physical and spiritual wounds. Before Friar Flatterer is summoned, Conscience recommends a skilled *leche* to those in the Barn of Unity who flee from their proper 'persons and parissh preestes' to 'the freres' because of their shame (B.20.281–85). This *leche*, Conscience explains, knows how to 'salve tho that sike were thorugh synne ywounded. / Shrift shoop sharp salve, and made men do penaunce' (B.20.306–07). The connection between confession and surgery is not a passing comment, but part of

---

58 Oxford, Bodleian Library, Douce 104, fol. 111ᵛ.
59 Kiefer, 'Uroscopy'.
60 All quotations from the C text are from Langland, *Piers Plowman*, ed. by Pearsall.
61 For more on this passage and the possible connections with William Jordan, see Friedman, 'Friar Portrait in Bodleian Library MS Douce 104', pp. 178–79.

a sustained comparison in medieval texts.[62] To treat a penitent with a 'sharp salve' is to prescribe a harsh penance for his or her past sins, which fester like wounds.[63] The links between penitence and medical treatment are strengthened by the fact that friars were sometimes licensed both to hear lay confessions and to treat patients. In 1398, for instance, the Dominican theologian and physician Geoffrey Launde was licensed to give both spiritual and medical services to the household of Edward, Duke of York. Launde became the confessor of Edward's son, the Duke of Aumale, and was permitted to practise medicine in his household and treat his friends and subordinates.[64]

Like Launde, the *leche* who is initially chosen by Conscience performs both spiritual and physical healing, yet he is rejected by the penitents in the Barn of Unity: 'Somme liked noght this leche, and lettres thei sent, / If any surgien were in the sege that softer koude plastre' (B.20.310–11). The penitents reject the *leche* because, much like the *sothsegger*, he prescribes a harsh treatment that causes pain before it cures. What the dissatisfied penitents want is 'any surgien' who can save them from the sorrow and sharpness of penance and offer a more agreeable remedy. As a consequence, the 'phisicien and surgien' Friar Flatterer, who is also licensed to hear confessions,[65] is summoned to the Barn of Unity. Conscience asks Flatterer when he arrives to treat Contrition:

> [...] 'kanstow heele sike?
> Here is Contricioun', quod Conscience, 'my cosyn, ywounded.
> Conforte hym', quod Conscience, 'and take kepe to hise soores.
> The plastres of the persoun and poudres ben to soore;
> And lat hem ligge overlonge and looth is to chaunge hem;
> Fro Lenten to Lenten he lat hise plastres bite'.
>
> (B.20.357–62)

---

62 The therapeutic processes of confession are discussed in Salisbury, *Narrating Medicine*, pp. 50–51, 55–56.
63 See Jones, 'Surgeon as Story-Teller', p. 86; McVaugh, 'Bedside Manners in the Middle Ages'. For the same tradition in the French context, see Jacquart, *Médicine médiévale dans le cadre Parisien*, pp. 50–82.
64 *Registrum litterarum Raymundi*, ed. by Reichert, p. 200.
65 The friar has the legal right granted by canon law to act as a confessor: 'To a lorde for a lettre leve to have / To curen as a curatour; and cam with his [lettre] / Baldly to the bisshop and his brief hadde / In contrees there he come in confessiouns to here' (B.20.325–28). With the acquisition of this document, Friar Flatterer enjoys the legal status of a *limitour* and has the right to hear confessions within the jurisdiction of the bishop who granted him the 'brief'. Although Friar Flatterer follows the established canonistic procedure of obtaining episcopal permission to hear the confessions of lay parishioners, he violates the procedures that require him first to elicit contrition from penitents and then to determine whether or not to grant absolution.

Contrition has already been prescribed harsh powders and plasters that burn his flesh and keep his wounds sore for the sake of enacting penance. There is, nonetheless, some discrepancy in the interpretation of the plasters that are applied from Lent to Lent. Derek Pearsall suggests that Contrition defies the parson's stringent measure by trying to get away with the minimum number of confessions as prescribed by the Fourth Lateran Council, namely each Easter, and thus his wounds have become reinfected.[66] Stephen Barney, by contrast, contends that the parson is 'unwilling to remit the penance due between the sinner's annual Lenten confessions'. In Barney's view, that Contrition wears the burning plasters from Lent to Lent seems to stress the long and arduous process of penance that lasts an entire year, as opposed to the more frequent changing of plasters prescribed by Friar Flatterer. The wounds of Contrition are not signs of his repeated sin, but rather a symbol of the continual need to repent for one's sins.[67] These differing interpretations reveal a tension in the text that is symbolized by wounds. Wounds are at once signs of sinful deviance and a means to enact a restorative penance. A wound can indicate the possible sinful nature of a character such as Contrition, but at the same time without a wound there is no means of representing the desire to atone for sin through the plasters of penance. Put simply, do Contrition's wounds linger because he is sinful in rejecting the parson's harsh treatment by taking confession only at the time of obligation, or do the wounds represent a need and desire to conduct a lasting penance year round? Whether Contrition does the bare minimum to atone for his sins or endures a lasting penance, the results seem to be unsatisfactory.

In contrast to the lengthy treatment prescribed by the parson, Friar Flatterer wishes to hasten to the solution before he has gathered evidence of the penitent's remorse, ignoring contrition and penance. Flatterer explains that Contrition has worn these plasters:

'[…] overlonge! […] I leve, I shal amende it' —
And gooth, gropeth Contricioun and gaf hym a plastre
Of 'a pryvee paiement, and I shal praye for yow,
And for al[le hem] that ye ben holden to, al my lif tyme,
And make yow [and] my Lady in masse and in matyns,
As freres of oure fraternytee for a litel silver'.
    Thus he gooth and gadereth, and gloseth there he shryveth —
Til Contricioun hadde clene foryeten to crye and to wepe,
And wake for hise wikked werkes as he was wont to doone.

---

66 *Piers Plowman*, ed. by Pearsall, p. 377, note to C.22.59–61.
67 Barney, *Penn Commentary*, p. 247.

> For confort of his confessour, contricioun he lafte,
> That is the soverayneste salve for alle kynne synnes.
>
> *(B.20.363–73)*

Whereas the ideal confessor poses questions to elicit signs of contrition, Friar Flatterer investigates in a physical manner: he 'gropeth' to procure a 'pryvee paiement'. This probing at once mocks the manual aspects of the craft of surgery and reveals the supposed desire of friars to exploit penitents for monetary gain. Flatterer here represents the opposite of the healing *sothsegger*, who never tries to hide the pain that his treatments will cause. Flatterer reduces penance to a monetary exchange, treating a donation as a sovereign salve to cure all sins.[68]

Friar Flatterer's treatments prove to be ineffective, and it does not take long for Contrition and Conscience to realize that they have been tricked by this surgeon *limitour*. Peace, who immediately recognizes Flatterer as a false friar, exclaims that the 'frere with his phisyk this folk hath enchaunted, / And plastred hem so esily [hii] drede no synne!' (B.20.379–80). The medicine of the friar is so mild that the patients no longer fear the consequences of sin. Clearly this attitude is far from the ideal of contrition. The poem ends with Conscience embarking on a journey to seek Piers, who is the only one who can purge his pride and reverse the damage of the false *leche*. A large part of the failing of Friar Flatterer is the manner in which the confession, or spiritual surgery, is administered. The healing provided by Flatterer is a financial exchange and it is because of the 'pryvee paiement' demanded that friars such as Flatterer are associated throughout the poem with the active life, which to antifraternal authors such as Langland, often constituted a life engaged in commerce. Friar Flatterer's customers pay him for an enjoined penance that is far softer than true penance.

Throughout the texts of the *Piers Plowman* tradition, there is a pervading antifraternal discourse that is used to criticize a supposedly transactional relationship with the laity.[69] *Pierce the Plowman's Crede* presents a layman who visits different religious orders, seeking someone to teach him the Creed. In the text, friars are depicted as little more than hawkers of pardons who fail to fulfil their duties: 'Thei ne prechen nought of Powel, ne penaunce for synne, / But all of mercy and mensk that Marie may helpen'.[70] Friars in *Pierce* downplay the harshness of penance to entice more people to come to them for their confessions. They present their

---

68 Thomas, '*Piers Plowman*' and the Reinvention of Church Law, p. 59.
69 See in particular Szittya, *Antifraternal Tradition*, especially pp. 247–87; Walling, 'Friar Flatterer', pp. 62–69; and Thomas, *Piers Plowman and the Reinvention of Church Law*, pp. 64–69.
70 *Pierce the Plowman's Crede* in '*Piers Plowman*' *Tradition*, ed. by Barr, p. 64, ll. 80–81.

services as if the penance they offer is gentler than that of a parish priest, yet just as effective. In fact, they offer parishioners a fee in exchange for a pardon and ignore penance altogether:

> For thei han of Bichopes ybought with her propre silver,
> And purchased of penaunce the puple to assoile.
> But money may maken mesur of the peyne,
> After that his power is to payen, his penance schal faile.
> God lene it be a good help for hele of the soules![71]

Just as with Friar Flatterer, who requests 'a litel silver', the exchange of money in *Pierce* seems to invalidate spiritual healing. As Nicholas Vincent has demonstrated, in late medieval society there was an emphasis on contrition rather than penance as the defining feature of repentance, and consequently pardons and indulgences came to be seen by some as an enjoined penance that functioned according to a transactional model.[72] Contrition, by contrast, was an interior process that could not be part of a monetary transaction; it was a state of sorrow reached only after reflection and rumination on one's sins.

In *Pierce* as in *Piers Plowman*, the friars' unsuccessful treatments point to the impossibility of a transactional route to spiritual and physical health. Unlike the *sothsegger*, who makes no attempt to hide the severity of his treatments, those who promise a painless penance trick penitents out of their money and worsen their spiritual health. Both ineffective confessors and *leches* compete for patients as they neglect *cura animarum* and *cura corporum* to focus on profit. They do not provide the services that they charge for, and indeed charging for them seems to indicate their inability to heal.

Hawkyn the Active Man and his Healers

The problems caused by a commercial attitude towards *lechecraft* are widespread in *Piers Plowman*. Nowhere is the scepticism towards this type of professionalized medicine shown more critically than in the depiction of Hawkyn the Active Man. Hawkyn is a lay 'wafrer' who bakes and sells wafers, though as Traugott Lawler explains, these wafers had no relation to the Eucharist but were savoury treats.[73] In fact, Langland may purposefully be contrasting the *wafrer* who makes these treats to those who make Eucharistic wafers: instead of offering a wafer that would be

---

71 *Pierce the Plowman's Crede* in '*Piers Plowman*' *Tradition*, ed. by Barr, p. 85, ll. 569–73.
72 Vincent, 'Some Pardoners' Tales', pp. 30–33.
73 Lawler, *Penn Commentary*, pp. 66–67.

turned into a spiritually healing part of the sacrament of the altar, Hawkyn provides wafers with no spiritual benefit, as he is entirely preoccupied with transactions in an urban marketplace.

Hawkyn's focus on commercial transactions is reflected in his attitude towards health. In the thirteenth passus of the B text, he imagines writing to the pope to ask for a pardon to protect him against 'pestilence' and 'bocches':

> I fynde payn for the Pope and provendre for his palfrey,
> And I hadde nevere of hym, have God my trouthe,
> Neither provendre ne parsonage yet of the Popes yifte,
> Save a pardon with a peis of leed and two polles amyddes!
> Hadde Ich a clerc that couthe write I wolde caste hym a bille
> That he sente me under his seel a salve for the pestilence,
> And that his blessynge and hise bulles bocches myghte destruye:
> *In nomine meo demonia ejicient, et super egros manus imponent, et bene habebunt.*
> And thanne wolde I be prest to peple, paast for to make,
> And buxom and busy aboute breed and drynke
> For hym and for alle hise, founde I that his pardoun
> Mighte lechen a man — as I bileve it shulde.
>
> (B.13.244–54)

Hawkyn desires a physical item to protect him from disease, 'the Popes yifte', and if he receives such a pardon, Hawkyn promises to produce more wafers for his clerical customers. This passage exposes Hawkyn's mercantile thought process in which services and goods are exchanged for one another even in a religious context. Hawkyn wishes to barter with the clergy rather than seeking their charitable, spiritual healing.[74] In contrast to the physical 'bille', Hawkyn seems to overlook the subtler *lechecraft* of Christ, which is dependent on a spiritual piety and has no physical form. Hawkyn's preference for the 'Popes yifte' leaves him vulnerable to all sorts of spiritual and bodily illnesses because pardons in *Piers Plowman* are often ineffective, especially in comparison to the healing power of Christ.[75]

Not all the medicine that Hawkyn seeks is prophylactic. He explains that he falls into a melancholy, caused by a build-up of choler or black

---

[74] Rodman Jones points to a similar moment in *Piers Plowman* (B.3.35, C.3.38) where a friar offers a full absolution of Meed's sins in exchange for wheat. In the B text, the friar then goes on to negotiate absolution for lecherous lords in exchange for enhancing and rebuilding his order's house (B.3.49–69). See Rodman Jones, *Radical Pastoral*, pp. 18–21.

[75] Orlemanski, 'Langland's Poetics of Animation', pp. 173–74; St-Jacques, 'Langland's *Christus medicus* Image', p. 120.

bile in his spleen,[76] when he considers 'mynstrals'.[77] Hawkyn condemns *mynstrals* for their inferior form of the active life and values his service far above theirs, despite the fact that he is paid less.[78] He enviously complains:

> And whan I may noght have the maistrie, swich malencolie I take
> That I cacche the crampe, the cardiacle som tyme,
> Or an ague in swich an angre, and som tyme a fevere
> That taketh me al a twelvemonthe, til that I despise
> Lechecraft of Oure Lord and leve on a wicche,
> And seye that no clerc ne kan — ne Crist, as I leve —
> To the Soutere of Southwerk, or of Shordych Dame Emme,
> And seye that [God ne] Goddes word gaf me nevere boote,
> But thorugh a charme hadde I chaunce and my chief heele.
>
> (B.13.334–42)

Hawkyn's sin of envy manifests itself in physical symptoms, indicating a tight connection between spiritual and physical illness as well as between spiritual and physical healing. He suffers from stomach cramps, indigestion, and an acute fever that lasts for twelve months, yet instead of turning to the 'Lechecraft of Oure Lord', he turns to a 'wicche', a male or female practitioner of healing magic such as the *Soutere* (cobbler) of Southwark or Dame Emme of Shoreditch.[79]

Langland here draws on the stereotype of cobblers as meddlers who had pretentions above their station. While cobblers had no training in medicine, they had a reputation for assuming competence. This stereotype is perhaps most famously reflected in the prologue to the *Reeve's Tale* in which Harry Bailey declares: 'The devel made a reve for to preche, / Or of a soutere a shipman or a leche'.[80] Through the charms offered by the cobbler and Dame Emme, Hawkyn relapses into the same chronic state of ill health. These two alternative 'wicche' healers prove to be just as exploitative as *leches* and friars, as they contribute to the same urban market of healing that looked to turn patient suffering into profit. Of course, a cobbler and Dame Emme may not have been *leches*, yet their willingness to sell charms makes them akin to other professional healers throughout the text. The healers also occupy the low end of the market. In late medieval London, status often dictated the type of healer that one would seek out, with university-trained physicians generally treating the aristocracy

---

[76] See Harvey, *Inward Wits*, pp. 4–30.
[77] As Lawler explains, the term 'mynstral' indicates one who provides a service or administers something such as food to their lord; see Lawler, *Penn Commentary*, p. 63.
[78] For more, see Steiner, *Reading 'Piers Plowman'*, p. 122.
[79] Galloway, *Penn Commentary*, p. 143.
[80] *Reeve's Tale*, 1.3903–04 in *The Riverside Chaucer*, ed. by Benson.

and gentry. The fact of the matter was that despite the complaints from physicians, surgeons, and master barbers about untrained healers, there were far too few trained practitioners to treat all of the gentry, let alone the entire populous of the country.[81] Yet in *Piers Plowman* whether a healer is formally trained at a university or sells charms to patients, when he or she profits from healing, it invariably leaves patients in a worse state of physical and spiritual health.

Through Hawkyn's illness and the treatments he receives, Langland presents scepticism towards pardons and medical charms, and in fact there are some similarities between them. Medical charms were often written on slips of parchment or paper and were frequently attached to amulets, combining the power of words with that of a physical object.[82] The Pope's pardon that Hawkyn desires has the same format, invoking the power of the written word on a piece of paper together with physical objects: 'a peis of leed and two polles amyddes' (B.13.247).[83] It would perhaps go too far to suggest that the pardon of the pope and the charms of Dame Emme and the cobbler are alike — for one thing the pardon is preventative rather than curative — but they are both presented as ineffective when compared to the healing of the Divine Physician.[84]

Directly following the mention of the cobbler and Dame Emme in the B text, the dreamer begins his gradual process of reading the sins that stain Hawkyn's coat. Will first notices that Hawkyn's coat is stained with lust and that to 'ech a maide that he mette, he made hire a signe / Semynge to synneward, and sometyme he gan taste / Aboute the mouth or bynethe bigynneth to grope' (B.13.345–47). The proximity of the description of Hawkyn's illness to the sin of lechery which immediately follows suggests a connection between 'harlotrye and horedom' (B.13.354) and the ineffective healers. Although there is no direct link between the *wicche* healers and sex work, their location in Southwark and Shoreditch, parts of London associated with the illicit, may indicate that these healers were situated near brothels.[85] In fact, there is a historical relation between barbers and

---

81 Rawcliffe, *Urban Bodies*, pp. 294–95.
82 Olsan, 'Charms and Prayers'; Rawcliffe, *Urban Bodies*, p. 90; Hunt, ed., *Popular Medicine*, pp. 84, 87–90, 92, 94–99.
83 The similarities between pardons, indulgences, and charms have been noted by Swanson, 'Praying for Pardon', pp. 215–40, and Edsall, '*Arma Christi* Rolls or Textual Amulets?', pp. 178–205.
84 Furthermore, it would be inaccurate to suggest that all medical charms were treated as spurious. Even university-educated physicians who advocated for the strictest rationalism used some charms, especially if they were associated with a particular authority. Nevertheless, the scepticism in *Piers Plowman* is aimed at charms used by unconventional healers. See Olsan, 'Marginality of Charms'; Garay and Jeay, 'Advice Concerning Pregnancy and Health'.
85 Sebastian Sobecki has considered the relationship between Southwark, poetry, and the illicit, in 'A Southwark Tale'.

brothels, because often barbers practised in similar parts of the city or even in the same buildings as sex workers, such as public bath houses. One of the earliest surviving references to the organized Company of Barbers in London was an attempt to disassociate themselves from brothels. In 1308, Richard le Barbour was tasked with seeking out barbers who were keeping brothels or disgracing the trade in any other 'unseemly way'.[86] In other words, the historical association between healers and sex work may have formed part of Langland's portrait of urban sin even if the cobbler and Dame Emme are not overtly connected with brothels.

Nevertheless, earlier in *Piers Plowman* healers are explicitly compared with sex workers. In passus 3 of the C text, Conscience condemns '*pre manibus*' payments, that is, payments in advance of work.[87] Conscience explains: 'Harlotes and hoores and alse fals leches / They asken here huyre ar thei hit haue deserued' (C.3.301–02). Arvind Thomas contends that it is not the type of work conducted that is the cause of condemnation, but rather when the payment is demanded. The moment at which the payment is given seems to distinguish good from bad 'huyre', as one should not receive a payment before one has earnt it.[88] *Leches* and *harlotes* are linked because they typically entered into a contract with the customer and may have been paid, either their full fee or a portion of it, upfront. Put simply, it is not the work itself that makes the *leches* false, but the fact that they demand a payment upfront — or perhaps the demand of a payment beforehand is a sure indicator of their falsity.

While the alternative healers that Hawkyn consults are neither explicitly *leches* nor clearly located in brothels, there is certainly an association between ill health and lechery. Rather than seeking out the Divine Physician who might balance his humours and heal his melancholy, Hawkyn goes to locations (or else he lives and works in these locations) that were somewhat notorious for the illicit and procures impotent charms. In purchasing medical charms, Hawkyn takes a transactional approach to spiritual and physical health and by indulging his lust, he further displaces his humours and increases his sin. Above all, we find that charms bought in a sinful urban marketplace are unable to heal Hawkyn's melancholy, which requires the *lechecraft* of Christ.

The equivalent passage on Hawkyn's illness comes much earlier in the C text (C.6.77–85) and in fact afflicts Envy rather than Hawkyn's C-text counterpart, Activa Vita. Envy's confession is explicitly medicalized, as the C text adapts B.5 by incorporating Hawkyn's melancholic illness from B.13. Nevertheless, the C version is more focused, collapsing the

---

86 *Annals of the Barber-Surgeons of London*, ed. by Young, p. 24; Bullough, 'Training of the Nonuniversity-Educated Medical Practitioners', p. 453.
87 Alford, 'Medicine in the Middle Ages', p. 393.
88 Thomas, *Piers Plowman and the Reinvention of Church Law*, pp. 92–94.

lengthy description of Envy from the B text (B.5.76–120) into three lines (C.6.63–65) before focusing on Envy's humoral illness.[89] Much like Hawkyn, Envy is unable to cure his melancholy and seems impatient in his confession to Repentance. In lines that are largely unchanged from the B text, he declares: 'May no sugre ne swete thyng aswage my swellynge, / Ne derworth drynke dryue hit fro myn herte, / Ne noþer shame ne shryfte, but hoso shrapede my mawe?' (C.6.88–90). Envy's question as to whether there is a sweet medication that can drive sin from his heart reveals his impatient attitude, as he believes he requires a surgeon to scrape his 'mawe'. The deeply imbedded nature of Envy's sin requires a more invasive procedure than the tonics, salves, and plasters that represent confession and penance.[90] His attitude and focus on physical surgery leads one to wonder whether Envy is capable of reaching a state of true contrition because spiritual remedies seem to be ineffective.

Hawkyn and Envy are far from equivalent characters. Hawkyn is widely regarded as a more sympathetic character than Envy, yet they are connected through the medicalized descriptions of their sins. They also demonstrate that healing in late medieval London was part of a marketplace where patients could shop around until they found the type of healer or treatment they desired. Whether they sought out a physician, such as those that grant Liar a licence to inspect urine, the surgeon who Envy requires to scrape his *mawe*, or an alternative healer like Dame Emme, patients were sure to suffer if the healer was more interested in profit than *lechecraft*. Yet there also appears to be some criticism placed on the patient, as Hawkyn rejects the omnipotent healing of *Christus medicus* and instead prefers those who facilitate further sin. Similarly, Envy feels he requires an invasive surgery rather than confession and penance. These patients demonstrate that the customer has just as much of a role in perpetuating this commercial marketplace of healing as those who seek out their business.

The Amateur *Lechecraft* of the Samaritan and Piers the Plowman

One would be forgiven for thinking that Langland was critical of all forms of *lechecraft* because, as we have seen, his characters accuse *leches*, friars, a cobbler, and Dame Emme of avarice and enabling sin in an urban marketplace. Yet Langland's characters recognize the benefits of medicine and surgery when practised under the correct conditions, namely, by an amateur healer with a charitable spirit. Perhaps the clearest example of

---

89 Hanna, *Penn Commentary*, pp. 91–92.
90 Hanna, *Penn Commentary*, p. 99.

charitable medicine is shown when the Samaritan approaches a wounded man, or *semivif*, on his way to Jerusalem. Faith and Hope abandon the half-dead man and it is only the Samaritan who is willing to help:

> And to the wye he wente hise woundes to biholde,
> And parceyved by his pous he was in peril to dye,
> And but if he hadde recoverer the rather, that rise sholde he nevere:
> And breide to hise boteles, and bothe he atamede.
> With wyn and with oille hise woundes he wasshed
>
> (B.17.66–69)

The Samaritan washes and salves the patient's wounds with oil and wine before wrapping them. These healing acts are both allegorical (the oil invoking baptism while the wine invokes the Eucharist) and literal: the Samaritan seeks to save the souls of Christendom and perform amateur *lechecraft* on the individual wounded man. Salving and wrapping wounds are treatments that numerous practitioners perform throughout *Piers Plowman*, but unlike the exploitative practitioners who charge for their treatments, the Samaritan provides his services in a spirit of charity, demanding no payment.

The Samaritan rides with his patient to a *graunge* — a farm, as modern editors have glossed it[91] — named *Lex Christi*. He pays for his patient's stay and even gives the *hostellere* silver 'for salve to hise woundes', explaining: 'What he [moore speneth] I make thee good herafter' (B.17.76–78). One might wonder why the Samaritan does not bring the patient to a hospital — after all, a hospital would seem to be the ideal location for convalescence. One factor is that the episode, at least in one sense, takes place during the life of Christ and thus there would have been no medieval hospitals. Another factor is that *Lex Christi* is akin to the inn to which the Samaritan brings the wounded man in Luke 10. 34. Although *Lex Christi* is a *graunge* rather than a hospital, it does not mean that it and its occupants are unfit to oversee a patient's convalescence. The term *graunge* has been taken to mean a farm, with Derek Pearsall arguing that its remote, agricultural setting contrasts the mercantile world of London, in turn demonstrating a need to separate Christian life from the world, 'at least for a therapeutic time'.[92] A *graunge* could equally denote a series of buildings on a monastic estate, however.[93] Such buildings were frequently used to house the sick poor, and so potentially *Lex Christi* would have been fit to see to the wounded man's physical and spiritual convalescence. Indeed, the Samaritan's payment for bandages and the care of the patient suggests that

---

91 See Langland, *Vision of Piers Plowman*, ed. by Schmidt; *Piers Plowman*, ed. by Pearsall.
92 Pearsall, 'Langland's London', p. 195.
93 *MED*, s.v. 'graunge'.

Lex Christi and its *hostellere* have adequate provisions to care for wounded patients even if it is not explicitly a hospital for the sick poor.

This Samaritan episode in *Piers Plowman* is a parable that stresses Christ's love for humanity, but it has additional implications.[94] The Samaritan symbolizes the New Law in the New Testament era and the *semivif* symbolizes all of humanity who are injured by the wounds of sin and are waiting for Christ to save them.[95] Although he is never explicitly named as such, the Samaritan is also the embodiment of Charity, the greatest of St Paul's three virtues in 1 Corinthians 13. 13, and a manifestation of Christ on his way to joust.[96] The dreamer looks to condemn Faith and Hope, who are Old Testament prophets,[97] for leaving the wounded man, but the Samaritan excuses their behaviour by insisting that their efforts would have been in vain. Only the blood of Christ and the plaster of penance can bring the wounded man back to full health. The Samaritan is thus unable to fully heal the wounded man, and hence humanity, with his medicines (B.17.95–100).[98] Raymond St-Jacques contends that this episode allows Langland to emphasize the supremacy of Christ's sacramental medicines of baptism, penance, and the Eucharist above all other treatments.[99] Still, the Samaritan performs a vital act of charitable medicine in salving and wrapping his patient's wounds, and without his help the *semivif* would be left for dead. The Samaritan's medicines are successful in preserving the patient's life until such time that Christ can heal him directly. There is never any suggestion that the Samaritan is a professional healer, but rather his wound treatment is part of his charitable attitude administered to a patient he happens upon rather than one he seeks out in an urban marketplace. Part of the difference, therefore, is whether the healer actively seeks out patients or not, as a commercial healer seeks out patients in a city marketplace whereas a charitable healer comes across patients in a variety of contexts.

Alongside this charitable attitude, the Samaritan is able to successfully help the wounded *semivif* because he has lived a humble life that contrasts with the avaricious nature of professional *leches*. A good *leche* in *Piers Plowman* seeks to live the *vita apostolica*, which was often manifested in the dress of practitioners. Andrew Galloway has demonstrated that the self-remaking and social signalling that clothes present can 'pose acute, even crisis-like challenges'.[100] Galloway's claim is certainly true for Physic,

---

94 Raschko, *Politics of Middle English Parables*, pp. 142–44.
95 Steiner, *Reading 'Piers Plowman'*, pp. 180–81.
96 Lawler, *Penn Commentary*, p. 384; Al Kaaoud, '"Caro", "caritas", and the role of Samaritan', p. 40.
97 Steiner, *Reading 'Piers Plowman'*, pp. 180–81.
98 Zeeman, *Arts of Disruption*, p. 320.
99 St-Jacques, 'Langland's *Christus medicus* Image', pp. 116–17.
100 Galloway, 'Langland and the Reinvention of Array', p. 609.

whose clothing becomes an indicator of his undeserved status and authority as a medical practitioner. In the sixth passus of the B text, Hunger criticizes the ornate clothing of Physic:

> That Phisik shal hise furred hodes for his fode selle,
> And his cloke of Calabre with alle the knappes of golde,
> And be fayn, by my feith, his phisik to lete,
> And lerne to laboure with lond [lest] liflode [hym faille].
>
> (B.6.268–71)

The furred hood and cloak of Physic may appear to be superficial, but his ornate appearance reflects his avaricious character. In fact, the extravagant dress of physicians was not merely a literary concern. John of Arderne wrote that surgeons must always dress and behave soberly and discreetly, avoiding boastful speech or dressing like a minstrel — that is, in extravagant clothes.[101] Hunger, then, presents a legitimate concern when he points to the dress of Physic because his dress defies the deontological standards for medical practitioners. Hunger seems to suggest that if Physic were practising medicine ethically, he would be able to afford only basic dress. This sentiment seems particularly characteristic of Hunger who, as Epstein shows, sees moderation, scarcity, and a just price for work as the solution to many moral problems caused by the labour market.[102]

Hunger's characterization of Physic foreshadows a later episode in B.20 and C.22 in which Life, under threat from advancing Eld, flees to a physician for protection:

> And bisoughte hym of socour, and of his salve hadde,
> And gaf hym golde good woon that gladede hir hertes;
> And thei gyven hym agayn a glazene howve.
> Lyf leeved that lechecraft lette sholde Elde,
> And dryven awey Deeth with dyas and drogges.
>   And Elde auntred hym on Lyf — and at the laste he hitte
> A phisicien with a furred hood, that he fel in a palsie,
> And there dyed that doctour er thre dayes after.
>
> (B.20.170–77; C.22.170–77)

---

101 Jones, 'Surgeon as Story-Teller', pp. 83–88. Arderne's standards derive from Hippocratic deontological treatises addressed to physicians, but over the course of the late medieval period, the standards came to apply also to barbers and surgeons. See Welborn, 'Long Tradition'; Leahy, '"To speke of phisik"', pp. 72, 111–32.

102 Epstein, 'Summoning Hunger', p. 66. For more on Hunger's ideas on moderation in relation to medicine, see Krug, 'Piers Plowman and the Secrets of Health', pp. 172–74.

Life approaches the physician seeking a salve, but Eld strikes the physician, who falls into a palsy and dies after three days. Life approaches the physician for help, receiving a salve and a glass cap or coif, a proverbial object that purports to provide protection but does not actually offer any safety. The physician himself proves to be equally vulnerable.[103]

Life's physician contrasts the self-healing *sothsegger* of *Mum and the Sothsegger*, as he is unable to heal himself. Not only does the physician fail to enact the proverb that Christ states in Luke 4. 23 to those who doubted him ('Medice cura teipsum'), but he also mirrors Christ's Passion by suffering for three days only to die rather than resurrect. The trope of the physician who cannot heal himself was not simply common in medical satires, but also invoked in pastoral texts. For instance, in the *Regula pastoralis*, Gregory the Great states that it would be a great stupidity for a patient to place their life in the hands of a physician who has a head wound, as it demonstrates his incompetence in healing. Gregory uses the image of the wounded physician to explain that just as it would be unwise for an injured physician to heal a patient before healing himself, so a spiritual physician needs to be free of sin to heal the souls of his congregants.[104] Similarly, the episode about Life in *Piers Plowman* continues a theme of the failure of those who attempt to escape the consequences of sin, old age, and death. The physician's death is illustrative not only of his untrustworthiness and incompetence but also of how sin, old age, and death are natural consequences of life and cannot be delayed forever with the treatments of physicians and indulgences of friars. By contrast, the wounds of sin can be cured according to penitential doctrine and death can be transformed into the ultimate reward in the afterlife through Christ the Divine Physician.

With Life's attempt to flee Eld a failure, it seems that Hunger's characterization of physicians proves to be accurate — that is, they are chiefly looking to make a profit from the suffering of their patients and do not offer healing. But Hunger is not so sceptical of physicians in all versions of *Piers Plowman*. While scholars have reached different conclusions on the Z text — that it could be a proto-A text, or a non-authorial version that borrows elements of the A and C texts[105]— its depiction of Hunger presents an intriguing perspective on the value of medicine. In the Z text, Hunger provides a more balanced account of medicine following his description of the extravagant clothing and lack of skill of Physic:

---

103 Barney, *Penn Commentary*, p. 218; Whiting and Whiting, *Proverbs, Sentences, and Proverbial Phrases*, p. 272, H 218.
104 Gregory the Great, *Regula pastoralis*, lib. 1, cap. 9, in PL 77: 22D.
105 Kerby-Fulton, *Piers Plowman*, pp. 518–19.

> I defame nat fysyk, for the science ys trewe,
> Ac vncunynge kaytyues that kannen nat rede a lettere
> Macuth hem maystres me for to hele.
> Ac hit ar maystres morthrares men for to quelle,
> Ant none leches but lyares — Lord hem amende!
> In Ecclesiasticis the clerc that can rede
> May se hit there hymsilf ant senes teche other:
> *Honora medicum*, he seyt, for *necessitatem*.
> For helthe from heuene, Y hope doth out springe,
> Ant therefor the Byble bit ant in ys bok techet
> That leches of lordus scholde here lower haute:
> *A regibus et principibus erit merces eorum*?
> Of princes ant prelatus here pencyoun schal aryse,
> Ant of no pore peple no peneworth gode take.
>
> (Z.7.255–73)[106]

It may seem to be contradictory of Hunger to follow his damning caricature of Physic with a statement on the truth of medicine. His logic is that 'fysyk' is a 'trewe' science but that it is practised by unknowing caitiffs who cannot read a letter of that which makes a physician a master. These illiterate physicians become masters of murder, killing their patients through their malpractice. The last two lines of the quotation are particularly telling, drawing a distinction between medicine in the active life and charitable medicine. Hunger explains that the wealthiest in society should pay for treatment and that the poor should receive it without any charge.[107] The payments of the wealthy, then, would not line the coffers of the physician, but would subsidize treatments for the less fortunate. Hunger does not condemn the idea of a practitioner charging a fee, rather that the fee should be commensurate with the patient's wealth.

Although Hunger's comment on different payments exists only in the Z text, similar sentiments can be found across the B and C texts. The benefit of treating poorer patients is emphasized in passus 16 of the B text, when Jesus learns *lechecraft* in preparation for the Crucifixion. Christ then seeks out the ill and practises healing until he perfects his craft. Piers the Plowman teaches Jesus *lechecraft* — although at this point in the text Piers is characterized as the human nature that Christ takes on through the Incarnation, and so it may be seen that Christ teaches himself:

---

106 Langland, *Piers Plowman*, ed. by Schmidt.
107 This same opinion, that richer patients should subsidize treatments for the poor, was expressed in Lanfranc of Milan's widely circulated *Cirurgie* and its Middle English translation. See *Lanfrank's 'Science of Cirurgie'*, ed. by Fleischhacker, p. 9.

> [... Piers] lered hym lechecraft, his lif for to save,
> That though he were wounded with his enemy, to warisshen hymselve;
> And dide hym assaie his surgerie on hem that sike were,
> Til he was parfit praktisour, if any peril fille;
> And soughte out the sike and synfulle bothe,
> And salvede sike and synfulle, bothe blynde and crokede,
> And commune wommen convertede and to goode turnede:
> *Non est sanis opus medicus, set male habentibus...*
>   Bothe meseles and mute, and in the menyson blody —
> Ofte he heeled swiche, he ne held it for no maistrie,
> Save tho he leched Lazar, that hadde yleye in grave
> *Quatriduanus* quelt — quyk dide hym walke.
>
>   *(B.16.104–14)*

St-Jacques notes that this passage signifies the healing of humanity's spiritual disease of sin, which Christ achieves through a series of miracles described in Langland's sketch of his life that ends with Christ's jousting in Jerusalem (B.161–66).[108] Piers's teaching of *lechecraft* also has an application for physical healers. As the Divine Physician who seeks out the ill in order to practise *lechecraft* until he gains mastery, *Christus medicus* provides an exemplar for earthly *leches*. Although Christ becomes the perfect practitioner, he first has to learn his craft by treating all he comes across. Christ therefore confirms that both knowledge and experience are vital in training physicians. By contrast, medieval *leches* who charged for their services were selective in the cases they took on. For instance, John of Arderne was particularly cautious in advising surgeons not to accept cases where the patient was likely to die, as the surgeon might be deemed to have caused the death. He also cautioned against treating a patient unless he knew how the patient would pay the fee. John of Arderne was not against the idea of charitable surgery, but rather recommended that a surgeon should exercise caution. He particularly feared the exploitation of the poor and the threat of disagreement arising between practitioner and patient.[109] Nonetheless, if *leches* were to treat patients without charge, their case loads would increase exponentially. What better way to perfect one's craft than by treating everyone one encounters? Charity is not simply beneficial for the soul of a physician, then, but also serves as a practical means of increasing mastery.

---

108 St-Jacques, 'Langland's *Christus medicus* Image', p. 122. This quick sketch of Christ's life is later expanded with the Crucifixion and Harrowing of Hell episodes in B.18. Christ's life is then summarized again in the story of Dowel in B.19. For more on the ways in which the poem presents Christ's life, see Steiner, *Reading 'Piers Plowman'*, pp. 174–78.

109 Arderne, *Treatises of Fistula in Ano*, pp. 5–6.

Lechecraft is not Christ's only role, but rather one part of his mission on earth. Similarly, the Samaritan is far removed from the other *leches* we have encountered. He treats the *semivif* as an act of charity because he is not a surgeon or barber and wound treatment is not his craft. For Langland not all medical practitioners are worthy of criticism because if they act charitably and reject the commercialization of healing in late medieval London, they are akin to the Divine Physician, the Samaritan, or Piers himself. While these characters are all healers, their *lechecraft* contrasts that sold in the marketplace; *lechecraft* is one aspect of their charitable duties.

***

In the final passus of the B and C Texts of *Piers Plowman*, the parallels between spiritual and physical health reach a pinnacle when Conscience prays to Kind for help to unite Holy Church. In what Nicolette Zeeman aptly defines as an 'extreme way of ending sin',[110] Kind sends a litany of diseases:

> [...] feveres and fluxes,
> Coughes and cardiacles, cramps and toothaches,
> Rewmes and radegundes and roynouse scales,
> Biles and bocches and brennynge agyes,
> Frenesies and foule yveles [...]
>
> (B.20.81–85; C.22.81–85)

As Barney explains, 'flourishing good health' becomes an obstacle to contrition and thus Kind sends these diseases in the hope that after having endured illness and death, the people of Holy Church will gain a new perspective on life.[111] These diseases act as reminders of the fragility of the human body and the need for a constant spiritual commitment.[112] At this moment, God is no longer a physician, but one who inflicts diseases. Following Friar Flatterer's subsequent ineffective healing, Conscience, who now rejects his false counsellors, prays again to Kind for 'heele' and then goes off on a spiritual pilgrimage in search of Piers the Plowman. At this point in the text, we find that professional healers are entirely powerless in the face of Kind, despite their pretentions of being able to cure such maladies. Piers is the only healer who can purge pride and lead the Church back to health. Yet rather than dreaming that Conscience finds Piers — who would presumably purge pride from the Barn of Unity — Will awakens, leaving the reader to wonder whether there is any hope of purging pride from the Church and healing it (B.20.385–87; C.22.384–86).

---

110 Zeeman, *Arts of Disruption*, p. 292.
111 Barney, *Penn Commentary*, p. 212.
112 Gasse, 'Practice of Medicine in *Piers Plowman*', p. 178.

Why would Piers's treatments be effective when those who present themselves as professional *leches* are impotent? It is his charitable attitude that leads Piers to exemplify the model established by Christ the Divine Physician. After all, Piers taught Christ *lechecraft*. The same charitable mission motivates *sothseggers*, who much like Piers the Plowman are the truth-telling barbers or surgeons of *Mum and the Sothsegger*. Throughout their critique of professional medicine, Langland and his contemporaries enter debates surrounding the development of professional medicine and surgery at a time in which authorities sought more stringent control over who practised in English cities. The sinful urban marketplace of healing, where Dame Emme, Friar Flatterer, and Physic all compete for the same clients, displays a particularly dismal view of *lechecraft* as an exploitative business. Yet among the sketch of commercialized *leches*, we find the *sothsegger*, the Samaritan, and Piers. These healers display no desire to seek a profit because they are not chiefly *leches*; they perform *lechecraft* as one part of their charitable duties rather than as a craft or profession.

Works Cited

Manuscript

Oxford, Bodleian Library, MS Douce 104 <https://digital.bodleian.ox.ac.uk/objects/e6865046-6257-4591-a731-548232c7c8dd/> [accessed 25 July 2022]

Primary Sources

Additional Material for the History of the Grey Friars, London, ed. by C. L. Kingsford (Manchester: Manchester University Press, 1922)
Annals of the Barber-Surgeons of London, Compiled from their Records and Other Sources, ed. by Sidney Young (London: Blades, East & Blases, 1890)
Biblia sacra vulgata, editio quinta, ed. by Robert Weber and Roger Gryson (Stuttgart: Deutsche Bibelgesellschaft, 2006)
Chaucer, Geoffrey, *The Riverside Chaucer*, ed. by Larry D. Benson, 3rd edn (Oxford: Oxford University Press, 1988)
Claudii Galeni Pergameni scripta minora, ed. by Johann Marquardt, Iwan von Müller, and Georg Helmreich, 3 vols (Leipzig: Bibliotheca Teubneriana, 1884–1893)
Daniel, Henry, *Liber uricrisiarum: A Reading Edition*, ed. by E. Ruth Harvey, M. Teresa Tavormina, and Sarah Star (Toronto: University of Toronto Press, 2020)
Gregory the Great [Gregorius Magnus], *Regula pastoralis*, ed. by Jacques-Paul Migne, Patrologiae cursus completus: series latina, 77 (Paris: 1844–1864), cols 13–125
The Guild Book of the Barbers and Surgeons of York (British Library, Egerton MS 2572): Study and Edition, ed. by Richard D. Wragg (York: York Medieval, 2022)
Hunt, Tony, ed., *Popular Medicine in Thirteenth-century England: Introduction and Texts* (Woodbridge: Boydell & Brewer, 1990)
John of Arderne, *Treatises of Fistula in Ano, Haemorrhoids, and Clysters*, ed. by D'Arcy Power, EETS, o.s. 139 (London: Oxford University Press, 1910; reprint 1968)
Lanfranc of Milan, *Lanfrank's 'Science of Cirurgie'*, ed. by R. V. Fleischhacker, EETS, o.s. 102 (Oxford: Oxford University Press, 1894; reprint 1988)
Langland, William, *Piers Plowman: A New Annotated Edition of the C-Text*, ed. by Derek Pearsall (Liverpool: Liverpool University Press, 2008)
———, *Piers Plowman: A Parallel-Text Edition of the A, B, C and Z Versions*, ed. by A. V. C. Schmidt, 2 vols (London: Longman, 1995 and 2008)
———, *The Vision of Piers Plowman: A Critical Edition of the B-Text Based on Trinity College Cambridge MS B.15.17*, ed. by A. V. C. Schmidt, 2nd edn (London: Dent, 1995)

Medieval English Political Writings, ed. by James M. Dean (Kalamazoo, MI: Medieval Institute Publications, 1996)

The 'Piers Plowman' Tradition: A Critical Edition of 'Pierce the Ploughman's Crede', 'Richard the Redeless', 'Mum and the Sothsegger', and the 'The Crowned King', ed. by Helen Barr (London: Everyman's Library, 1993)

Registrum litterarum Raymundi de Capua, 1386–1399: [et] Leonardi di Mansuetis, 1474–1480, ed. by Maria Benedikt Reichert (Leipzig: Harrassowitz, 1911)

Richard the Redeless and Mum and the Sothsegger, ed. by James M. Dean (Kalamazoo, MI: Medieval Institute, 2000)

Whiting, Bartlett Jere, and Helen Wescott Whiting, ed., *Proverbs, Sentences, and Proverbial Phrases from English Writings Mainly Before 1500* (Cambridge, MA: Harvard University Press, 1968)

Secondary Sources

Aers, David, 'Justice and Wage-Labor after the Black Death: Some Perplexities for William Langland', in *The Work of Work: Servitude, Slavery, and Labor in Medieval England*, ed. by Allen J. Frantzen and Douglas Moffat (Glasgow: Cruithne, 1994), pp. 169–90

Alford, John, 'Medicine in the Middle Ages: The Theory of a Profession', *Centennial Review*, 23.4 (1979), 377–96

Al Kaaoud, Elizabeth, '"Caro", "caritas", and the Role of Samaritan in *Piers Plowman*', *Proceedings of the PMR Conference*, 7 (1982), 39–45

Barney, Stephen A., *The Penn Commentary on 'Piers Plowman': C Passus 20–22; B Passus 18–20*, vol. v (Philadelphia: University of Pennsylvania Press, 2006)

Beck, R. Theodore, *The Cutting Edge: Early History of the Surgeons of London* (London: Lund Humphries, 1974)

Bullough, Vern L., 'The Medieval Medical School at Cambridge', *Medieval Studies*, 27 (1962), 161–68

——, 'Training of the Nonuniversity-Educated Medical Practitioners in the Later Middle Ages', *Journal of the History of Medicine and Allied Sciences*, 14.4 (1959), 446–58

Butler, Sara M., 'Portrait of a Surgeon in Fifteenth-Century England', in *Medicine and the Law in the Middle Ages*, ed. by Wendy J. Turner and Sara M. Butler (Leiden: Brill, 2014), pp. 243–66

Colson, Justin, and Robert Ralley, 'Medical Practice, Urban Politics and Patronage: The London "Commonalty" of Physicians and Surgeons of the 1420s', *English Historical Review*, 130.546 (2015), 1102–31

Edsall, Mary Agnes, '*Arma Christi* Rolls or Textual Amulets? The Narrow Roll Format Manuscripts of "O Vernicle"', *Magic, Ritual, and Witchcraft*, 9.2 (2014), 178–205

Epstein, Robert, 'Summoning Hunger: Polanyi, *Piers Plowman*, and the Labor Market', in *Money, Commerce, and Economics in Late Medieval English Literature*, ed. by Craig E. Bertolet and Robert Epstein (London: Palgrave Macmillan, 2018), pp. 59–76

Friedman, John B., 'The Friar Portrait in Bodleian Library MS Douce 104: Contemporary Satire?', *Yearbook of Langland Studies*, 8 (1994), 177–85

Galloway, Andrew, 'The Economy of Need in Late Medieval English Literature', *Viator*, 40 (2009), 309–31

——, 'Langland and the Reinvention of Array in Late-Medieval England', *Review of English Studies, New Studies*, 71.301 (2019), 607–29

——, *The Penn Commentary on 'Piers Plowman': C Prologue–Passus 4; B Prologue–Passus 4; A Prologue–Passus*, vol. I (Philadelphia: University of Pennsylvania Press, 2006)

Garay, Kathleen, and Madeleine Jeay, 'Advice Concerning Pregnancy and Health in Late Medieval Europe: Peasant Women's Wisdom in *The Distaff Gospels*', *Canadian Bulletin of Medical History – Bulletin canadien d'histoire de la médecine*, 24.2 (2007), 423–43

Gasse, Roseanne, 'The Practice of Medicine in *Piers Plowman*', *Chaucer Review*, 39 (2004), 177–97

Getz, Faye M., 'Medical Education in England', in *The History of Medical Education in Britain*, ed. by Vivian Nutton and Roy Porter (Amsterdam: Rodopi, 1995), pp. 76–93

——, *Medicine in the English Middle Ages* (Princeton: Princeton University Press, 1998)

Grigsby, Bryon, 'The Social Position of the Surgeon in London, 1350–1450', *Essays in Medieval Studies*, 13 (1996), 71–80

Hanna, Ralph, *The Penn Commentary on 'Piers Plowman': C Passus 4–9; B Passus 5–7; A Passus 5–8*, vol. II (Philadelphia: University of Pennsylvania Press, 2006)

Harvey, E. Ruth, *The Inward Wits: Psychological Theory in the Middle Ages and the Renaissance*, Warburg Institute Surveys 6 (London: Warburg Institute, 1975)

Jacquart, Danielle, *La Médecine médiévale dans le cadre Parisien XIVe–XVe siècle* (Paris: Fayard, 1998)

Jones, Peter Murray, 'John of Arderne and the Mediterranean Tradition of Scholastic Surgery', in *Practical Medicine from Salerno to the Black Death*, ed. by Luis García-Ballester, Roger French, Jon Arrizabalaga, and Andrew Cunningham (Cambridge: Cambridge University Press, 1994), pp. 289–321

——, 'The Surgeon as Story-Teller', *Poetica*, 72 (2009), 77–92

Kantorowicz, Ernst H., *The King's Two Bodies: A Study in Medieval Political Theology*, 2nd edn (Princeton: Princeton University Press, 1997)

Kean, P. M., 'Love, Law, and Lewte in *Piers Plowman*', *Review of English Studies*, 15.59 (1964), 241–61

Kerby-Fulton, Kathryn, 'Piers Plowman', in *The Cambridge History of Medieval English Literature*, ed. by David Wallace (Cambridge: Cambridge University Press, 1999), pp. 513–38

Kiefer, Joseph H., 'Uroscopy: The Artist's Portrayal of the Physician', *Bulletin of the New York Academy of Medicine*, 40 (1964), 759–66

Krug, Rebecca, '*Piers Plowman* and the Secrets of Health', *Chaucer Review*, 46 (2011), 166–81

Kudlien, Fridolf, 'Medicine as a "Liberal Art" and the Question of the Physician's Income', *Journal of the History of Medicine*, 31 (1976), 448–59

Langholm, Odd, *The Merchant in the Confessional: Trade and Price in the Pre-Reformation Penitential Handbooks* (Leiden: Brill, 2003)

Lawler, Traugott, *The Penn Commentary on 'Piers Plowman': C Passus 15–19; B Passus 13–17*, vol. IV (Philadelphia: University of Pennsylvania Press, 2018)

Leahy, Michael, '"To speke of phisik": Medical Discourse in Late Medieval English Culture' (unpublished doctoral dissertation, Birkbeck, University of London, 2015)

Mann, Jill, *Chaucer and Medieval Estates Satire* (Cambridge: Cambridge University Press, 1973)

McVaugh, Michael R., 'Bedside Manners in the Middle Ages', *Bulletin of the History of Medicine*, 71 (1997), 201–33

——, *The Rational Surgery of the Middle Ages* (Florence: Sismel, Edizioni del Galluzzo, 2006)

Moir Bryce, William, *The Black Friars of Edinburgh* (Edinburgh: Constable, 1911)

Montford, Angela, *Health, Sickness, Medicine and the Friars in the Thirteenth and Fourteenth Centuries* (Aldershot: Ashgate, 2004)

O'Boyle, Cornelius, *The Art of Medicine: Medical Teaching at the University of Paris 1250–1400* (Leiden: Brill, 1998)

Olsan, Lea T., 'Charms and Prayers in Medieval Medical Theory and Practice', *Social History of Medicine*, 16.3 (2003), 343–66

——, 'The Marginality of Charms in Medieval England', in *The Power of Words: Studies on Charms and Charming in Europe*, ed. by James Kapaló, Éva Pócs, and William Ryan (Budapest: Central European University Press, 2013), pp. 135–64

Orlemanski, Julie, 'Langland's Poetics of Animation: Body, Soul, Personification', *Yearbook of Langland Studies*, 33 (2019), 159–83

——, *Symptomatic Subjects: Bodies, Medicine, and Causation in the Literature of Late Medieval England* (Pennsylvania: University of Philadelphia Press, 2019)

Pearsall, Derek, 'Langland's London', in *Written Work: Langland, Labor, and Authorship*, ed. by Steven Justice and Kathryn Kerby-Fulton (Philadelphia: University of Pennsylvania Press, 1997), pp. 185–207

Pelling, Margaret, *Medical Conflicts in Early Modern London: Patronage, Physicians and Irregular Practitioners, 1550–1640* (Oxford: Oxford University Press, 2003)

Raschko, Mary, *The Politics of Middle English Parables: Fiction, Theology, and Social Practice* (Manchester: Manchester University Press, 2019)

Rawcliffe, Carole, 'A Crisis of Confidence? Parliament and the Demand for Hospital Reform in Early-15th and Early-16th Century England', *Parliamentary History*, 35 (2016), 85–110

——, *Medicine and Society in Later Medieval England* (Stroud: Sutton Publishing, 1995)

——, *Urban Bodies: Communal Health in Late Medieval English Towns and Cities* (Woodbridge: Boydell & Brewer, 2013)

Rodman Jones, Mike, *Radical Pastoral, 1381–1594: Appropriation and the Writing of Religious Controversy* (Farnham: Ashgate, 2011)

Salisbury, Eve, *Narrating Medicine in Middle English Poetry: Poets, Practitioners, and the Plague* (London: Bloomsbury, 2022)

Smith, D. Vance, *Arts of Possession: The Middle English Household Imaginary* (Minneapolis: University of Minnesota Press, 2002)

Sobecki, Sebastian, 'A Southwark Tale: Gower, the 1381 Poll Tax, and Chaucer's *The Canterbury Tales*', *Speculum*, 92.3 (2017), 630–60

Star, Sarah, 'Introduction: Reading Henry Daniel', in *Henry Daniel and the Rise of Middle English Medical Writing*, ed. by Sarah Star (Toronto: University of Toronto Press, 2022), pp. 3–14

Steiner, Emily, *Documentary Culture and the Making of Medieval English Literature* (Cambridge: Cambridge University Press, 2003)

——, *Reading 'Piers Plowman'* (Cambridge: Cambridge University Press, 2013)

St-Jacques, Raymond, 'Langland's *Christus medicus* Image and the Structure of *Piers Plowman*', *Yearbook of Langland Studies*, 5 (1991), 111–27

Swanson, Robert N., 'Praying for Pardon: Devotional Indulgences in Late Medieval England', in *Promissory Notes on the Treasury of Merits: Indulgences in Late-Medieval Europe*, ed. by Robert N. Swanson, Brill's Companions to the Christian Tradition, 5 (Leiden: Brill, 2006), pp. 215–40

Szittya, Penn R., *The Antifraternal Tradition in Medieval Literature* (Princeton: Princeton University Press, 1986)

Talbot, C. H., *Medicine in Medieval England* (London: Oldbourne, 1967)

Theilmann, J. M., 'The Regulation of Public Health in Late Medieval England', in *The Age of Richard II*, ed. by James L. Gillespie (Stroud: Alan Sutton; New York: St Martin's Press, 1997), pp. 205–23

Thomas, Arvind, *'Piers Plowman' and the Reinvention of Church Law in the Late Middle Ages* (Toronto: University of Toronto Press, 2019)

Vincent, Nicholas, 'Some Pardoners' Tales: The Earliest English Indulgences', *Transactions of the Royal Historical Society*, 6.12 (2002), 23–58

Walling, Amanda, 'Friar Flatterer: Glossing and the Hermeneutics of Flattery in *Piers Plowman*', *Yearbook of Langland Studies*, 21 (2007), 57–76

Wallis, Faith, 'Pre-modern Surgery: Wounds, Words, and the Paradox of "Tradition"', in *The Palgrave Handbook of the History of Surgery*, ed. by Thomas Schlich (London: Palgrave Macmillan, 2018), pp. 49–70

Welborn, Mary Catherine, 'The Long Tradition: A Study in Fourteenth-Century Medical Deontology', in *Medieval and Historiographical Essays in Honour of James Westfall Thompson*, ed. by James Lea Cate and Eugene Newton Anderson (Chicago: University of Chicago Press, 1938), pp. 344–60

Yeager, Stephen M., *From Lawmen to Plowmen: Anglo-Saxon Legal Tradition and the School of Langland* (Toronto: University of Toronto Press, 2014)

Zeeman, Nicolette, *The Arts of Disruption: Allegory and 'Piers Plowman'* (Oxford: Oxford University Press, 2020)

GRACE CATHERINE GREINER

'Meddling with Making'

Speech, Poetic Craft, and the Spectre of Imaginatif in Piers Plowman A

▼ **ABSTRACT** Taking energy from the addition of the B-text phrase 'meddling with making' to the A-text ending in Oxford, Bodleian Library, MS Rawlinson poetry 137 composed by the medieval reader John But, this article argues that a renewed attention to the reception history of *Piers Plowman* and to the correspondences between certain moments in the A text and Imaginatif's passūs in the B and C texts corroborates a genetic reading of the poem's development. Such an approach, I contend, shows the poet to have thought about Imaginatif even before writing him as a character in the poem, and further sheds light on medieval readers' responses to and engagement with *Piers* as a multi-text literary phenomenon centred around issues of speech, craft, and the intellectual and spiritual value of poetic making.

▼ **KEYWORDS** Imaginatif, John But, Oxford Bodleian MS Rawlinson poetry 137, *Piers Plowman* A, reception history

Grace Catherine Greiner is a Visiting Lecturer in the Department of Literatures in English at Cornell University, where she specializes in medieval and early modern literature, with a focus on premodern poetics, book history, and theories of materiality. Prior to coming to Cornell, she completed a postdoctoral fellowship at the University of Texas of Austin. She holds a PhD and MA from Cornell University, an MPhil from the University of Cambridge, and a BA from Columbia University.

Of the many divergences between the A, B, and C versions of *Piers Plowman*, the absence of Imaginatif in the A text is particularly noticeable when compared to his presence in the later B and C versions. In both the B and C texts, Imaginatif receives an entire passus to himself, nestled between the dreamer's encounters with Reason and Conscience.[1] In these versions, he is arguably one of the most active and exuberant personifications in the poem. His dramatic entrance and exit are worthy of comment in their own right; he is the only character whom the dreamer has to actively follow (he 'shoop hym for to walken. / And I aroos up right with that and [raughte] hym after', B.11.437b–38), and who 'vanysshe[s]' (12.295b) once his discourse is complete. Will, in the B text, in fact suggests that the reader also ought to have been surprised and perplexed by Imaginatif's curious exit; when he wakes at the beginning of the next passus, he 'of this metyng many tymes muche thought [...] hadde' (13.4), and 'whan he [Imaginatif] hadde seide so, how sodeynliche he passed' (13.20). Just as striking is the way in which Imaginatif stages a dramatic, legalistic defence of Clergy, which ultimately bears on the dreamer's sense of his own poetic craft. Both for Langland and for scholars since, Imaginatif proves an obvious choice for explorations of poetic invention, the poem's distinctions between 'lettred and lewed' (15.353a), and the institutional assortment of legal, clerical, and ecclesiastical undertones — all popular ideas examined by scholars in reference to other moments in the poem.[2] And yet, curiously, in the A text, there is no character that goes by this name; Imaginatif is, apparently, nowhere to be found.

And yet, Imaginatif's absence from the A text of *Piers Plowman* is not, in fact, totalizing; there are, as I will argue in this essay, subtler poetic workings in play that can help account for his apparent absence in the earliest version of the poem and also shed light on his role in later versions first as a critic and then as an advocate for poetic craft, or

---

1 Both the B and C texts have proved fertile fields for contemplating which fourteenth-century sources might have informed Langland's Imaginatif, generally agreed to be 'a faculty mediating between the senses and reason'. See White, 'Langland's Ymaginatif', p. 241. See, for instance: Jones, 'Imaginatif in Piers Plowman'; Quirk, 'vis imaginativa'; Kaulbach, '"vis imaginativa" and the Reasoning Powers'; Kaulbach, '"vis imaginativa secundum Avicennam"'; and Eldredge, 'Some Medical Evidence'.

2 Several scholars who work on medieval faculty psychology, cognition, memory, and the rhetorical arts have given Imaginatif space in their discussions. Alastair Minnis and Michelle Karnes both discuss *Piers Plowman* and Imaginatif in relation to late medieval intellectual history. See Minnis, 'Langland's Ymaginatif', and Karnes, 'Will's Imagination'. Nicolette Zeeman discusses Imaginatif in her chapter on Clergy and Kynde before considering the figure in a more sustained manner in the following chapter on Imaginatif and the Feast of Patience. See Zeeman, *Piers Plowman*, pp. 201–62. McDermott, '"beatus qui verba vertit in opera"', comments briefly on Imaginatif's view of poetic making in the context of a larger investigation into the poet-dreamer's ethical invention and tropology. Hanna, 'Langland's Ymaginatif', examines Imaginatif in relation to questions of poetic making.

'meddling with making', as he puts it in the B text.[3] Focusing on moments in the A-text Vita that contain lexical, stylistic, and thematic relations to Imaginatif's passūs in the B and C texts, I will demonstrate how an Imaginatif-like presence seems to lurk in the poet's mind as he writes the A text, arguing that the spectre of Imaginatif hovers in A-text sites where Langland tries and tests the characteristic discursive moves of the fully fleshed-out personification of the B and C texts, but through the words and activities of A-text characters. Accordingly, my goal in this essay is to trace one possible story of textual development that corroborates an evolutionary, genetic approach to *Piers Plowman* by taking heed of Imaginatif's apparent absence from the A text, while also attending to the poem's reception history as emblematized in one manuscript that contains what Míceál Vaughan calls the 'A-plus' version of the poem: Oxford, Bodleian Library, MS Rawlinson poetry 137.[4]

In this manuscript, somewhere in the final passus, the scribe appears to break from the A text as written by Langland and offers an account of how Will, the dreamer and also the poet, dies ('And whan this werk was wrought, ere Wille myghte aspie, / Deth delt him a dent, and drof him to the erthe', *Piers Plowman* A.12.100–01), leaving one John But to complete the poem.[5] In these final moments, But imports a phrase that appears in Imaginatif's passus in the B text to describe his A-text intervention. 'And so bad Johan But', the manuscript reads,

> busily wel ofte,
> When he saw thes sawes busyly allegged
> By James and by Jerom, by Jop and by othere;
> And for he medleth of makyng, he made this ende.
>
> (*A.12.103–06*)

But's continuation — his A-text meddling with making — I would suggest not only implies his familiarity with *Piers Plowman* as a multi-version textual phenomenon,[6] but also connotes his status as a reader attuned to

---

3 Compelling arguments for the A text's composition prior to the B and C versions are set out by Hanna, *Pursuing History*, pp. 195–243. Alternative textual orders place A after B or after the so-called Z text. See *Piers Plowman*, ed. by Rigg and Brewer (Z), and Mann, 'Power of the Alphabet' (A after B). I follow Hanna's placement of A.
4 *Piers Plowman*, ed. by Vaughan, p. 3.
5 Throughout, I reference Vaughan's classroom A-text edition because Vaughan, like myself, is interested in the poem as attested by Rawlinson poet. 137. Vaughan's text also includes John But's conclusion as part of the main text, whereas George Kane's Athlone edition relegates this conclusion to an appendix.
6 A suggestion also put forward by Middleton, 'Making a Good End', p. 247, on the basis of the same evidence. In her view, John But's making, 'becomes a way to stabilize and unify the moral truth of the text that he knew circulated in the world in more than one form'.

Langland's theorizations of poetic craft and to the proto-presence of Imaginatif in the A text because of his familiarity with later versions of the poem. In other words, But's poetic intervention, I will contend, provides the means and motive for modern readers to meddle not, as But or Imaginatif do, with Will's making, but rather with Langland's, considering the ways in which But's imported B-text phrase reminds us of *Piers Plowman*'s status as a multi-version text composed in stages. When we work both forwards and backwards in time from the A text to the B and C texts, our focus trained on instances where Imaginatif *might* be but is not *yet*, Langland's poetic process retrospectively comes into view, his making (as mediated by his own imagination) on display, paradoxically, wherever Imaginatif is not.

See Middleton, 'Making a Good End', p. 262. Warner, 'John But', p. 17, citing Middleton and Hanna, also notes the 'strong evidence that John But knew *Piers Plowman* B'. '[H]is accommodation of B matter within his own A-continuation', Warner observes, 'is perfectly in keeping with the behaviour of the many other scribes who conflated or combined texts from the various versions'. Further evidence that supports the claim that But knew other versions of the poem and, what's more, purposefully zeroed in on the B-text phrase *meddling with making* as it occurs in the B-text Imaginatif passus, comes in both scribal and textual forms. As Horobin, 'Scribe of Rawlinson Poetry 137', pp. 4 and 13, demonstrates, the hand of the scribe can be identified as belonging to one Thomas Tilot, who worked or was trained in South Sussex, and likely had ties to Chichester Cathedral where he was installed as a vicar. Horobin's identification, which draws evidence from But's conclusion and a scribal subscription, not only gives us a name and a place with which we might associate the beginnings of Rawlinson poet. 137; it also gives us a sociohistorical context for reading this particular witness of the A text that includes But's imported B-text phrase ('medlest thee with makynge' in B). Assuming an early readership (or, at the very least, a point of origin) for Rawlinson poet. 137 with ties to the office of the vicar, this witness and its expanded ending, as copied by Tilot and supposedly originating from But, become entangled with aspects of vicarial training, particularly the probationary year in which candidates were expected to learn the psalter, antiphonary, hymnary, and histories by heart. Since the B-text instance of 'meddling with making' occurs in (oppositional) relation to 'seye[ing] thi Sauter' (and in Imaginatif's speech, at that), Tilot's rationale for retaining it in this copy of the poem (or, possibly, selecting this version for copying) becomes a little clearer, especially if we assume that Tilot was familiar with the B-text moment that But seemed to know. Assuming this — a not entirely unreasonable assumption, given the proliferation of *Piers Plowman* manuscripts by Tilot's time and their popularity within ecclesiastical settings — But's mention of 'meddling with making' may have caught Tilot's eye precisely because of its vocational resonance; that is, Tilot's own vicarial training, which required saying the psalter, likely would have made the B-text Imaginatif's juxtaposition of poetic craft against devotional exercise a striking moment in his reading experience. But even leaving aside the possibility that Tilot knew the B-text moment alluded to by But, we must remember that Tilot was himself someone evidently interested in making, insofar as scribal copying constitutes a form of making. That is, the appeal of But's ending for Tilot may have lain simply in its metatextual reflection on poetic composition and 'making an end' to a poetic work, as Tilot himself completed his scribal labours and finished copying the poem.

Taking as a fulcrum, then, But's imported B-text phrase 'meddling with making' in his A-text ending,[7] throughout this essay I will examine moments in the A-text Vita, most often concerned with different kinds of speech, that parallel Imaginatif's discursive strategies in the B and C texts — those moments, I suggest, where his spectral presence is most present — and explore how Langland offers them as an inroad to contemplating the nature and significance of a material poetic making: when poetry (though characterized as 'meddling') itself becomes intellectually and spiritually valuable. I will show Imaginatif's proto-presence in *Piers Plowman* A to be evoked most strongly at times when the activities of speech and poetic craft are put into conversation; this A-text spectre, I will argue, ultimately anticipates Langland's vision of a material, ethical, and spiritually valuable poetics as articulated in later versions of the poem — of a poetics that (to elaborate on Anne Middleton's reading) utilizes both the poet's and the reader's imagination to join 'doings' and 'makings' in order to 'inscribe one's life usefully in the book of the world's history'.[8] As I will suggest in the final moments of this essay, contemplating Langland's material poetics and the A-text spectre of Imaginatif in light of scribal and readerly interventions in *Piers Plowman*'s manuscript history, its material afterlives, invites us to think about how that poetics and Langland's attendant imagination *of* the imagination as perpetually continuing the poem's making have been borne out by readers' engagements with the poem since it first was made.

***

The John But who fiddles with the ending of Langland's text in Oxford, Bodleian Library, MS Rawlinson poet. 137 (hereafter Rawlinson poet. 137) is one such reader whose textual meddling recalls to us the importance of attending closely to readerly and scribal textual additions and interventions in the study of medieval texts, especially those like *Piers Plowman* that enjoyed a vibrant material history, reception, and continual remaking both during and after their authors' lives. Indeed, as Simon

---

7 This focus has a precedent in a seminal essay by Anne Middleton, in which Middleton not only offers a reading of the B-text Imaginatif passages examined here, but also identifies the term *medlyng* as integral to Langland's poetic project insofar as it is related to the disrupted episode. 'Medlying', she stresses, not only describes the episodic structure of the poem — a structure characterized by disruption 'either by the "medlyng" subject or one of his rebuking informants [like Imaginatif]' — it is also 'used to describe the enterprise of "making" the poem itself'. For this reason, she argues, 'the disruption of the episode becomes doubly an artistic signature. It releases the energy by which the poem not only *makes* itself, but *defends* itself'. See Middleton, 'Narration and the Invention of Experience', p. 110.
8 Middleton, 'Narration and the Invention of Experience', p. 115. The B-text Imaginatif, Middleton suggests, privileges 'verbal "doings"' such as 'prayer and penance' over Will's poetic '"makings"'.

Horobin reminds us, the 'identification of scribes of manuscripts of *Piers Plowman* can provide important insights into the study of the poem's reception', and furthermore, this is 'particularly true of amateur scribes [such as Thomas Tilot, whom Horobin identifies as the scribe of Rawlinson poet. 137] who were unlikely to have been guided by the external demands of a bespoke book trade, and who would produce copies of *Piers Plowman* reflecting their own personal responses to the poem'.[9] Middleton argues that precisely this kind of response-oriented reception and compilation practice is at work within Rawlinson poet. 137, and furthermore, takes But's poetic intervention as the first case of the autobiographical fallacy in *Piers Plowman* readership.[10] But's subscription, she stresses, should be interpreted not as 'a scribal *explicit* but a tribute in kind, a "making" about a making, an act of both literary criticism and literary imitation'.[11] But, as 'grateful and discriminating reader and amateur versifier', thus 'borrows' the B-text author's phrase *medleth with makyng* as a means of embedding his readerly response to the other longer version in the shorter A text. Middleton suggests that But's borrowing proves that he was familiar with other versions of the poem.[12] This suggestion makes sense especially in light of the fact that many of the A-text manuscripts of *Piers Plowman* date later than most extant B- and C-text manuscripts;[13] this phenomenon supports the theory that someone like But or Tilot, as A-text copiers, would have had encountered B- and C-text forms of the poem prior to sitting down to complete or copy the A text. In Middleton's view, But's making, which she identifies as starting around A.12.55, 'thus becomes a way to stabilize and unify the moral truth of the text that he knew circulated in the world in more than one form'.[14]

Following in Middleton's footsteps, we can zero in on the 'meddling with making' moment in Rawlinson poet. 137 as a form of

---

9 Horobin, 'Scribe of Rawlinson Poetry 137', p. 7. Wood, *Piers Plowman*, 97–118, focusing less on scribal identification and more on manuscript compilation and *Piers Plowman* companion texts, has recently made a compelling case for John But as a reader trained in the ethical and affective modes of romance reading, a claim she makes on the basis of *Piers Plowman*'s frequent appearance in manuscript alongside popular medieval romances such as the *Wars of Alisaunder*. My thanks to the *YLS* editors for pointing me to Wood's monograph.
10 Middleton, 'Making a Good End', p. 243, observes: 'If the "autobiographical fallacy" is a critical error, it is not exclusively a modern one. The first of Langland's readers committed to the "autobiographical fallacy" was, I believe, also the first of his critics to leave us his name: the poet's contemporary John But, who "made an end" to the A version some time before 1399, and in doing so held out to us the hope of discovering, through his addendum to the text, factual truths concerning a poet whose life is otherwise virtually undocumented in surviving records'.
11 Middleton, 'Making a Good End', p. 246.
12 Middleton, 'Making a Good End', p. 247.
13 *Piers Plowman*, ed. by Vaughan, p. 8.
14 Middleton, 'Making a Good End', p. 262.

reader-response-oriented writing and copying that thematizes Langland's making alongside that of But the reader/scribe, while also provoking us to turn our attention to the B text of *Piers Plowman*, where the phrase originated. Imaginatif's B-text opposition of 'meddling with making' to 'saying your psalter' occurs as part of Imaginatif's rebuke of the dreamer for choosing the less spiritually useful activity of writing poetry in lieu of engaging in devotional activities. Imaginatif's rebuke is not entirely surprising coming from a figure who imparts very set ideas about what kinds of made words — particularly, Clergy, or revealed kinds of book-learning — are spiritually valuable. Nonetheless, 'meddling with making' in the B text comes across as, in Middleton's words, 'perhaps the most devastating systematic indictment of "making" anywhere in Middle English literature'.[15] When But employs the phrase in his subscription, however, he does so unironically, according to Middleton. If But truly uses the phrase in earnestness to describe his own writerly activity, then perhaps it is the case that But was familiar not only with what we know as the B text, but also the C text. For in the C text, Imaginatif's poetic rebuke vanishes and his discourse seems, if anything, as much a defence of making as it is a defence of Clergy. And what is more, poetic making in the C text (and even in certain moments in B) is further vindicated when thought of in material terms, and so can be deemed ethical and spiritually useful. It is here that I diverge from Middleton in my thinking on how Imaginatif actually conceptualizes making. While Middleton suggests a reading in which making for Imaginatif is 'the mental equivalent of material "wasting" on the half-acre' (although, it must be noted, she considers making primarily in the B text), I believe that Imaginatif ultimately doubles back on his initial reproach and instead develops a case for poetry as a potentially fruitful kind of spiritual doing.[16]

Oddly, we see this development nowhere so clearly as in the A text, in which the Vita — just the place that in the B and C texts would occasion Imaginatif's meditation on poetry — grows increasingly physical and material as more and more examples of doing crowd the text (recall, for example, the catalogues of craftsmen in *Piers Plowman* A.11). Vaughan is quick to note this feature of the A text:

> Given the emphasis on various forms of Do-ing in this section of the poem, the concept of 'life' implies a form of 'action', of practicing

---

15 Middleton, 'Making a Good End', p. 247. Middleton, 'Narration and the Invention of Experience', p. 114, repeats this view of B.12.16–19, describing Imaginatif's rebuke as 'the most absolute challenge to the poetic enterprise to appear in either the A or the B texts, for it attacks both the product and the profession of "making"'. Hanna, 'Langland's Ymaginatif', p. 82, concurs with this view, asserting that 'the B-version Ymaginatif, more strenuously than any other figure in the poem, rejects Wille Langland's entire poetic project'.

16 Middleton, 'Making a Good End', p. 248.

(for instance) what one has contemplated in vision. In the moral universe of this poem, and of medieval Christian theology, knowledge and intentions are important; however, it is only when they are enacted in real life that they can become the decisive expression of a moral life.[17]

The importance of doing posited by the A text, alongside Imaginatif's B- and C-text advancements of poetic making as one such kind of spiritual activity, may lead us finally to conclude that But was even more sensitive a reader of *Piers Plowman* than Middleton gives him credit for. He may use the phrase 'meddling with making' unironically when referring to his own poetic response to the poem's various versions, yet he does so not simply as a means of synthesizing these versions or via a naïve misreading that narrows in on the phrase for its alliterative aesthetic pleasure. Rather, But seems acutely aware of the ways in which different versions of the poem set out to problematize, and then recuperate, a notion of poetic making as spiritual doing.[18] That he was writing, most eminently, in response to the A text's recuperation of poetry and its concurrent nascent conceptualization of Imaginatif only further reinforces a sense of But as a highly attentive reader and practitioner of poetic making, and so now it is to the A-text Vita that I turn.

But's lines in Rawlinson poet. 137, while an enlightening example of readerly-comment-turned-poetry, are by no means the first instance of speech transforming into verse that *Piers Plowman* A offers. Langland devotes much of A.9 and A.10 to exploring how various kinds of speech literally materialize, and so become more spiritually productive, when reconfigured into alliterative verse. The examples through which he proceeds in this exploration each recall — or more properly, envisage — many of the same discursive methods that characterize Imaginatif's speech in the B and C texts. In passus 9, the emphasis is on earthly forms of poetic making, but at its end and leading into passus 10, the poet turns towards more explicitly spiritual varieties of speech and poetry. Over the course of these two passūs, the A text stages an argument for poetry as material craft originating from human and divine forms of speech.

A.9 opens with the dreamer's encounter with the two friars amidst his search for Dowel. When they claim that Dowel resides with them, the dreamer takes the opportunity to show off his logical reasoning skills and refute their claim:

---

17 *Piers Plowman*, ed. by Vaughan, p. 12.
18 As Middleton, 'Narration and the Invention of Experience', p. 110, notes, 'only in what may be the last addition to the C text — the so-called "autobiographical" interlude between the first and second visions — is this defense before the authorities even provisionally successful'.

> '*Contra,*' quod I as a clerk, and gan to disputen:
> '*Sepcies in die cadet iustus et cetera.*
> "Sevene sythes on the day," seyth the Booke, "falleth the rytful."
> And whoso synnes,' I sayde, 'certes, me thinkes,
> 9.20 That Dowel and Do-evel mow not duelle togederes;
> *Ergo,* he is nowt alway at hom among you freres;
> He is otherwhile elleswher to wissen the peple.'
>
> (Langland, Piers Plowman A.9.16–22)

While this episode is familiar from the B and C versions of the text, the dreamer's disputational language stands out in this instance because of the ways in which it corresponds to Imaginatif's own legalistic discourse in the other versions.[19] Whereas Imaginatif offers a defence of Clergy in B and C, here it is the dreamer who linguistically styles himself 'as a clerk'. Also like the later Imaginatif, the dreamer attributes argumentational value to biblical citation (and here, notably, a speaking book). But the language that most closely reflects that of Imaginatif is the dreamer's Latin debate lexis: *contra* and *ergo*, both of which Imaginatif himself employs at a key moment in B.12. The context for Imaginatif's legalistic Latin deployment is Will's overreaching desire to know whether pre-Christian pagans can possibly be saved. In response to these ruminations, which Imaginatif deems both unwise and spiritually unproductive, he issues a *contra*, goes on to quote a passage from Peter ('The just man shall scarcely be saved on the day of judgement; therefore — he shall be saved! [*Salvabitur vix iustus in die iudicii;* / *Ergo – salvabitur!*]', B.12.277–78; translation A. V. C. Schmidt's), and shortly thereafter 'seide no moore Latyn' (B.12.279b). The dreamer's parallel move in the A text suggests an early trial, of sorts, of Imaginatif's discursive strategies in later versions of the poem. At the same time, it offers a glimpse at a specific kind of speech — here, the language of dispute — being made into what, for the dreamer, is a meaningful poetic articulation of scripturally based reasoning.

While such legal-poetic articulation occasions, in the B and C texts, Imaginatif's vanishing act (for him, the Latin functions as a linguistic flourish that punctuates his dramatic exit — one of those characteristic disrupted episodes Middleton identifies),[20] in the A text it elicits another kind of speech-turned-poetry. The dreamer's rebuttal causes one of the friars to respond: 'I shal sey the my sawe' (*Piers Plowman* A.9.23a). *Sawe,* according to the *Middle English Dictionary,* may equally mean 'what is said,

---

19 For a detailed study of Will's and Imaginatif's deployment of the language of dispute and its connections to Clergy, see Somerset, *Clerical Discourse,* esp. pp. 3–21 and 22–61.
20 Middleton, 'Narration and the Invention of Experience', p. 119: 'the disrupted episode [is] Langland's poetic signature in the sense that it is deeply characteristic of his way of composing narration'.

talk, words, speech, discourse, the word of God'; a 'statement, declaration, claim'; an 'opinion, idea, belief'; an 'old saying, proverb, biblical saying or quotation'; or a 'story, narrative, parable, account, history, or *poem*' (my emphasis). This 'sawe' or poem, as it turns out, reappears in the B and C texts as the friar's exemplum and accompanying exegesis of the 'man in a bot, amyddes a brod water' (9.26). The boat's rocking, as the friar describes, 'Maketh the man many tyme to falle and to stande; / For stonde he nevere so styf, he stumbleth in the wagging' (9.28–29). The man in the boat, the friar glosses, is in fact a parable for the experience of 'folk here on erthe' trying to avoid sin:

> 9.35 The water is lyk to this world, that waxeth and wanyes;
> The godes of the grounde beth lyk to the wawes,
> And as wyndes and wateres wawes abowte;
> The bot is lik to the body, that brotel is of kinde,
> And thorw the fend and the flesh, and the falce world,
> 9.40 Syneth the sadde man sevene sithes on the day.
> [...]
> Ay is the soule saf, but thou thiself wilt
> Folwe thi fleschly wil, and the fend after,
> And do dedly synne, and drenche thy soule.
> God wil suffre the to deye so, for thou hast the maystry.
>
> (9.35–40, 45–48)

The conclusion of the friar's 'sawe' proves significant for two reasons: first, it recalls the dynamic of 'following' that frames Imaginatif's B and C passūs; and second, the imagery of the 'sawe' itself, especially the 'drenching' of the soul, corresponds to Imaginatif's own illustrative exemplum of the two men cast into the Thames. Once again, Langland seems to be experimenting with Imaginatif-like forms of discourse and their translatability into poetry; with the friar's 'sawe', the spiritual value of this kind of poetic making is made clear.

This putting of poetry to imaginative spiritual use may be apparent to the reader at this point, but the dreamer still struggles to recognize this kind of making for what it is. In his usual manner, he insists that he has 'no kinde knowyng' to 'conseyve' the friar's words (Langland, *Piers Plowman* A.9.49), and sets off again in search of Dowel. Lulled to sleep by the 'layes the lovely bryddes madyn' (9.58), he then wakes within another dream vision in which he meets Thought, who, according to the dreamer, is meek, mild, and 'lyk to myselven' (9.62b). Like Imaginatif in the B and C texts, Thought says he has followed the dreamer for some time during his life ('I have served the this sevene yere', 9.67a). Also like Imaginatif, Thought offers a definition of the three lives (Dowel, Dobet, and Dobest) that depends largely upon using speech and language well:

> Whoso is meke of his mouth, and mylde of his speche,
> Trewe of tounge and of his two handis,
> And thorw the labour of his handes his lyflode wynneth,
> 9.75 And trosty of his taylende, taketh but his owyn,
> And is not drunkelew ne deynous, Dowel hym folwyth.
> Dobet thus doth, ac he doth moche more:
> He is as low as a lomb, and lovely of speche.
>
> *(9.72–78)*

The crucial part of Thought's definition of 'doing well' is the way in which he joins being 'meke of [...] mouth', 'mylde of [...] speche', 'trewe of tounge', and 'lovely of speche' with honest manual labour and winning ('of his two handis, / And thorw the labour of his handes his lyflode wynneth'). This is perhaps the first explicit manifestation of Langland's A-text attempt to recuperate poetry in such a way as to emphasize its engagement with speech as a skilled, manual, material kind of craft or doing.[21] That poetry, thus conceived, can now be thought of in relation to doing well clearly interests and influences the dreamer. Langland marks the dreamer's intellectual stimulation by this idea of poetic activity by having him dispute with Thought for another three days, putting into practice, as it were, the emerging principles of imaginatively turning speech, via poetry, towards spiritually productive ends ('Thought and I thus thre dayes we yede, / Disputyng on Dowel day after other', 9.109–10).

After the debate with Thought (which we only hear of from the narrator), the dreamer is introduced to Wit, who is meant to tell him where the three *Do*s dwell. Wit begins to depict the castle of Kynde in which 'Sire Dowel dwelleth' (Langland, *Piers Plowman* A.10.1a) and, before long, takes the opportunity to describe Kynde, who is in fact 'creatour of alle kynnes bestes; / Fader and formere, the furste of alle thinges' and 'grete God, that gynnyng hadde nevere, / The lord of lyf and of lyt, of blysse and of peyne' (10.27–30). Wit's elaboration soon lapses into a Pauline treatise on the *imago dei* and a miniature history of Creation:

> And man is him most lyk of mark and of shappe;
> For thurgh the word that he warp waxe forth bestes,
> And al, at his wille, was wrought with a speche:
> 10.35 *Dixit et facta sunt, et cetera.*
> Save man that he made ymage to himselven,

---

21 Gallacher, 'Imaginatif and the *sensus communis*', also identifies a link between Imaginatif and craft.

>   Gaf him of his godhede, and graunted him blysse,
>   Lyf that ay shal laste, and al his lynage after.
>
>   (10.32–38)

Wit reduces the entire seven-day Creation story into three precise lines that nonetheless highlight the most important part of this divine analogue for human craft or creativity: namely, the equivalence of speaking with making. God 'wrought' the world 'with a speche' and 'thurgh the word', notably described in the Latin phrase *Dixit et facta sunt*. Divine speaking *is* doing and making. So too, Langland posits, human speech can constitute a kind of poetic making that qualifies as doing in an active spiritual sense via its mirroring of the divine creative act. God and the poet are both craftsmen who meddle with making in a speech-oriented, poetic fashion.[22]

Wit's usage of the word *mark* may also be interpreted as an instance of Imaginatif's proto-presence lurking in the A text. The first cited usage of *mark* to mean 'the trademark of a craftsman' in the *MED* is in fact *Piers Plowman* B.15.349a (in Schmidt's lineation). Anima is speaking:

>   The merk of that monee is good, ac the metal is feble,
> 15.350 And so it fareth by som folk now; thei han a fair speche.
>   Crowne and Cristendom, the kynges mark of hevene,
>   Ac the metal, that is mannes soule, [myd] synne is foule alayed:
>   Bothe lettred and lewed beth alayed now with synne,
>   That no lif loveth oother, ne Oure Lord, as it semeth.
>
>   (B.15.349–54)

That Anima speaks of the 'merk' of the 'feble' metal of 'mannes soule' in the B text, and that in the same breath he invokes one of Imaginatif's much belaboured points (the ambiguous distinction between 'lettred and lewed') is pertinent to our purposes because, in A.10, Wit goes on from discussing man's 'mark' to talking about Anima. It is in the context of discussing God's

---

22 The idea of God as master craftsman comes across in Wit's history especially with his lexicographical choice of the word *mark* in describing man's creaturely relation to God. *Middle English Dictionary* Online, 'mark(e (n.(1))', 5, confirms a craft-related sense of the word. Specifically, *mark* can mean 'the trademark of a craftsman or tradesman set on products, merchandise, and the like for purposes of identification and guarantee of quality'; 'the badge or insignia of a sovereign lord'; 'a personal or familial badge stamped on vessels, flatware, etc.'; 'a seal, confirmation (as with covenants)'; 'a written symbol such as an asterisk, letter, or character'; or 'a musical note'. When Wit uses the term *mark* to signal man's created nature, he does so with a term that connotes, in the first instance, an idea of divine craft achieved through speech, and in the second, a craft-like making that is made manifest by a written symbol, which again provokes associations between speech, written poetic craft, and physical products or records of making. (It is no coincidence that, in the B and C Imaginatif passūs, God and Christ both engage in highly materialized acts of writing).

making of man in an 'ymage [like] to himselven' (A.10.36b), impressed with his 'mark' and 'shappe' (A.10.32b), that Wit describes the body, 'the castel of Kynde made' (A.10.39a), as a space wherein 'Inwit and alle wittes' are 'enclosed' (A.10.43). Within this space, Anima 'wandreth', ranging 'over al the body' (A.10.45b), helped all the while by Inwit, that faculty that 'in the hed is an help to the soule' (A.10.50). 'Inwit', Wit asserts, 'is the help that *Anima* desyret; / After the grace of God, Inwit is the grettest' (A.10.48–49).

I would submit that Langland's usage of the word *mark* across these two moments in A and B, both of which involve Anima and some of the central concerns that circulate around Imaginatif in the later versions, forges a lexical and thematic correspondence. In the B text of *Piers Plowman*, two passūs are interposed between Imaginatif's appearance and Anima's exposition of man's coin-like divine stamp, which enable Clergy and Conscience to take up and expand the debate about the distinctions between 'lettred and lewed' that so preoccupy Imaginatif. In the A text, meanwhile, the *imago dei* doctrine receives a concise yet dense summary from Wit, who suggests for the first time what may well be the closest thing we get to an Imaginatif-like personification in the A text: Anima's 'help' Inwit. 'Of speche and of going he [Inwit] is bygynnere', Wit says (10.48). In other words, Inwit (whom Vaughan defines as 'the faculty of [natural or intuitive] human understanding aligned with Divine Reason') is the motive force behind the two concepts Langland has been interested in throughout the A-text Vita: speaking (*speche*) and manifest, productive activity or labour (here captured in the term *going*).[23] And so, even in Wit's succinct description, Inwit becomes a distillation of Imaginatif's figuration and rhetorical force in later versions of the poem: he is a figure who both speaks and goes, who is related to divine craft and creation through his habitation within the divinely wrought human body, and who thus embodies — whether as Imaginatif, Inwit, or the mobile combination of language and material that gathers around his presence from A to B to C — the very notion of active, material poetic making that Langland first questions, and ultimately defends.

***

In the final moments of this essay, I would like to return to Rawlinson poet. 137 and to John But's B- and C-text-inflected conclusion to the A text:

> Wille thurgh inwit tho wot wel the sothe –
> That this speche was spedelich — and sped him wel faste;
> And wroughthe that here is wryten, and other werkes bothe –

---

23 *Piers Plowman*, ed. by Vaughan, p. 20.

>   Of Peres the plowman and mechel puple also.
> 12.100 And whan this werk was wrought, ere Wille myghte aspie,
>   Deth delt him a dent, and drof him to the erthe,
>   As is closed under clour — Crist have his soule!
>   And so bad Johan But, busily wel ofte,
>   When he saw thes sawes busyly allegged
> 12.105 By James and by Jerom, by Jop and by othere;
>   And for he medleth of makyng, he made this ende.
>
>   (Piers Plowman A.12.96–106)

I observed earlier that this passage has been the subject of much scholarly speculation for its compelling portrait of early *Piers* readership, whether viewed as a meditation on scribal making like Tilot's or amateur, reader-response-oriented making like But's. I return to it here because of the ways in which But fashions himself in these lines both as an astute, multi-version reader of *Piers Plowman* and as a poetic maker in his own right, but, crucially, in the craftsman-like mode urged by Inwit and Imaginatif across the A, B, and C texts. Again, as a reader, But seems to have been familiar with more than one version of the poem, and it seems likely, given his language in this passage, that he, too, made the connection between the Imaginatif-like Inwit of the A text and the Imaginatif of later versions, and also identified the relationship between speech, poetic 'making', and spiritual activity that runs throughout the Vita and the Imaginatif passūs in the B and C texts. Here, But's ending to *Piers Plowman* in fact identifies 'inwit' as the final 'sothe'-giving faculty by which the dreamer acquires understanding. This understanding comes through 'speche' and is translated by the dreamer into poetry: he 'wrought that here is wryten, and other werkes bothe — / Of Peres the plowman and muchel puple also'. It seems no accident that But deploys precisely those terms that have been the cornerstones of the earlier Vita argument for speech-derived, materially wrought poetic making. Even *wrought(he)*, which But uses twice within three lines, is exactly the term used to describe God's great speech-act in A.10. But's description of Will's writing is not the only instance in which he reproduces material from other parts of the text; when he begins to discuss his own editorial, poetic intervention, he refers to *Piers Plowman* as 'thes sawes', the same term meaning tale, parable, or poem that the friar uses in A.9, and which here seems to refer just as much to the multiple versions of *Piers Plowman* as to the multiple visions and passūs within it.[24]

---

24 On the question of whether the 'other werkes' that John But writes about in this passage refer to other versions of *Piers Plowman* (as medieval readers would have been familiar with them) or to other texts written by But's 'Wille', see Warner, 'John But'.

In short, But seems as attuned to the issues of poetic craft present in the A text of *Piers Plowman* that circulate around moments where Imaginatif's proto-presence lurks as he is to Imaginatif's B-text rebuke of and C-text revised attitude towards the dreamer's meddling with making. Specifically, he seems especially aware of Langland's emphasis on poetic craft and making as becoming spiritually valuable when thought of in material terms. This awareness in turn, I have suggested, should light the way for our attempts as scholars to better understand how Langland's early readers encountered *Piers Plowman* as a multi-version text, but one moored to and revolving around recurrent thematic, stylistic, and lexical features from A to B to C. As discussed earlier (and as John But seems to have noticed), the A text, like Imaginatif's lessons in B and C, gets increasingly material in its meditations, and while the A text does not telescope outwards from the Vita portion as much as in the B and C versions, A.11 does begin to dwell considerably both on a material understanding of the word (as something to be consumed, 'carped', and kept always in one's mouth — eucharistically and verbally) and on material craft and physical labour. These material emphases on word and craft come to a head with But's A-text continuation, when he enacts the last instance of meddling with making in Rawlinson poet. 137. The *Piers Plowman* A of Rawlinson poet. 137 thus stands out among texts of *Piers Plowman* for its complex poetic, material performance of what we might call, in a reformulation of a B-text phrase, 'faith *with* feat'. It is a text that speaks, that crafts its verbal utterances into a material poetic object, and so becomes a physical record of the reading, and writing, of multiple craftsmen in a mode first imagined by Imaginatif's spectre in the A text.

The broader implications of the spectral A-text presence of Imaginatif and But's meddling with making for A-text scholarship and *Piers Plowman* scholarship writ large are several. For one thing, as I have suggested throughout this essay, Imaginatif's proleptic presence in the A text corroborates the evolutionary approach to the poem traditionally championed by scholars; we can detect Langland working out his characteristic moves, metaphors, and speech patterns in the words and actions of A-text characters. But's sensitivity to and apparent knowledge of both B- and C-text matters pertaining to Imaginatif, of the *Piers Plowman* multiverse and the poem's multi-versionality, meanwhile remind us of the rewards of attending closely to readerly and scribal textual additions and interventions in the study of medieval texts — partly, by demonstrating that our modern scholarly concerns with Langland's making of the poem were in fact shared by *Piers Plowman*'s earliest readers. We're reminded, too, of the inextricable relationship, in many medieval authors', scribes', and readers' minds, between literature and the material contexts in which it circulated, and of a conception of poets (and scribes and readers) as makers and doers who intervene in the creation and imagination of texts via their material forms, leaving their 'marks' on texts in a variety of ways.

According to this reading, the A text itself, as imagined and investigated by scholars (whether in sleek, modern editions or via its vital material afterlives in archives), becomes an active, material reflection on (Langland's) poetic making, spiritual doing, and reader response — one that, like Imaginatif, both speaks and moves. Experimental in a highly experiential sense (to go back to these words' shared origins), Langland's A text works a particular kind of material — speech, language, and discourse — honing, expanding, and contracting an initially diffuse, but increasingly connected array of meaning and ideas. The experimental moves of the experiential A-text Vita gradually move Langland and his early readers towards the making of meaningful and readily identifiable personae — those we get in the B and C texts. It remains only to say that it seems fitting that Langland's earliest forays into the creation of something like the imagination (or someone like Imaginatif) appear in the A-text Vita, the site of life and lived experience, of doing as well as saying — of meddling, in as many ways as possible, with making. Imaginatif is here, and already he is doing exactly what imagination does: moving, changing, developing before our eyes in the subtle, dynamic, and ineluctable ways spectres — or poets' and readers' imaginations — do.

Works Cited

Manuscript

Oxford, Bodleian Library, MS Rawlinson poetry 137 [sigil R of A]

Primary Sources

Langland, William, *The Vision of Piers Plowman*, ed. by A. V. C. Schmidt (London: Dent, 1995) [B text]
———, *Piers Plowman: The A Version*, ed. by Míceál Vaughan (Baltimore: Johns Hopkins University Press, 2011)
———, *Piers Plowman: The Z Version*, ed. by A. G. Rigg and Charlotte Brewer (Toronto: University of Toronto Press, 1983)

Secondary Sources

Eldredge, L. M., 'Some Medical Evidence on Langland's Imaginatif', *Yearbook of Langland Studies*, 3 (1989), 131–36
Gallacher, Patrick J., 'Imaginatif and the *sensus communis*', *Yearbook of Langland Studies*, 6 (1992), 51–60
Hanna, Ralph III, 'Langland's Ymaginatif: Images and the Limits of Poetry', in *Images, Idolatry, and Iconoclasm in Late Medieval England: Textuality and the Visual Image*, ed. by Jeremy Dimmick, James Simpson, and Nicolette Zeeman (Oxford: Oxford University Press, 2002), pp. 81–94
———, *Pursuing History: Middle English Manuscripts and Their Texts* (Stanford: Stanford University Press, 1996)
Horobin, Simon, 'The Scribe of Rawlinson Poetry 137 and the Copying and Circulation of *Piers Plowman*', *Yearbook of Langland Studies*, 19 (2005), 3–26
Jones, H. S. V., 'Imaginatif in Piers Plowman', *Journal of English and Germanic Philology*, 13 (1914), 583–88
Karnes, Michelle, 'Will's Imagination in *Piers Plowman*', *Journal of English and Germanic Philology*, 108 (2009), 27–58
Kaulbach, Ernest N., 'The "vis imaginativa" and the Reasoning Powers of Ymaginatif in the B-Text of *Piers Plowman*', *Journal of English and Germanic Philology*, 84 (1985), 16–29
———, 'The "vis imaginativa secundum Avicennam" and the Naturally Prophetic Powers of Ymaginatif in the B-Text of *Piers Plowman*', *Journal of English and Germanic Philology*, 86 (1987), 496–514
Mann, Jill, 'The Power of the Alphabet: A Reassessment of the Relation between the A and B Versions of *Piers Plowman*', *Yearbook of Langland Studies*, 8 (1994), 21–50

McDermott, Ryan, '"beatus qui verba vertit in opera": Langland's Ethical Invention and the Tropological Sense', *Yearbook of Langland Studies*, 24 (2010), 169–204

Middleton, Anne, 'Making a Good End: John But as a Reader of *Piers Plowman*', in *Medieval English Studies Presented to George Kane*, ed. by Edward Donald Kennedy, Ronald Waldron, and Joseph S. Wittig (Cambridge: Brewer, 1988), pp. 243–66

——, 'Narration and the Invention of Experience: Episodic Form in *Piers Plowman*', in *The Wisdom of Poetry: Essays in Early English Literature in Honor of Morton W. Bloomfield*, ed. by Larry D. Benson and Siegfried Wenzel (Kalamazoo, MI: Medieval Institute, 1982), pp. 91–122

Minnis, Alastair J., 'Langland's Ymaginatif and Late-Medieval Theories of Imagination', *Comparative Criticism*, 3 (1981), 71–104

Quirk, Randolph, 'Vis imaginativa', *Journal of English and Germanic Philology*, 53 (1954), 81–83

Somerset, Fiona, *Clerical Discourse and Lay Audience in Late Medieval England* (Cambridge: Cambridge University Press, 1998)

Warner, Lawrence, 'John But and the Other Works That Will Wrought (*Piers Plowman* A XII 101–2)', *Notes and Queries*, 52 (2005), 13–18

White, Hugh, 'Langland's Ymaginatif, Kynde and the *Benjamin major*', *Medium Ævum*, 55 (1986), 241–48

Wood, Sarah, *'Piers Plowman' and its Manuscript Tradition* (Cambridge: Brewer, 2022)

Zeeman, Nicolette, *'Piers Plowman' and the Medieval Discourse of Desire* (Cambridge: Cambridge University Press, 2006)

Reviews

Daniel Wakelin, *Immaterial Texts in Late Medieval England: Making English Literary Manuscripts, 1400–1500.* Cambridge: Cambridge University Press, 2022. Pp. xv + 284.

The material forms of medieval texts are important to their interpretation. Lively scholarship in manuscript studies over the last fifty years has demonstrated repeatedly how valuable it can be to take the physical forms of medieval works into account. But do scholarly interests in the twenty-first century map neatly onto the interests of makers and readers of manuscripts in the fifteenth century? Daniel Wakelin suspects not, and in a brilliant new study that is both careful and bold, he challenges others who work with medieval books to value anew the perspectives of the medieval craftspeople who made them.

In reaction to the now-established view that the physical text is always the most important version of the text, Wakelin proposes that materiality is, in fact, *not* as important as we think. Or, more specifically, that it was not as important to those who designed and wrote medieval manuscripts. The medieval literary text, in particular, was imagined to transcend its own material form. Although the physicality of the book asserts itself through holes in parchment, uneven rulings, and inconvenient page breaks, these material details that so fascinate manuscript scholars more often than not created annoyances and posed problems for medieval scribes. By analysing scribes' efforts to overcome the challenges of materiality, Wakelin uncovers some of the basic expectations that shaped the culture of the medieval book: 'that pages are mostly rectangles', 'that reading will be continuous and sequential', 'that one copy of a text will have the same words as another' (p. 5). These expectations may seem unsurprising, as they align so easily with modern assumptions about books and reading. But in fact they unsettle some of the most foundational concepts of manuscript studies: that the variable *ordinatio* of a material text is key to its meaning, that discontinuous reading is the principal affordance of the codex as a form, that *variance* and *mouvance* are the deep structures of textuality in a manuscript culture. The field will need to reckon with Wakelin's fruitfully revisionary argument.

One of the particular challenges Wakelin mounts is to new materialism, an 'object-oriented' ontology that explores the agency that materials can have in relation to human actors. He delineates the useful distinction between 'hylomorphism', the idea that makers impose their ideas on the materials they make, and 'morphogenesis', the contrary idea that materials impose their ideas on people, or that 'matter dictates what minds can do' (p. 68). Always judicious, Wakelin acknowledges the interest of morphogenesis, but he warns that there are risks, as well, to underestimating human agency. Inspired by the perspectives of modern craftspeople (since medieval ones did not leave much in the way of theorizing), he seeks the 'modes of craft-thinking' revealed in the construction of fifteenth-century manuscripts (p. 21). In multiple contexts, he demonstrates that the material choices of scribes and book makers reflect powerfully idealist conceptions of the literary text. The medieval manuscript, for all its physicality, is — and here Wakelin quotes 'roof carpenter and philosopher' Arthur Lochmann — 'un trésor immatériel' (p. 6).

To understand this immaterial treasure, Wakelin paradoxically must comb through the material evidence presented by the manuscripts in his archive. Writing in a colloquial voice about the 'umpteen' 'fiddly' details of medieval bookmaking, while also sometimes sending this reader, at least, to the dictionary ('fissiparous', 'nous'), he invariably presents the technical side of medieval bibliography in accessible, engaging terms. Chapter 2, for example, analyses myriad kinds of imperfections in parchment, revealing that parchmenters and scribes did their level best to obscure such challenges to the regular rectangles of the page and text block. The problems they encounter include the awkward *lisières* (or irregular margins) that plague large bifolia, irregular and damaged pages that need patching, and holes sewn closed by parchmenters or thoughtfully written around by scribes. In working around such difficulties, manuscript artisans sought to suppress the creaturely aspects of medieval bookmaking that are so compelling to those of us accustomed to reading on paper; again and again, they aim to erase all traces of their books' animal origins.

Chapter 3 investigates the ruled layout of pages as another site of the complex struggle between scribes' immaterial ideas and their stubbornly material texts. Here, Wakelin demonstrates that ruling is not a careful articulation of textual form so often as a set of conventions inherited from exemplars. Often, ruling sets up regular forms into which the surprisingly irregular texts do not fit. And problems arise even when — as in the case of the stanzas in rhyme royal — the verse forms of the text produce consistent numbers of lines. Scribes' accommodations to these inconsistencies repeatedly show that, to them, 'literary form was more important than material format' (p. 105).

The page itself might be described as the most important of the codex's material forms, but again Wakelin sees bookmakers working around and against, rather than with, the opportunities a turning leaf might offer. Chapter 4 addresses the problem of page breaks, noting the ways in which scribes often try to smooth the potential for interruption that comes with the physical segmentation of literary works into individual leaves — which, moreover, have two sides. Those who wrote lengthy texts into codices do not celebrate the potential of the form for discontinuous reading; instead, they seem to imagine that the process of reading should be continuous and sustained. In this way, they aspire to transcend the divisions of the page, which pose a potential threat to understanding.

Scholars have understandably been interested in annotation and marginalia as traces of medieval reading habits; nowhere else is the potential payoff of the material text for literary interpretation clearer. Wakelin points out that — regrettably — there is actually little annotation in medieval books, and almost none around the edges of literary narrative texts. Chapter 5 explores the implications of this absence. Extending the idea that the page is a regular rectangle, undisturbed even by marginal annotation, Wakelin suggests that the emptiness of the margin itself implies certain kinds of reading: continuous, immersive, directed towards narrative pleasure rather than scholarly study. These are modes of reading that have most often been associated with more recent literary forms such as the novel, but the bare margins of medieval literary texts suggest that earlier readers might have engaged with texts in equally immaterial ways.

Chapter 6 addresses perhaps the most obvious feature of medieval books, and one that has been hiding in plain sight. As Wakelin rightly insists, the scribes who created medieval manuscripts attempted to copy texts accurately, and for the most part they were successful. By contrast, the material features of a single book — such details as its page breaks and even its illuminations — were very rarely copied. Scribes, that is, sought to replicate, not duplicate, their exemplars. The combination of verbal likeness with material difference in most copies makes a persuasive case that scribes cared more about the text of the manuscript than the look of it. Wakelin demonstrates the care taken in copying through analysing the constancy of interjections (*lo*, for example), as the unnecessary words most likely to fall out of a copy without damaging the sense of a text. Another useful case study in copying-while-revising is the 'spurious' links added to the *Canterbury Tales*, which testify to scribes' idealization of the *Tales* as a complete and unified work. As Wakelin puts it, 'copying is the ultimate pursuit of texts as things that transcend materiality — and that is why it is the endpoint of this study' (p. 195).

There is much to admire in this truly innovative book, not least the hard facts and concrete details Wakelin gives us to think with. In deriving transcendent ideas about the text from the material particulars of many manuscripts, *Immaterial Texts* offers a usefully quantitative approach, tallying numerous data points across a large archive to reach conclusions that are both well-informed and durable. Of course, the quantitative archive must be manageable, as well, and so Wakelin sets some necessary limits to his inquiry, explicitly omitting some reading matter that is arguably more materially interested, such as 'trophies' of illumination (p. 16) and 'practical books' (p. 18). He also deliberately chooses to concentrate on the perspective of those who made manuscript books in the fifteenth century, rather than, for example, those who were reading them. These decisions might possibly underplay some evidence for the agency of the material object; books act on their readers, even as their makers have acted on them. But in focusing on the scribes who crafted long narrative literary texts — namely Chaucer's *Canterbury Tales* and *Troilus and Criseyde*, Hoccleve's *Regiment of Princes*, and Lydgate's *Troy Book* and *Siege of Thebes* — Wakelin discovers a great deal about an important category of late medieval manuscript production, and one that will specially interest many scholars. Because his examples are so well-chosen, they allow him to sketch a large field satisfyingly, and to use it to raise still more far-reaching questions about the idea of the medieval book.

Much of the energy in the opposing view — that materiality is the definitive feature of medieval books — has come from scholars keen to push against the assumptions of print culture. If printed books teach modern readers to expect that the page and the text block will be regular rectangles, or that one copy of the text will be identical to just about every other, it has been worth emphasizing that manuscript culture is different in some ways. But, in *Immaterial Texts*, Wakelin pulls the pendulum usefully back in the other direction, reminding us that, free of the comparison with print, those who made medieval manuscripts aspired to instantiate assumptions about their texts that were every bit as immaterial as ours. Medieval scribes had no idea their decisions would be so closely parsed; they 'thought that others would not look as closely as codicologists do' (p. 98). I am grateful to Daniel Wakelin for looking as closely as he has, and for advancing an innovative and persuasive argument about the ways in which the makers of medieval literary manuscripts believed their work exceeded the limits of physicality. *Immaterial Texts in Late Medieval England* destabilizes the status of the material in late medieval reading and writing cultures, and it will undoubtedly recalibrate the presumptions of manuscript studies in the future.

Jessica Brantley
Yale University
jessica.brantley@yale.edu

Thorlac Turville-Petre, ed. and trans., *Pearl*. Exeter Medieval Texts and Studies. Liverpool: Liverpool University Press, 2021. Pp. x + 210.

Thorlac Turville-Petre's new book contributes a singular approach to the web of perspectives on one of the most extraordinary poems in the English language. This edition and translation of *Pearl* is the latest book to emerge from this important scholar's learning and philological acumen. While many editions of *Pearl* already exist — and those of E. V. Gordon (1953) and Malcolm Andrew and Ronald Waldron (2007, 5th edn) remain essential — Turville-Petre's addition to the field is both welcome and novel in its own way. Listed in the same series, Exeter Medieval Texts and Studies, this edition is clearly not intended to supplant Andrew and Waldron's magisterial critical edition, *The Poems of the Pearl Manuscript*. It is, instead, ideally suited to introduce *Pearl* to readers who are new to it, and to give non-specialists who love poetry ready access to its Middle English.

An expert on Middle English alliterative verse, Turville-Petre has written two books on the subject — *The Alliterative Revival* (1977) and *Description and Narrative in Middle English Alliterative Poetry* (2018). He has also produced the useful *Alliterative Poetry of the Later Middle Ages: An Anthology* (1989), along with a fine student anthology, *A Book of Middle English*, (2021, 4th edn; with J. A. Burrow). On single poems or manuscripts, Turville-Petre has edited, for EETS, *Poems from BL MS Harley 913: 'The Kildare Manuscript'* (2015) and *The Wars of Alexander* (1989; with H. N. Duggan); for SEENET, *Piers Plowman: The B-Version Archetype (Bx)* (2018; with Burrow). Amid this high-quality corpus, there is also his influential — in its day, ground-breaking — *England the Nation: Language, Literature and National Identity, 1290–1340* (1996).

The originality of Turville-Petre's contribution to *Pearl* scholarship lies in how he serves up this Middle English poem in a way similar to how Dante scholars often deliver *The Divine Comedy* to students first reading it. His method resembles, in particular, the still-useful, often reprinted edition of John D. Sinclair (1939), wherein Dante's Italian appears beside facing-page English translations and is followed by direct, charmingly accessible commentaries. With this method applied to *Pearl*, Turville-Petre's edition encourages a ruminative, slow and steady absorption of the poem's verbal subtleties, its sensorial and emotive cues, and its theological nuances. It encourages the new reader of *Pearl* to read and reread, with barriers to understanding the basic sense of each stanza either removed or delicately explained. The very method underscores the greatness of *Pearl*.

The edition itself is sound and unfussy. Archaic letter-forms are preserved. Modern punctuation and capitalization are added. Emendations to the text (sparse in number) are set beneath the Middle English, given merely as lemmata without comment, implicitly inviting the philologically curious to consult Gordon and/or Andrew and Waldron to learn more about a crux. More striking than the editorial treatment of *Pearl*, though, is the offering of *Pearl* by its metrical sections — that is, the twenty stanza-groups with echoic refrains. Each stanza-group of five (in one case, six) receives a thematic title, for example, 'I. The Garden' (stanzas 1–5), 'II. The Dream Landscape' (stanzas 6–10), and so on. At the beginning of each section, Turville-Petre provides a brief headnote, which orients a reader as to link-words and semantic play, as well as to the narrative progress and the dreamer's responses. *Pearl*'s stanzas with same-page translations follow, with the translations rendered in closely literal prose. After each edited/translated stanza-group, Turville-Petre offers a few pages of cogent, stanza-by-stanza commentary. To give a taste of Turville-Petre's explications, here are his comments on stanza-group 'VI. Reprimand', after a dissection of the link-word *deme*: 'Who is to judge? In his arrogance the dreamer thinks his views are enough to determine the matter, but, says the maiden, he should consider whether he should address God in that way. He supposes himself to be condemned to unrelieved grief, yet his anger, kicking against the comfort of God's love, is utterly pointless, since he is bound by what God ordains' (p. 81). *Pearl* remains, of course, a challenging poem, especially for the novice, but Turville-Petre's commentaries attempt to anticipate difficulties and to explain them in clear language, often referencing medieval analogues, patristic and biblical sources, and key critical views. When reading *Pearl* in this edition, one feels led by a well-travelled guide.

Because Turville-Petre translates and also discusses numerous words and shifting wordplays, this edition of *Pearl* lacks a glossary. Given the book's scope and purpose, the decision is reasonable. Lacking too, however, is an index — an unfortunate choice because having one would help a reader track medieval sources and authors cited in the introduction, headnotes, and commentaries. Preparing an index would have caught, presumably, the rare instances where an analogue is cited without a corresponding bibliographical listing, as happens for William Dunbar (p. 67). The bibliography itself (pp. 21–27) seems rather too restricted. It covers most classic literature on *Pearl*, but in its list of other editions of the poem, I was sorry to see the solid, sensitive edition by Sarah Stanbury (2001) omitted. Also missing is Stanbury's important *Seeing the Gawain Poet: Description and the Act of Perception* (1991), as are many recent studies of interest, for example, Ann R. Meyer, *Medieval Allegory and the Building of the New Jerusalem* (2003); Jessica Barr, *Willing to Know God: Dreamers and Visionaries in the Later Middle Ages* (2010); and David K. Coley, *Death and the Pearl Maiden: Plague, Poetry, England* (2019). While no edition should aspire to be a variorum of all criticism, a judicious sifting of newer scholarship would have imbued this book with a more up-to-date sense of *Pearl*'s present critical reception.

For a poem like *Pearl*, there are, however, no drawbacks to having another edition, especially one so well suited for a graduate seminar or an upper-level undergraduate class. It is refreshing to see *Pearl* being treated like Dante's epic, as a brilliantly malleable, allegorical/symbolic word-object, representative of a high aesthetic, guided by devotional aspirations, and rewarding deep study. That this edition also conveys Thorlac Turville-Petre's long-considered, graceful thinking on the poem carries another valuable benefit.

Susanna Fein
Kent State University
sfein@kent.edu

Sarah Wood, *'Piers Plowman' and its Manuscript Tradition*. York Manuscript and Early Print Studies 5. Woodbridge, Suffolk: York Medieval Press / The Boydell Press, 2022. Pp. xiv + 243.

Sarah Wood has written an important book for Langland studies. At the risk of oversimplifying what is not a simple argument, I suggest that two of the book's most oft-repeated phrases provide a shorthand way to grasp its main concerns: these phrases are 'earliest readers' and 'exemplary lives'. The first refers to the collective work of the copyists who transmitted Langland's text, including copies that do not survive but whose traces are still discernible in the manuscript record. The second refers to the idea that these earliest readers were very unlike modern readers (especially perhaps professional readers) in their affective and intellectual responses to the text. They were much more likely, that is, to make sense of Langland's poem and the represented *vitae* of both Will and Piers by assimilating them to the more familiar and less literary genres of 'exemplary lives' — including hagiography, travel narrative, and pseudo-historical romance. The two phrases also correspond roughly to the distinction between textual and codicological approaches to the interpretation of the complex manuscript tradition of *Piers Plowman*, and it is in the grafting together of these approaches that Wood most fruitfully extends an already extensive body of scholarship.

By her own account, Wood has examined at first hand forty-six of the fifty-two complete manuscript copies of *Piers*, not counting fragments and excerpts. She provides a helpful list of the manuscripts and their sigla in the front matter. This extensive archival work has allowed her to see aspects of the corpus that few other scholars have tried, or cared, to see. Her interest is not editorial; she has no axe to grind here in the ongoing debates about establishment of the authorial text or the relationships among the versions. In the latter case, her analysis will muddy the waters further, since she gives multiple examples of early copyists' near-total ambivalence concerning what modern scholarship calls the 'versions'. Instead, Wood organizes her reading of the evidence into two large categories that help to structure the book: textual evidence (including scribal 'editing' and transmission of paratextual schemes of marginalia, etc.) and codicological evidence (with emphasis on those texts that are the poem's most frequent fellow travellers in manuscript books, especially less-studied ones). But of course, these two approaches cannot be held in isolation from one another. In expressing the 'desirability of recoupling codicological and textual approaches', Wood acknowledges that the 'democratisation of manuscript studies' (p. 8) made possible by digital facsimiles has made it easier for Langlandians who are not trained as textual scholars to access, to analyse, and to draw conclusions from the corpus of surviving books in ways that were not possible a few decades ago. The caveat implicit in Wood's approval of this democratization, however, is that it still matters 'what was transmitted, in *and alongside* the text' (emphasis mine). 'What was transmitted' includes, in Wood's capacious re-reading of the evidence, not only a maddeningly complex textual tradition marked by scribal interventions ranging from brilliant to bonkers, but also the paratextual schema that organized the transmitted text into units comprehensible to its earliest readers. 'When scribes responded to *Piers Plowman*', she writes, 'they responded not just to a poem, but to inherited forms of textual display' (p. 9).

The book includes an introduction and six chapters, along with an epilogue and an extensive appendix with comparative tables showing original schemes of marginalia across six manuscript groups, including all three of the main textual traditions (A, B, and C).

Chapter 1, 'Scribal Texts and Multivocal Manuscripts', focuses on textual interventions by individual scribes through case studies of the A-text copy found in Dublin, Trinity College, MS 213 (sigil E) and the C-text copy in Cambridge, Corpus Christi College, MS 293 (Sc). In Wood's telling, both scribes made emendations designed to foreground the 'life' of Piers the Plowman. These are not merely examples of isolated 'maverick scribes' (a favourite figure in Langland studies), but rather show evidence of transmission of such interventions across genetic groupings of manuscripts. The case studies are therefore in service of a larger point that is one of Wood's major emphases: 'The relatively unstudied books that I reexamine here', she writes, 'offer examples of the complexity of *all* manuscripts as the product not of a single moment or single agent, but of a multi-layered history. Each copy reflects, in fact, some mixture of accident and deliberation, the exact contours of which can be difficult to define' (p. 20). The case study of Sc, a copy deemed 'of minimal value' by editors because of its defective text, nevertheless provides Wood an opportunity to make her point about the 'mixture of accident and deliberation'. She attributes the Sc scribe's omission of a huge chunk of the poem (passūs 16–20) not to an accident in copying or a defective exemplar, but rather to deliberate suppression by an earlier redactor in Sc's textual tradition. This same redactor then cleverly covered his tracks by suturing lines from the end of passus 15 with related lines (on dreaming and waking) from the beginning of passus 21. With the renumbering of the affected passus headings, no visible material trace was left of the redactor's redacting.

Here I want to remark on a general aspect of the experience of reading this book that applies to most of its case studies. I found it much easier and more satisfying to follow Wood's arguments about particular manuscript copies if I had images of the book under discussion in front of me. As she points out with the inclusion of numerous URLs in her footnotes, many of these books, even the 'unstudied' ones, can now be accessed via the internet in high-resolution colour facsimiles. This fact makes the inclusion of six monochrome images in the hard copy of the book seem like an afterthought. The limitations of the material form of the printed academic monograph are evident on every page. This is not a criticism of Wood's book but rather an expression of desire for a future — not far off — in which such arguments can be made via seamless integration of digital open-access resources. Wood gestures toward this future in her epilogue. But we are not quite there yet.

Chapter 2, 'Marginalia and the *Piers Plowman* Manuscript Tradition', analyses the evidence collected in tabular form in the appendix, in support of Wood's argument that Langland's earliest readers were not merely transmitting the text but responding to it. These responses were not perhaps as idiosyncratic as proponents of the 'maverick scribe' theory have insisted. Indeed, she says, 'when the *Piers* manuscripts are grouped by their textual affiliations, it becomes clear that while there is room for innovation and reinvention by individual scribes, imitation or adaptation of earlier schemes of marginal annotation is in fact the norm' (p. 41); and further 'when these manuscript producers respond to *Piers Plowman*, they are responding also to one or more traditional presentations that may influence their understanding of Langland's work as much as inherent properties of the poetry itself' (p. 42). The case studies in this chapter focus less on individual manuscripts than on genetic groupings (copies that can be shown via the process of recension to have a shared ancestor); or on reconstructed archetypes (such as Burrow and Turville-Petre's edition of Bx, the lost ancestor of all surviving copies of B). For example, Wood's analysis of the *p*-group family of C-text manuscripts shows a remarkable level of scribal coherence to the marginalia of their shared exemplar, and she argues persuasively that this coherence marks a scribal commitment to the structure of the text and not just to its content. This claim sets the stage for the next three chapters, which form a cluster examining the generic affiliations of *Piers Plowman*. It is here that the book's emphasis shifts from 'earliest readers' to 'exemplary lives'.

Chapter 3, 'Legends and Lives', looks at hagiographical writings, arguing that the copy of *Piers Plowman* in the famous Vernon manuscript (Oxford, Bodleian Library, MS Eng. poet. a. 1) needs to be understood as part of a cluster of texts that form a 'miniature legendary' (p. 78) whose compiler would have understood the 'life' of Langland's dreamer as another instantiation of an exemplary *vita*, like those in the *South English Legendary* or the *Legenda aurea*. A close study of the illustration of Emperor Trajan in Oxford, Bodleian Library, MS Douce 104 (sigil Dc) links Langland's version of the righteous heathen to the life of St Gregory in the *Golden Legend*, suggesting provocatively that 'the illustrator outdoes the poet' in correcting the poem's account to agree with its source (p. 87). Chapter 4, 'The Romance of Will and Alexander', covers the manuscript associations of *Piers Plowman* with the genre Wood calls 'pseudo-historical romance', focusing especially on *King Alisaunder* and the *Wars of Alexander*. Chapter 5, 'Piers Plowman and His Travelling Companions', explores the relatively well-known fact of the frequent manuscript pairing of *Piers Plowman* with *Mandeville's Travels*, but now seen through the wider lens of Wood's category of 'exemplary lives'. The chapter's two case studies on Cambridge, University Library, MS Dd.1.17 (sigil C of B) and London, British Library, MS Harley 3954 (H) show in extraordinary detail how two very different compilers reacted to the pairing of Mandeville and Langland. In such contexts, Wood writes, '*Piers Plowman*'s affinities with the *Travels* as a popularized and experiential mode of knowledge becomes freshly visible to the reader today' (p. 119).

The final chapter, 'The Anonymous Huntington Scribe and Public *Piers Plowman*', focuses on the work of a single copyist whose literary compilations provide Wood the opportunity to fully explore the tension between individual scribal intervention and the public transmission of materials that were understood to be 'standard'. This scribe's *Piers Plowman* manuscript, San Marino, CA, Huntington Library, MS HM 114 (sigil Ht), again puts Langland's poem together with Mandeville in highly idiosyncratic versions of both texts. In Wood's words, the copy of *Piers Plowman* in Ht is a 'notorious splice of materials from all three versions of Langland's poem interspersed with unique verses probably of [the scribe's] own invention' (p. 154). Recent scholarship has usually identified the Ht scribe as the early fifteenth-century London Guildhall clerk Richard Osbarn (following Linne R. Mooney and Estelle Stubbs, *Scribes and the City: London Guildhall Clerks and the Dissemination of Middle English Literature 1375–1425* [York: York Medieval Press, 2013]). Wood is sceptical of the attribution and would return the Ht scribe to anonymity. She likewise rejects the idea that Ht's eclectic *Piers Plowman* text is the product of an elite coterie of London readers with special access to early exemplars; to the contrary, it reflects 'the public transmission of the poem in the metropolitan book trade' and 'silently incorporates the work of many earlier, anonymous hands' across several decades (p. 155). The chapter goes on to analyse the fascinating and unexpected ways in which the Ht scribe's literary activities overlap with his more mundane day job of copying documentary texts like the *Liber albus*.

I hope I have successfully conveyed my admiration for this project. My few reservations therefore reflect a desire for a more robust proclamation of its stakes for the field, beyond the relatively small number of scholars active in *Piers Plowman* manuscript studies. In her brief epilogue to the book, Wood takes aim at the conventional scholarly view that treats *Piers Plowman* as merely a 'collection of institutional discourses' (p. 186) that eschews narrative sense-making. She claims instead, now based on the evidence of the previous six chapters, that 'the manuscript contexts suggest that the twenty-first century [sic] audience might consider the possibility that it has exaggerated Langland's narrative oddities in the service of a fashionable scepticism that any sense might be made of the text by the effort of reading' (p. 188). This is a strong claim and perhaps a justifiable one — but its justification will depend ultimately on those same 'sceptics' seeing the text anew in the light of Wood's presentation of the manuscript evidence. But will they? I think herein lies my main complaint: I worry that the inherent technicality of the kinds of evidence Wood presents will prevent scholars who are not manuscript or textual studies people from engaging with it fully, if at all, and that its far-reaching consequences for our understanding of Langland's poem will not be taken up as fully as they might have been. More, and earlier, explanation of how the technical trees add up to a field-altering forest would have been helpful. Even so, it is indicative of Wood's modesty and scrupulousness as a scholar that she never overstates her case; where the evidence is mixed and complicated, she admits that firm conclusions are hard to draw. The book is generous in its citation of previous scholarship, even when it disagrees; it engages directly on several occasions with unpublished or in-progress work by junior scholars, a practice much rarer in our field than it should be, given the state of the job market.

Finally, on the idea of 'exemplary lives', I have one small quibble of a different kind. The late Anne Middleton is a frequent interlocutor in these pages, as one might expect given her trenchant analyses of textual and codicological cruxes as portals into whole worlds of literary, historical, and theological meaning. And since more than half of Wood's book is concerned with the intersection between *Piers Plowman* and the genres of 'exemplary lives', one might have wished for more nuanced reflection on the complexities of the word 'life' and its forms as Langland's poem understood them. As Middleton points out, the 'insistent ambiguity of the word [*life*] in [Langland's] hands appears to be the reason that both the *OED* and the *MED* avoid citing the poem's several memorable occurrences of it in support of any of the several common senses of the word in the fourteenth century: virtually all of its interesting uses in the poem are *extremely treacherous*' ('Langland's Lives: Reflections on Late-Medieval Religious and Literary Vocabulary', in *The Idea of Medieval Literature: New Essays on Chaucer and Medieval Culture in Honor of Donald R. Howard*, ed. by James M. Dean and Christian K. Zacher [Newark: University of Delaware Press, 1992], pp. 227–42, at p. 229; emphasis mine). My own desires aside, however, this book is a major accomplishment. I very much hope that the field of Langland studies will take up the challenges posed both by its methods and its conclusions.

Jim Knowles
North Carolina State University
jrknowle@ncsu.edu

Andrew Kraebel, *Biblical Commentary and Translation in Later Medieval England: Experiments in Interpretation*. Cambridge: Cambridge University Press, 2020. Pp. xiv + 302.

Andrew Kraebel's book is complex and important. While it is fundamentally and finally concerned with works well studied by readers of Middle English — Rolle's *English Psalter* (chapter 3) and the Wycliffite Glossed Gospels (chapter 4) — it approaches them through Latin texts altogether less frequented, working from primary manuscript sources throughout. Chapter 1 looks at three quite divergent Latin commentaries on the Psalms from the 1310s and the 1320s, by Thomas Waleys OP, Nicholas Trevet OP, and Henry Cossey OFM, and shows that 'late medieval biblical commentaries were more intricately and diversely experimental than the familiar narrative of the rise of the literal sense would suggest' (p. 52). Chapter 2 looks in depth at Wyclif's Psalter commentary and biblical exegesis, the *Opus Evangelicum* and the *Postilla*, which are generally judged from printed extracts, and at William Woodford's postill on Matthew (the subject of Jeremy Catto's unpublished DPhil thesis in 1969). To some of these texts Kraebel has devoted more productive time than any or all but a handful of living scholars, as the book's appendices exemplify. Appendix A presents the detailed evidence that Wyclif adopted a system of subject matter symbols and cross-reference from the *Media Glosatura* of Gilbert of Poitiers, the point being to demonstrate Wyclif's 'interpretive eclecticism' (p. 65) and both his and Woodford's response to Lyre by way of a return to earlier commentaries. Appendix B develops the substantial evidence for two distinct versions of Rolle's Latin Psalter, in support of Kraebel's case in chapter 3 that Rolle's revisions enact his own growing understanding of the contemplative life and so prepare the ground for the yet more innovative English Psalter. Appendix C is Kraebel's edition of the prologue to a Latin commentary on Matthew prepared at Durham priory in the early twelfth century which served as the basis for the 'almost unstudied' late fourteenth-century commentary-translation of Matthew in BL Egerton MS 842 and CUL MS Ii 2.12; Kraebel's edition of the English prologue is to be found in *Traditio* 69 (2014), 87–123 (the reference is wrongly given in the book's bibliography), but would have been worth repeating here. The point again is to show the eclectic turn in the fourteenth century in both Latin and English to earlier commentary materials. It is an index of the book's specialization that the Latin text is provided, to my mind unhelpfully, without an English translation.

This degree of specialization has two consequences. First, and less important, is that a reviewer, at least this reviewer, must scrabble to find solid ground from which to assess Kraebel's extensive presentation of commentary material in which Kraebel himself is uniquely well-versed, except to say that it is lucidly written, careful and nuanced in the inferences drawn, and throughout persuasively argued, not least in redrawing scholarly frameworks. The second, and greater consequence, is that some readers, especially those better qualified in vernacular theology than in scholastic exegesis, may find themselves in the position of this reviewer. There is the more reason, then, to emphasize that — for all its necessary and often exhilarating textual complexity, and by virtue of it — Kraebel's book is important to the whole field in its re-orienting of scholarship on late medieval biblical commentary-translation in both Middle English and Latin, and in its detailed support for its literary and religious centrality. (The book is emphatic that work in the two languages should not be separated and speaks of a context that is 'multilingual and predominantly Latin', p. 9). Kraebel's chapters and appendices deploy a weight of textual work that has often been overlooked as scholarship ran with inherited premises. This is not to say that Kraebel adopts the role of prophet. Rather, he plays the scholar-exegete of the ambitious but modest kind he describes, drawing on a huge body of existing commentary and edging it in new directions, marking his point of origin early on in the work of Beryl Smalley and conversing along the way with Hudson, Hanna, Gillespie, Copeland, Cole, Ghosh, Somerset, Watson and others; his thesis is particularly anticipated in the late work of Mary Dove, to whose influence Kraebel pays tribute in the *Traditio* piece. Yet the new evidence and analysis Kraebel brings to bear gives his study an immediate and pressing impact. This is effectively and clearly outlined in his excellent Introduction.

The key term 'commentary-translation' originates not with Kraebel but with Alastair Minnis, whose mentorship is warmly acknowledged; but Kraebel gives full weight and meaning to the hyphen. He uses it particularly to refer to distinctive interpretive developments in fourteenth-century England, in both Latin and English, that seek to meet the needs of readers beyond the universities. Though it does not trip off the tongue, the term has a corrective function; in Kraebel's view of such work it is not possible to maintain a distinction between translation and commentary. Later medieval commentators seek to unlock the full potential meaning of Scripture, which is illimitable; like the range of Latin commentators discussed in Chapter 1, the translator-commentator is responsive to a sense of multiple possibility inherent in each single word or phrase or sentence, and the aim is to document and add judiciously, rarely to fix a single meaning. Crucially, this is equally true of Wyclif and the Wycliffite Glossed Gospels. It follows that to speak of the Wycliffite project as liberating text from gloss is a false representation — derived, as Kraebel would have it, from the rhetoric of Tudor Reformers, though he is at pains in his epilogue, 'John Bale's dilemma', to show that the issue was not a simple one, certainly not for Bale. Kraebel aims to redress a residual prejudice against commentary as somehow falsifying translation or inimical to it; he describes a multiform project in which they are indivisible and shows Wycliffite texts to be its inheritor. In such a project, the proposition that the Scriptural text should be 'plain' or 'open' means something quite different from its post-Reformation sense (p. 162); it means open to interpretation, so that commentary-translation becomes a disciplined search for multiplicity, not for the pseudo-singular fixity of what is left of a translation when shorn of gloss. The movement beyond the universities shifts attention towards devotion as well as study in the unfolding of divine wisdom. Kraebel's account is sensitive and attentive to the various manuscript formats which structure the forms of that unfolding in commentary-translations.

Another force for diversity in fourteenth-century commentaries, seen clearly in each of the three studied in Kraebel's first chapter, is their recognition of difference among books of the Bible and their insistence, pushing back against Lyre and totalizing Thomistic exegesis, on the need for commentary to be book-specific. The biblical book offering most scope for multiplicity is of course Psalms, and Kraebel's account of their exegetical strategies is a useful complement to Annie Sutherland's 2015 book and to other recent scholarship. He shows how the categories of author and voice diverge sharply as historical and moral readings play together: there is no contradiction between maintaining that all the Psalms are the work of David as single author and ascribing an individual *vox* or multiple voices to each — of king, sinner, Church, righteous Christian and the like. Yet the Psalms also offer a register of voices that allow an interpreter 'oblique' (p. 3) scope to authorize his own voice, or hers (I regret that Eleanor

Hull apparently falls outside the chronological boundaries of this study; her work would have provided richer soil than, say, Richard Maidstone, for whom see pages 118–22). The Psalms commentary-translations model the kinds of exegetical free play — Kraebel's 'experiments in interpretation' — that are then shown at work on the gospels later in the century.

These are what Kraebel terms 'moral experiments' because their readings reconcile the historical/literal and the tropological; they bring together the academic and the devotional in a synthesis. There is no desire here 'to shake off the yoke of scholasticism' (p. 20). This is a crucial finding of Kraebel's book. Its hero, immediately proclaimed, is Richard Rolle, who 'turns commentary into a form of writing that is at once scholastic and devotional' (p. 3). As well as his mystical '*canor*', Kraebel emphasizes Rolle's academic credentials and the subsequent influence of his work in Oxford at just the time of biblical translation in the late fourteenth century. The English Psalter is not a diminution of his scholastic enterprise in the cause of dumbing down for a vernacular audience but rather a unique and creative fusion, 'for the sake of an ambitiously learned form of devotional reading' (p. 93), between the meditative and the intellectual, scholastic commentaries and the affective voice work of the Psalms. With deft examples generally focused on Rolle's additions to or departures from Peter Lombard in the Latin Psalter, for example in his treatment of Psalm 9 (p. 98–99) and Psalm 54.8 (p. 101), Kraebel shows Rolle's 'assumption of a psalmic voice', that of one who 'should be numbered among the *perfecti*' (p. 99) — a register of voice which is offered in the English Psalter as a set of scripts for a 'perfyt mane or womman' (p. 110). In pairing vernacular commentary with close translation, and with the Latin included on the page, Rolle invents a 'wholly new' form of multilingual commentary-translation, catering both for those who have no Latin and those who have the Latin and access required to follow up the citations. It is a hybrid (though Kraebel avoids the word), 'neither simply a rendering of the Latin nor a vernacular gloss' (p. 113–14), and exerts a commanding influence over succeeding work, towering as tall as Wyclif.

Kraebel's account goes far to bridge the distance between Latin and English, scholastic and devout, and has far-reaching implications for the ways in which we approach vernacular religious texts. There is a good deal at stake here for readers of *Piers Plowman*, who work on manuscripts whose multilingual *ordinatio* marks their resemblance to commentary-translations. It has never seemed adequate to the poem's many facets to embrace prior invitations to read the English as mere commentary on the Latin it cites and often translates, but Kraebel's intertwining of text and gloss, of scholarly and spiritual, of biblical text and multivocality, might encourage us to look again and differently. And we might also look at the poem's version of 'hermit hermeneutics' (p. 95), and at its narratorial voice that aspires to 'parfitnesse' but falls short of its own pretensions. Much of the work has already been done by many hands, and more yet is dispersed through the Penn commentary volumes, but in view of Kraebel's revaluation might we look forward to a detailed and concentrated presentation of *Piers Plowman* as a Rollean text or, as is still conceivable in this new light, critique?

David Lawton
Durham University
lawtonda@gmail.com

Jordan Kirk, *Medieval Nonsense: Signifying Nothing in Fourteenth-Century England*. New York: Fordham University Press, 2021. Pp. 187.

In its broadest sense, Jordan Kirk's book, *Medieval Nonsense: Signifying Nothing in Fourteenth-Century England*, asks what constitutes literary language and probes the purpose of reading it. Literature, he argues, offers 'an experience of a very particular kind of unknowing' (p. 25) through which the mind slips into states of productive confusion. *Medieval Nonsense* offers a lineage of techniques of unknowing, beginning with the early grammatical thought of Priscian, Boethius, and Augustine, then extending into the linguistic philosophy the early thirteenth-century Oxford philosopher Walter Burley, then the later Middle English *Cloud of Unknowing*, and finally to the anonymous poem, *St Erkenwald*. With his emphasis on what he calls an 'engineering of awareness' (p. 7), Kirk's book joins other recent work in medieval literary studies by scholars like Katharine Breen, Seeta Chaganti, Eleanor Johnson, and others — all of which amplifies the experiential nature of language and literary form and explores how texts produce a range of modes of cognition (or for Kirk, perhaps *de*-cognition). Kirk extends such scholarship into the realms of medieval grammar and sign theory, drawing from the work of scholars like Rita Copeland and Eugene Vance in conversation with contemporary linguistic thought.

Though it delves into the earlier lineages of thinking on the nonsignifying *vox* (primarily in Chapter 1) and accentuates the global context of many of his sources, *Medieval Nonsense* directs its attention to fourteenth-century England, where, Kirk argues, an efflorescence of nonsignifying practices arose just as Middle English was emerging as a written language. The organization of this book is not chronological, but around a 'constellation of paradigms' (p. 20) arranged according to what Boethius called the *orandi ordo*, a fourfold scheme delineating the course of an act of speech, moving from external referents, to mental conception, to spoken words, and finally to written words. Kirk examines 1) definitions of the *vox sola* (bare utterance) as a 'thing' among early theorists of *vox* Priscian, Boethius, and Augustine, 2) the philosophy of Walter Burley on how mental concepts could be adequate to external things, 3) how the spoken word could correspond to mental conceptions in the late medieval contemplative text *The Cloud of Unknowing*, and 4) how the enigmatic fourteenth-century alliterative poem *St Erkenwald* approaches problems of inscription. Proceeding in this order enacts the medieval theories of linguistic cognition that lie at the heart of this study, offsetting the sense that each chapter is a discrete essay.

In the introduction, Kirk demonstrates how medieval thinkers re-imagined the integumental model of language through an extended reading of a little-noticed moment of *tregetrie* or sleight of hand in Chaucer's *House of Fame*. In this reconsideration, words can not only be vehicles for meaning, but also technologies for the destruction of meaning, offering a 'contemplative practice' (p. 7). For Kirk, this moment in Chaucer anticipates a similar preoccupation among modernist thinkers: Walter Benjamin, Lewis Carroll, James Joyce, Gertrude Stein, Knut Hamsun, as well as more recent theorists like Roland Barthes, Jacques Lacan, and Julia Kristeva. All of these thinkers, and others, explore how language can not only represent the world, but also facilitate unknowing, offering a tool of experience.

Next, Kirk shows how *vox* is fundamental to the three elementary branches of medieval education (grammar, logic, and rhetoric), teasing apart the sometimes contradictory ways that Priscian, Boethius, and Augustine theorized *vox*. Far from dismissing the non-signifying voice, Kirk shows how all three influential thinkers sought to understand it, and even considered meaninglessness to be an inherent property of *vox*. Together, these paradigmatic theorists of *vox* accentuate how the material properties of language — its 'basic stuff' (p. 29) — exist whether or not it is meaningful. Acknowledging such existence, moreover, attests to a doctrine of non-signification woven into early grammatical theories of *vox* (discussed further below).

Kirk then sketches the next stage of debate about the nature of *vox* among thirteenth-century philosophers and excavates the traces of a theory of non-signification submerged beneath that debate as it was expressed in a commentary on Aristotle's *De interpretatione* by Walter Burley, a logician and scholar of Oxford's Merton College, the same Mertonians known to have influenced Chaucer and the author of *The Cloud of Unknowing*. Kirk argues that Burley's commentary might productively be read as a 'collage' of the earlier debates about whether *vox* was referent for things or concepts: Burley 'expropriates their elements and recombines them in a new form' (p. 53). To fully contextualize his thought, Kirk situates Burley's collage in relation to a twelfth- and thirteenth-century history of the *vox non-significativa* in a range of works on logic by Oxford thinkers. For Kirk, this context enables a reading of Burley's commentary that accentuates how he embraces the incoherencies of earlier linguistic thought and transforms them into a logic of non-signification through which the reduction of a word to its 'bare utterance' produces a failure of knowledge that becomes its opposite: a knowledge of that failure. In Burley's commentary, this process is the 'highest calling' (p. 74) and the foundation of logic.

After exploring theories of *vox* among these Latin writers and thinkers, Kirk turns to Middle English writers and to the ways that the spiritual pursuit of unknowing undergirds the contemplative programme laid out in the Middle English *Cloud of Unknowing*. Offering an extended gloss of the 'litil worde of o syllable' repeatedly mentioned by the *Cloud*-author, this chapter shows how the terms of debate around *vox* in the medieval linguistic sciences were assimilated into the discourse of late medieval affective apophaticism that inform the procedure of prayer outlined in the *Cloud*. Through this assimilation, they formed a *sui generis* contemplative programme different from other schemes that advocate the meditative repetition of a single name, e.g. those by Hilton and Rolle. For Kirk, the *Cloud*-author's prayer calls for the production of an utterance that is simultaneously both a syllable and word and also neither. Refuting the importance scholars have placed on the vernacularity of the words offered by the Cloud-author as examples — *god, loue, synne*, and *oute* — Kirk accentuates the *Cloud*-author's preoccupation with the 'hoelnes' (i.e., 'wholeness') of the syllable, amplifying how it is the 'crie' or sound of the word — not its meaning — that offers the 'loue put' (or 'love thrust') that reaches God. Such a cry must take place in silence, however, for vocalized sound always indicates a will to meaning that must be escaped in order to produce the unknowing that is knowledge of God. For the *Cloud*-author, the repetition of such a word, Kirk explains, is concerned with producing the cognitive confusion or 'unknowing' that occurs in the mind of a person repeating a word to the point of nonsense.

Finally, Kirk turns to nonsense in its written form. He notes that the central formal feature of the Middle English alliterative poem *St Erkenwald* — a line break in precisely the middle — separates the poem into two sections, each of which is fundamentally concerned with signs. The first section centres on the 'roynyshe [...] resones' — the mysterious signs or *caracters* inscribed on the tomb of the virtuous pagan, excavated by masons at the opening of the poem. The second section deals with Saint Erkenwald's miraculous baptism of the corpse, a sacrament that worked through performative language that effected a baptismal character: a mark or tattoo on the soul. Contextualizing the poem in the history of *caracters* or runish figures associated with magic and necromancy and the treatment of signs in medieval debates about baptismal theology, Kirk argues that these two treatments of the character — the necromantic and the baptismal — demand to be read in relation to each other, offering a 'riddle' or 'thought experiment' through which the poem poses a chiastic relationship between the two. As a mark on the interior, the soul, that signals a point of entry into the Christian community, the baptismal character is 'intelligible but not sensible'. As a mark that is visible, but incomprehensible, the necromantic *caracter* is 'sensible but not intelligible' (p. 123). Because a sign is fundamentally defined as something sensible that brings to mind something intelligible, neither the baptismal character nor the necromantic *caracter* is a sign on its own. Rather, each can operate as a sign only in relation to the other: they bring about meaning only to the extent that they fail to signify and so mark how the poem maintains its own mystery.

Medieval Nonsense is a carefully observed exploration of a range of sources that rarely get treated with the depth and breadth that Kirk brings to this book. To my mind, it has two great strengths. First, it is extremely valuable in highlighting the attention that early medieval thinkers such as Priscian and Boethius brought to the non-signifying utterance, even going so far as to argue that such work is 'grounded in a theory of meaninglessness' (p. 21). What emerges from the first chapter's argument is that medieval theories of *vox* are also, sometimes, theories of what we might call noise, emitted from things both animate and inanimate: Priscian, for example, insists on the fundamental sameness of human and animal *vox*. In making this claim, Kirk challenges scholarship that has accentuated the hierarchical nature of medieval *vox* — its privilege of human, non-foreign, learned male discourse over the voices of others. Aside from a fairly broad footnote in the introduction covering work on animal studies, medieval zoosemiotics, and idle talk, he makes no mention of such work and his argument would undoubtedly be strengthened by more direct engagement with it. A full exploration of the implications of a fundamental medieval theory of *vox* that accommodates the sounds of animals and objects is beyond the scope of the book. But *Medieval Nonsense* offers promising avenues of research along these lines for scholars interested in questions around mind, matter, and the post- or inhuman in medieval studies.

Second, *Medieval Nonsense* accentuates conceptual and aesthetic continuities between medieval and modernist/contemporary thought with precision and imagination. Through several forays into modernist theory on linguistics and poetics, Kirk demonstrates a reciprocal relationship between the medieval and the modern. If modernist nonsense must be read within a longer history of medieval literary theory and practice of nonsignification, medieval literature must also be read in terms of the modernist *avante garde*. Most of Kirk's discussion of modernist thought is concentrated in the introduction where he discusses, for example, Walter Benjamin's *reine sprache* or 'pure language', Knut Hamsen's invented word 'Kuboa', and Gertrude Stein's attention to the ways Chaucer's poetics 'sounds as sounds'. At the close of the book, as a kind of 'postgraph' to prompt further thought, Kirk places a provocative quotation from Samuel

Beckett on 'knowing nothing'. With such a rich set of resonances between medieval and modernist thought established, one wishes Kirk had added an epilogue to expand upon and explore the implications of this overlap and its significance: what does it mean for literary language to cultivate unknowing and how might this perspective help us defend literature? Perhaps holding back on these questions was a formal choice calculated to produce the same kind of gap in knowledge that he explores among medieval thinkers.

Medieval Nonsense will be of interest to scholars of medieval linguistics and poetics, medieval theories of cognition, devotional and contemplative technique and practice, the history of the senses, and modernist medievalism. Though there is no mention of *Piers Plowman* in the book, Kirk's arguments may be enormously generative for considering some of the poem's more confounding questions, perhaps especially its central question: what kind of work can language and poetic craft do? In the introduction, Kirk's reading of Chaucer's *tregetour* is illustrative. This *tregetour* performs a wonder — 'an uncouth thyng to telle' — placing a windmill under a walnut shell. For Kirk, this moment offers an example in miniature of the entire mechanism of the poem. The tregetour's sleight of hand is a metaphor for the various transmissions and transformations of language thematized and undertaken in the poem: the translation of Virgil and others, the movements of *vox* through space, and more. Each transmission 'turn[s] back on itself to circulate in a void, inoperative' (p. 4). The walnut and the windmill re-envisions the integumental model of language: words can not only be vehicles for meaning, but also technologies for the destruction of meaning, offering a contemplative practice that leads to wisdom. Central to *Piers* is the 'craft' Will seeks to cultivate the 'kynde knowyng that kenneth in [his] heart'. Perhaps this craft is, in part, a technique of unknowing.

Adin E. Lears
Virginia Commonwealth University
alears@vcu.edu

David Aers, *Versions of Election: From Langland and Aquinas to Calvin and Milton*. Notre Dame: Notre Dame University Press, 2020. Pp. xvii + 330.

The doctrines of predestination and reprobation have always been difficult to accept, and perhaps even more difficult to justify. How do we understand the repeated biblical claim that God is merciful, or any of the scriptural or ecclesial dicta to be virtuous and obedient, if it is in fact the case that God had, at the beginning of time, elected some humans for eternal salvation in heaven and others for eternal punishment in hell? The Augustinian tradition that established the contours of the Christian doctrines of predestination and reprobation attended closely to Paul's counterintuitive suggestion in Romans 9. 11–14 that God had meted out eternal justice for Jacob and Esau while they were still *in utero*, 'the children being not yet born, neither having done any good or evil'. Paul had himself turned to scripture to justify his shocking suggestion that divine justice unfolded with perfect disregard of any good or evil human exercise of will. His claim is founded on the chilling statement of divine will as revealed in the Book of Malachi, quoted here from the Authorized Version: 'I loved Jacob, and I hated Esau, and laid his [Esau's] mountains and his heritage waste for the dragons of the wilderness' (Malachi 1. 1–3). But where Malachi permits the reader to imagine that God may have loved Jacob and hated Esau in response to their respective actions during the early years of their lives, Paul takes on the more difficult task of asserting that God's eternally binding election of man is unrelated to the good or evil performed by any particular individual. Paul focuses resolutely on God's, not man's, will: 'that the purpose of God [...] might stand, not of [man's] works, but of him that calleth' (Romans 9. 11).

It is the overwhelming intellectual, emotional, and spiritual challenge with which the doctrine of election confronts the believer that David Aers analyses with precision and panache in his *Versions of Election: From Langland and Aquinas to Calvin and Milton*. The subtitle boldly presents the central ambitions of the book. It pursues the problems attending the doctrines of predestination and reprobation in two distinct historical periods, the late medieval period and early modernity. And it studies the logical and rhetorical subtlety of the theologians Thomas Aquinas, Robert Holcot, John Calvin, and William Twisse with the same intense scrutiny that it brings to the poetry of William Langland and John Milton. As one might imagine, this aggressively transdisciplinary book can feel somewhat ponderous, with its densely argued treatment of all its writers: it is all the more challenging to read for its refusal to present the hugely complex works of its theologians as a neatly packaged intellectual background against which we can more clearly discern the literary foreground of the more familiar poets. For Aers, the discursive universe of Christian doctrine looks a lot like the discursive world of poetry: '[W]hether medieval or Reformation, [it] is many-stranded, replete with contradictions and as unstable as it is dynamic' (p. 162).

In the book's first chapter, on the C text of *Piers Plowman*, it is Langland's feeling for the instability, even the inadequacy, of settled soteriological doctrine that is seen to motivate Will's struggle for an answer to the question originally posed in Acts 16. 30: 'what must I do to be saved?' Much as John Bunyan's *Pilgrim's Progress* will open with Christian's cry, 'What shall I do to be saved', so Langland's Will asks Holy Church in passus 1: 'How Y may save my soule?' The medieval period, as Aers writes later in the book, was committed in general to the answerability of that question; it was an age dependent on an understanding of the 'intimate relations between scripture, tradition, church, and reason, each an essential and interrelated vector through which the Holy Spirit guided humanity' (p. 184). But for Langland, these authorities fail to cohere as essential and interrelated, and Will is left to engage in idiosyncratic, thorny encounters with the disparate teachers 'Holy Churche, Conscience, Reason, Repentance, Piers the Plowman, Wit, Studie, Clergie, and Scripture' (p. 3). The prospect of the unchangeable predetermination of the fate of one's soul induces in Will a spiritual terror and panic that Langland weaves into a 'brilliantly conceived dramatic process that is cultural and ecclesiological, social and theological' (p. 27). The result of that process seems to be a stout resistance to the unyielding metaphysical abstraction of an Augustinian claim for divine election. The absolutist God who preemptively adjudicates the ultimate status of the soul is countered by Langland's alternative, softer vision of a merciful and loving Christ made available to believers by means of the Church: 'Langland's poetic theology is exuberantly Christocentric as it weaves together the past, present, and future with an account of the sacraments of baptism, eucharist, and penance in the divinely given ways of salvation' (p. 43).

Aers follows that chapter focused on the anxiety-induced theological searching of Langland's Will with a clever thought experiment. If the poetic character Will had actually studied in a later fourteenth-century university, what would his theological education have looked like? To what intellectual resources, in other words, would a university-trained Will have had access as he struggled to arrive at an understanding of election that gave space to the pious individual's virtuous and obedient works? Here, Aers introduces his reader to a group of fourteenth-century theologians who resisted the orthodox doctrines of predestination and reprobation bequeathed by the Augustinian tradition. He draws on the work of James Halverson, who singles out Peter Aureol, William of Ockham, and Holcot as figures committed to a robust attempt to establish theories of election that rival the Augustinian orthodoxy that had been so capably defended in the previous century by Aquinas. Aureol has no choice but to maintain *some* doctrine of election, but in Aureol's account, according to Aers, 'God's electing will is "general" [...] God does not predestine and reprobate particular individuals like the unborn twins Esau and Jacob. Rather, God offers saving grace to *all* who do not place an obstacle in the way of this grace but simply receive it' (p. 81).

For students of early modern theology and literature like myself, this chapter holds some wonderful surprises. Scholars of late sixteenth- and early seventeenth-century Protestant controversy are familiar with the anti-Calvinist arguments of that period for the universality of God's calling of the elect. Those arguments are typically understood to have been generated by Jacobus Arminius (1560–1609), the Dutch theologian who took on Calvin by insisting that God's predestinating will doesn't *cause* salvation or damnation; the omniscient God, rather, *foresees* who will ultimately deserve the reward of salvation and who the penalty of damnation. But as Aers makes clear, what may seem to be a unique feature of Reformation controversy, Arminius's radical opposition to the Calvinist insistence on an absolute predestination and reprobation, isn't really unique or revolutionary at all. Rather, Arminius and the Dutch Remonstrants who followed and expanded his anti-Calvinist theology of election appear to have been replaying a set of argumentative moves that had been established some two hundred years prior. As Aers writes, 'the Reformation did not cause this pluralism [in the matter of predestination]; it merely reinforced a diversity that was already present in theological discussion' (p. 82).

It could be argued that in my mention of 'Arminius' I am distorting somewhat Aers's own position on the recurrence, in the Reformation, of preexisting arguments for and against God's 'general' or 'particular' election of souls. And that is owing to a striking feature of *Versions of Election*. Aers doesn't actually mention Arminius more than a single time in the main text of his study. He is determined, it would seem, to take a wider-angled perspective on the relation of medieval to Reformation theological controversy, avoiding what he may consider to be the incautious limiting move of identifying theological positions too closely with individual writers, as well as the limitations of tying Reformation ideas too closely to their medieval precursors. Aers is more comfortable with formulations that emphasize the dynamism of doctrinal history. But Aers's reader, responding to the striking similarity of the anti-predestination arguments of Aureol and Holcot with those of Arminius and his Remonstrant heirs, may well imagine that the theologies of the fourteenth century had an as yet undefinable intellectual half-life, mediated possibly by university education, that enabled them to serve, in whatever whole or fragmentary form, as conceptual resources for the controversialists of the late sixteenth and early seventeenth centuries. I, for one, now eagerly await a study that aspires to trace an intellectual genealogy between these two closely related moments of intense theological foment.

The third chapter offers a fascinating account of the ways in which, in both historical periods, a doctrine of 'assurance' arose to assuage the anxiety of believers who took seriously the orthodox position that God had long before our existence determined who was bound for heaven and who for hell. The attempts to explain theologically how we are to experience ourselves as elect for salvation were always tricky, especially given the fact that it could be impossible to determine whether one felt truly assured of one's status as predestined, or merely transitorily assured, as in the case of a reprobate's blind, delusory assurance of divine grace.

This chapter argues brilliantly as well for the positive distinctness of the Reformation's invention of the theory of 'penal substitution'. What would become in seventeenth-century England the dominant Puritan theory of the meaning of Christ's crucifixion had no precedent at all in the medieval period: for the Reformed, the wrathful Father subjects the Son to a punishment equivalent to an eternity of burning in hell. Calvin and Calvin's God were in fact certain that the Son 'knew that he stood accursed before God's judgment seat', and that Christ knowingly entered 'the state of reprobates' (p. 135).

After a chapter focused on the entanglements of confident assurance and despondent doubt in Arthur Dent's homely *Plaine Man's Path-way to Heaven* (1601), Aers produces a splendid finale in his discussion of election, predestination, and reprobation in Milton's posthumously published *De doctrina Christiana*. He rightly takes to task the editors of the recent Oxford edition of the treatise who have placed Milton squarely 'in the theological mainstream' of Protestant thought on questions of soteriology (pp. 184–86). Far from the mainstream indeed, Milton, as Aers notes, goes much further than Arminius did, arguing that God decrees 'whoever wants to be saved must have a personal faith of their own', a faith to be derived from scripture, because every Christian 'has the spirit, the guide into truth; he has the mind of Christ'. That's not to suggest that Milton took the reliance on scripture to be uncomplicated, since, as Aers interestingly emphasizes, Milton wobbles on the question of the possible corruption of scriptural transmission: the Bible, or 'external' scripture, which is seen to be corrupt in *De doctrina*, is confidently asserted in *Paradise Lost* to be an uncontaminated assembly of 'written records pure' (12.513). On the matter of assurance, Milton is unquestionably a standout figure in this study: the consolation of assurance for Milton has less to do with affect or feeling than with will. The seventeenth-century poet 'argues that the assurance we need comes not from endless introspective searching for signs of election or reprobation but rather from our sustained decision to practice the virtues of faith and charity, a practice replete with the consolations of hope' (p. 207). Indeed, almost every discussion of faith in Milton's treatise quickly morphs into a nuanced celebration of works.

Milton had suggested in book 7 of *Paradise Lost* that the 'fit' or ideal readers of the epic were all too 'few'. The same might be said of *Versions of Election*. Surely few scholars (and certainly I exclude myself from this category) are sufficiently versed in the institutionally segregated fields of Langland and Milton studies to be able judiciously to assess the wisdom of Aers's pronouncements on both of those poets and their diverse intellectual lineages. But it's the boldness and idiosyncrasy of Aers's period-hopping analysis that gives this book its energy and insight. I can't speak for Langlandians, but students of seventeenth-century literature and religious controversy will find this doggedly transdisciplinary book of great interest and value.

John Rogers
University of Toronto
johnd.rogers@utoronto.ca

Eve Salisbury, *Narrating Medicine in Middle English Poetry: Poets, Practitioners, and the Plague*. London: Bloomsbury, 2022. Pp. xii + 224.

This is a time of global public health crisis. An infectious disease has killed millions of people around the world and inflicted a social trauma so deep that its reach has not yet been fully understood. It has spread alongside a new medical consciousness that increasingly translates specialist scientific discourse into popular expression and practice and seeks to find new ways for communities to live, heal, and connect. This is the fourteenth and fifteenth century, of course. And it's the subject of Eve Salisbury's new book, which starts with a question as timely for our own crisis moment of COVID-19: how do the stories we tell — including those told in poetry and prose — represent the experience of a society transformed by the trauma of a deadly pathogen?

Salisbury builds on the work of Marion Turner, Julie Orlemanski, and many others in analysing the significance of a change at the end of the fourteenth century: the rapid rise in the number and diversity of medical texts written in English and England. These texts, Salisbury suggests, encouraged innovations in medical treatment, both within and beyond the traditions of Galen and Hippocrates, and they opened a new medical discourse increasingly accessible to non-professional and vernacular audiences. Medical practitioners took notice. And so did poets.

Salisbury shows that literary texts belong to this same discourse of innovation and experimentation. They use medical terminology, tell stories of illness, and share medical treatments. They also reflect the visceral experience of their world's public health crisis: the Black Death, which first hit England in 1348 and continued to shape lives and literature for hundreds of years after. Salisbury finds that impact beyond the usual suspects of medieval plague literature, such as Giovanni Boccaccio's *Decameron* and Guillaume de Machaut's *Jugement dou Roy de Navarre*, across a larger archive of Middle English poetry and prose. It spans from Geoffrey Chaucer and William Langland to John Lydgate and Thomas Hoccleve to Julian of Norwich and Margery Kempe — and many others, too, who often represent the experience of a deadly pestilence in individuated stories and subtle, even unspoken, ways.

To examine these stories of illness, Salisbury draws on the heuristic of narrative medicine, pioneered in the late twentieth century by American physician Rita Charon, who sought a diagnostic approach that would enter imaginatively into other points of view. The idea is for patients to tell their own stories and for medical professionals to listen to them in all their complexity, trying to understand their ambiguity and allusions, their images and contradictions, and to follow their themes into worlds different from their own. The practice works to create connections — among people, languages, and worlds — and to build communities that link the personal with the public, individual illness with broader narrative threads of social trauma. Salisbury applies this heuristic to Middle English poetry and prose, finding in fictional narratives of illness a way to recover the individual experiences of a society living in a time of plague.

She analyses these experiences over five chapters, each of which directs attention to the literal and metaphoric roles of medical language, including the word *pestilence* itself. Chapter 1 links Chaucer's poetic art to the art of healing. It positions the poet and his persona in the *Canterbury Tales* as a practitioner responsible for listening to and diagnosing the pilgrims through their tales and shows that the pilgrims are all concerned with bodily and spiritual health. Chapter 2 puts John Gower and Langland in conversation, demonstrating how each poet uses confession as an intersubjective mode of communication to enable healing. Salisbury suggests that both Gower and Langland amplify individual and collective voices in their texts. In doing so, they evoke not just metaphorical but also literal analyses of pestilence and highlight the persistence of plague in their own times.

Chapter 3 studies the medical consciousness of Lydgate and Hoccleve, suggesting that their work gives voice to medical concerns in its self-reflexivity and illuminates for a modern audience the significance of patient storytellers. Chapter 4 reads Robert Thornton's codices through a medical perspective and as medical collections, whose narratives promote 'deeper understanding of what it means to be human and what it takes to stay alive during an epidemic' (pp. 122–23).

Chapter 5 contains the most wide-ranging analysis. It argues that women writers such as Margaret Paston, Julian of Norwich, and Margery Kempe, as well as fictional characters, including Josian from *Bevis of Hamptoun*, the *Pearl* maiden, and Morgan le Fay, are healers. Even when vilified, Salisbury shows, women find ways to 'participate in delivering health care' (p. 187).

There's a lot to learn from here: the broad cross-genre scope of texts covered; the productive expansion of what counts as medical discourse; the sustained, empathetic attention to individual experiences of epidemic life. The book shows persuasively that the Black Death, however infrequently acknowledged explicitly, shaped Middle English literature. And so it extends work that points in a similar direction, such as David Coley's *Death and the Pearl Maiden: Plague, Poetry, England* (Columbus: The Ohio State University Press, 2019), in providing new ways to hear 'pestilence whispered' (from the title of Coley's conclusion), i.e., the impact of plague on texts that tangentially address it.

The book also has some opportunities for development, especially in the scope of its theoretical framework. Given her emphasis on the relation between trauma and narrative, for example, Salisbury might have engaged more consistently with the field of trauma studies, both medieval and modern. The tradition of psychoanalytic scholarship about the roles of trauma in Chaucer is one prominent case in point, which might help complement or complicate arguments here about the work of memory in, and cross-temporal relevance of, illness narratives.

The same opportunity applies to the field of disability studies, toward which, like trauma studies, Salisbury gestures only occasionally. But its insights might have broader application throughout, including as a heuristic to inform the book's treatment of 'frenesy', impairment, and embodied experience in Hoccleve. Salisbury points to these and other approaches intermittently, especially in the afterword, which celebrates the breadth of medical humanities scholarship and suggests directions for future research. But I wondered if some of these directions might have helped shape the present conversation, too, as ways complementary to Charon's to listen to what makes a body and to think about what counts as medical discourse.

So, there's room to say more, and that's to the book's credit. It has brought to the surface a new medical consciousness in Middle English plague-time literature, and it will spark new work in the medical humanities about personal stories told amid a global health crisis.

Sarah Star
University of Toronto
sarah.star@utoronto.ca

Eric Weiskott, *Meter and Modernity in English Verse, 1350–1650*. Philadelphia: University of Pennsylvania Press, 2021. Pp. xviii + 297.

This is a highly unusual and very interesting study of the different metres in which verse was written in England between 1350 and 1650. I have called it a 'study' rather than a 'history', because the author himself introduces his material by subjecting received literary 'history' to a searching critique, taking issue with what are seen as the distortions produced by (especially) the binary division into 'medieval' and 'modern' phases and an over-emphasis on the emergence and development of pentameter. He thus deliberately suspends periodization and provides instead three interlinked disquisitions. Part I concentrates on the popularity between 1450 and 1650 of a genre of verse that is now little read, prophetic verse, and the metres in which it was written: largely alliterative verse and/or tetrameter, with hardly any specimens in pentameter. Parts II and III take up the various metres that have appeared in Part I. Part II investigates alliterative metre and pentameter blank verse (verse forms which, the book points out, were once perceived as linked to each other and to classical verse in their common rhymelessness) and the metre of *Piers Plowman*, the most influential and best-known alliterative poem after 1450. Part III gives an account of tetrameter, once the only alternative to alliterative metre for vernacular verse, and of the pentameter verse produced by and after Chaucer, who first introduced that metre into English verse.

The investigation into these 'relatively independent literary-historical shapes' (p. 197) leads in the Conclusion to an outlining of the overlapping sequence, or metrical chronology, that emerges. This chronology is exemplified through the contents of four manuscripts arranged in chronological order. The successive periods discerned from the successive manuscripts are: a phase characterized by the dominance of alliterative and/or tetrameter verse (Digby 102, which contains *Piers Plowman*, alliterative-stanzaic verse in tetrameter and other tetrameter poems); a phase in which 'prophecy, alliterative meter, tetrameter, and pentameter coexisted and overlapped' (CUL, MS Kk.I.5, which contains a number of prophetic poems as well as other verse); a phase in which alliterative verse no longer appears and in which 'pentameter and prophecy were authoritative but nonintersecting forms' and in which tetrameter was still 'an attractive option' (the commonplace book of Francis Castillion (1561–1638)); and finally a poetic culture in which pentameter was 'dominant', but when tetrameter was clearly still 'available' (Rawlinson poet. 26, a verse miscellany compiled over the first half of the seventeenth century). There follow appendices relating to prophetic verse that will prove useful to those working in this area, which is one not well documented: lists (of English prophecy books; of verse texts not noted in *NIMEV*; of compilers, scribes, and owners of relevant manuscripts) and an edited text of the *Ireland Prophecy*.

This account of the wide range of the book and its novel *dispositio* cannot do justice to its density in factual and literary detail. It is unfailingly interesting and informative, even where one might disagree with particular interpretations or emphases. There are some predictable notes struck in the conduct of the negative part of the argument. The pejoratives 'middle-class' and 'bourgeois' make their due appearance in generalizations about the history and structure of traditional literary studies, which are represented (plausibly) as over-emphasizing the pentameter tradition. Pentameter verse is, in the body of the book, characterized in similar terms: it is narrowly based geographically, emanating from within a seventy-mile radius round London, and so skews attention to the south, and its exponents, starting with the 'middle-manager, Geoffrey Chaucer' (p. 153), resemble one another sociologically, tending to be in government employment (p. 190) and being nearly all male. That last fact naturally has little significance in differentiating this group from other writers — and is added in plainly only to reinforce the implicit alignment with modern derogatory designations of an undesirably un-diverse profile. The author does have a point, but it is made in tendentious terms not characterizing other regional and demographic observations.

It is also questionable whether distinctions between 'medieval' and 'modern' really do influence literary responses quite as much or as crudely as is sometimes implied, and that issue impressed itself as something of a straw man in the section on prophetic verse. The section begins with a well-chosen reference to a nineteenth-century note in the Bodleian manuscript Ashmole 1835 (a collection of political prophecies). The annotator surmises (correctly) that Ashmole himself copied out parts of it: 'He was exceedingly superstitious, and believed in prophecies, visions, and various absurdities. Yet this man was the founder of the Ashmolean Museum at Oxford' (p. 25). We are certainly confronted at once, very pertinently, with an example, in Ashmole, of the seriousness with which such literature could be taken by educated men. But the opposition between 'a collection of *medieval* arcana' (my italics) and the 'modernity' of the 'scientific institution' of the Museum is one read into the remark by Weiskott himself. The incongruity registered by the annotator is simply that of the co-existence in one man of superstition and signal contribution to knowledge. Prophetic verse, it emerges, had its origins in the Welsh-descended *Prophetie Merlini* inserted by Geoffrey of Monmouth into his *Historia regum Brittaniae* and in the prophetic passages in *Piers Plowman*, but was at its peak well into the modern era. But it is not because it thus defies classification as either 'medieval' or 'modern' (p. 26) or because 'being both nonnarrative and nonlyric, [it] stymies modern reading habits' (p. 28) that this body of writing has proved to be an 'underappreciated literary archive' (p. 26). It is because the examples they have encountered strike many readers as tedious and/or unintelligible and as having an absurd and phoney portentousness, arousing in them the same impatience with 'this skimble-skamble stuff' as was felt by Hotspur. The question is, however, in every sense academic, as Weiskott's survey is bound to modify those prejudices. He clearly demonstrates that the genre did have a rhetoric and a register of its own and that, skilfully handled, it could produce effective and interesting verse. His account of the understanding with which the alliterative metre is handled in the *Ireland Prophecy* is especially persuasive, and among the other highlights are the arresting opening lines from Bridlington's *Prophecy* (in Latin hexameters) and a strangely haunting lyric in trimeter stanzas beginning 'When Wealth is walkt awaye'.

One aspect of its thesis on which the book is particularly convincing is the need to read metrical choices in their precise historical context, and not in the context of a future that had not yet occurred (p. xvii). Poets were responding to 'modern' conditions and chose and adapted their metres in response to their own 'modern' perspectives. Striking illustration comes in the two texts that book-end Part II. George Gascoigne's *Steele Glas*, a social satire heavily influenced by *Piers Plowman*, was written in blank verse. It was published in 1576, when blank verse was still a very recent innovation (p. 104), before both it and alliterative verse had acquired a certain cachet of antique austerity by being equated, by reason of their rhymelessness, with classical verse (pp. 112–13), and well before blank verse had become associated with epic. It does not here bring those associations with it. In fact, being a new form striking for its rhymelessness, it is presented by Gascoigne as having a certain brute plainness suited to the ungarnished 'reason' with which his satire will attack vice, whose walls will be breached through 'reasons force' and the 'battring' cannon shot of 'rymelesse verse' (see the lines quoted on p. 105). Though he could not know it, Gascoigne is making a metrical choice comparable with Langland's own partial de-poeticization of the alliterative mode he inherited. A few years earlier, blank verse would not have been available to Gascoigne as an option, and a few years later it would have come with different connotations. The precise context in the history of metre in which Langland chose his alliterative metre is likewise carefully explicated. The only other form then available for vernacular verse was tetrameter (pp. 123–24). His choice would thus have had a slightly different significance once pentameter had, a little later, entered English verse. Weiskott pays special attention, however, to Langland's choices within, as well as of, the rhymeless option: to the adaptations and innovations which he made to the alliterative metre as he inherited it and which turned that metre into a vehicle suited to address modern issues and one with a wider range of registers.

The book will, I believe, meet its objectives. Readers may not emerge from it eager to make their way through all the prophecy books listed in Appendix A, nor (I hope) will they have learned to regard the pentameter poets as merely further depressing examples of the undue influence wielded by middle-class males. But in both these areas they will have had their views significantly modified and they will certainly have discovered that English metrical history is much richer and more complex than they had imagined.

Myra Stokes
University of Bristol
myrastokes@talktalk.net

Joëlle Rollo-Koster, *The Great Western Schism, 1378–1417: Performing Legitimacy, Performing Unity*. Cambridge: Cambridge University Press, 2022. Pp. xiv + 406.

Joëlle Rollo-Koster's new book makes no mention of Middle English literature, much less Langland's *Piers Plowman*. And yet Rollo-Koster's dynamic new account of the central ecclesiological crisis of the later Middle Ages not only merits review in the *Yearbook of Langland Studies*, but should also take an immediate place in any shortlist of essential contextual reading for all Langlandians. Why? There are three reasons.

First, the Western Schism defined the culture in which Langland revised *Piers Plowman*, scribes copied the text, and readers read it. Unfortunately, English literary history generally adopts the view of the cultural resonance of the Schism expressed by Howard Kaminsky, 'The Great Schism', in *New Cambridge Medieval History, Volume 6: c. 1300– c. 1415*, ed. by Michael Jones (Cambridge: Cambridge University Press, 2000), pp. 674–96: the crisis was more or less irrelevant to everyday life and, by extension, vernacular literature. Likewise, other prominent English-language accounts of the crisis like Walter Ullman's *The Origins of the Schism: A Study in Fourteenth-Century Ecclesiastical History* (London: Burns, Oats, & Washburne, 1948) and R. N. Swanson's *Universities, Academics and the Great Schism* (Cambridge: Cambridge University Press, 1979) focus on specific topics or debates and neglect the larger cultural stakes of the Schism. More recently, the most generative analyses of the Schism have either taken place in French, Italian, or German or focused on topics off the radar of most scholars of Middle English. As such, readers of *Piers Plowman* will benefit from Rollo-Koster's magisterial synthesis of several decades' worth of interdisciplinary scholarship in French, German, Italian, and, yes, even English. For these readers, Chapter 1, 'The Great Western Schism: A Social Drama', will provide a succinct and modern account of the crisis that should enlumine their understanding of Langland's account of the church as an institution. Indeed, it should be the new starting point for Anglophone literary critics interested in learning more about the Schism or, perhaps more likely, understanding just enough to get by without embarrassment.

Second, as the subtitles of Rollo-Koster's book and her first chapter suggest, she takes a radically capacious approach to analysing the Schism. Until very recently, most histories of the Schism have focused on the ecclesiological or political aspects of the crisis. This approach necessarily centres such histories on the religious and political elite — so much so that several influential scholars have denied its relevance to the day-to-day lives of non-elites. This attitude continues to inform the Schism's persistent absence from English literary history. While the 'elite-only' thesis has been heavily critiqued and more recent scholarship on it has widened in scope, Rollo-Koster's analysis of the Schism as a 'social drama' reconfigures the crisis in ways particularly hospitable to literary criticism. Drawing on the work of Victor Turner, Rollo-Koster centres her account of the Schism on 'the grammars of social drama, underpinned by various forms of performance' (p. 23). This is not to say that Rollo-Koster ignores the concerns and texts that have informed generations of scholarship on the Schism but rather that she reframes key texts like Antonio Baldana's *De magno Schismate* and debates like the French subtraction of obedience in a wider performative context that focuses less on historical adjudication — who did what, when, and why — and more on modes of representation.

Focusing on performance, in turn, results in analysis that, on the one hand, greatly expands the intellectual history of the Schism and, on the other, is uniquely relevant to students of English literature. For example, in Chapter 4, 'Conflicting Legitimacy: The Schism and the Rhetoric of Tyrannicide', Rollo-Koster deftly reassembles a common language of legitimacy and dissent that unites the deposition of and execution of Richard II, the decision of France to 'subtract' its obedience from the Clementine papacy, and the murder of Louis of Orléans. 'Discussions of legitimacy, tyrannicide, the authority of a ruler vis à vis subjects or of the one vis à vis the many can', she convincingly argues, 'be productively located within the study of the Great Western Schism' (p. 186). The relevance of this line of thought to the study of *Piers Plowman* or Middle English at large hardly needs reiteration: one need only glance at the place Richard II occupies in English literary history to grasp the import. While this specific chapter may have particular relevance to English literature, Rollo-Koster's methodological approach to the Schism renders other, more surprising, aspects of the crisis directly relevant to the reading of Langland and his contemporaries.

In fact — and this is the third and final reason why Langlandians ought to engage with Rollo-Koster's account of the Schism — each chapter illuminates or contextualizes some aspect of *Piers Plowman*. Beyond the chapters discussed above, Langlandians will be most interested in Chapter 5, 'Finding Unity in the Liturgy: Papal Funerals and the Political

Theology of the Pope's One Body'. *Piers Plowman* concludes with — or perhaps collapses into — the question of unity and ecclesiological governance. As I have argued elsewhere in this journal (33 [2019], 69–109), the Schism was basic to Langland's ecclesiological imagination. In this respect, Langland's Barn of Unity must be understood as part of a much larger conversation about the basic nature of the church that connects *Piers Plowman* to the liturgical texts discussed by Rollo-Koster. While the remaining chapters may not, at first glance, seem as directly relevant to *Piers*, each merits close reading by scholars interested in particular aspects of Langland's poem.

For example, Rollo-Koster's virtuoso reading of the administrative performativity of papal *bullae* in Chapter 2, 'Performing the Papacy, Performing the Schism', could cast fresh light on the much-discussed pardon scene in *Piers Plowman*. Likewise, while Chapter 3, 'Images and Responses', focuses on visual representations of the crisis, Rollo-Koster's analysis of these depictions surfaces a welter of terms and ideas that speak directly to Langland's concerns. For example, Rollo-Koster's recontextualization of the *Apocalypse Tapestry of Angers* in terms of the Schism models how Langlandians might understand the apocalyptic aspects of *Piers Plowman* in relation to an ecclesiological situation that many contemporaries viewed as apocalyptic itself. The final two chapters focus on the geographic poles of the Schism: Rome and Avignon. Of these, the second chapter, especially its discussion of the debates surrounding France's first and second subtractions of obedience, will likely be of most value to Langlandians, especially those invested in the ecclesiological positions taken in *Piers Plowman*.

Historians will certainly find something to critique in Rollo-Koster's account of the Schism — that is what historians do — but those critiques are unlikely to change the book's merits for literary critics. For us, Rollo-Koster's work will remain a profoundly generous and generative resource precisely because it opens so many interpretive doors and closes so few. While Rollo-Koster offers no explicit engagement with the text of *Piers Plowman*, the contents of her book and the nature of her argument will deepen and enrich our understanding of Langland's historical context, ecclesiological commitments, and poetic vision.

Zachary E. Stone
Independent scholar
zachary.e.stone@gmail.com

Philip Knox, *The 'Romance of the Rose' and the Making of Fourteenth-Century English Literature*. Oxford: Oxford University Press, 2022. Pp. viii + 320.

Philip Knox's monograph offers an exciting contribution to the recent trend in Middle English studies that underscores late medieval England's ongoing cultural contact with the whole European continent. But where excellent recent studies, such as Olivia Robinson's *Contest, Translation, and the Chaucerian Text* or Stephanie Viereck Gibbs Kamath's *Authorship and First-Person Allegory in Late Medieval France and England*, have mainly focused on the relationship between late medieval English poets and their Continental contemporaries, Knox reaches further back. He argues that late medieval English and Continental poets define their relationship to one another through the lens of their mutual reception of the *Romance of the Rose*, that mid/late thirteenth-century *magnum opus* of weighty philosophical thought and scurrilous irony. To offer a prime example, Eustache Deschamps's *Ballade to Chaucer*, the only known acknowledgement by a contemporary of the English poet's literary practice, has French poet Deschamps famously praising Geoffrey Chaucer for his translation of the *Rose* into English. As Knox concludes, 'any account of fourteenth-century English literary history must include the *Rose* [...] [and] any attempt to understand the complexities of the European afterlife of the *Rose* must include England' (p. 2).

But Knox eschews the well-worn narrative, familiar to Anglo-French scholars, that starts by tracking the *Rose*'s influence on fourteenth-century French poets such as Guillaume de Machaut and Jean Froissart and then those poets' influence on their fourteenth-century English contemporaries like Chaucer and John Gower. Centred on courtly poetry in the French *dit amoureux* tradition, this narrative has read the *Rose*'s influence on England as primarily filtered through that text's later French treatments. By contrast, Knox returns to the *Rose* itself, and he examines the many more places, besides courtly poetry, where it emerges in late medieval English literature. He thus brings in a host of literary works whose relationship to French literature has remained sorely understudied, such as *Pearl* and *Cleanness*, Langland's *Piers Plowman*, and Chaucer's *Physician's Tale*. Knox generatively expands our understanding of English literature's debt to French literature.

As his chapter-length introduction details, Knox's investigative focus is not on individual authors' treatment of the French text. Instead, he examines the ways in which a 'rhizomatic' (p. 12) text like the *Rose* invites reading communities to coalesce around it, variously defining themselves by it, or, by contrast, against it. The popularity of the *Rose* allows it to function for some communities as a textual standard, or cultural common ground, around which to calibrate a sense of literary value. But the text's multidimensionality also invites literary debate, which allows communities to make and unmake themselves in opposition to the dissenting side. The remainder of Knox's monograph takes three main features of the *Rose*'s role within fourteenth-century reading communities under its purview: the *Rose*'s capacity to stimulate a discussion about literary value; its originary position as a philosophical poem in the vernacular; and its own treatment of its dual-authored status that provokes later meditations on vernacular self-authorization.

In his first chapter, Knox explores the ways in which literary communities get constructed around 'shared cultural objects' (p. 33) of 'collective consensus or collective dispute' (p. 96). (And here I would have loved more theorization of the circulation of cultural objects, the construction of value, and the social workings of cultural capital). Beginning with what he terms 'domesticating' (p. 50) interpretations of the *Rose*, Knox suggests that *Pearl* contains a programme of *Rose* references that encodes the limitations of the secular world and, by extension, the dreamer's limited understanding of eternal life. This representation, Knox argues, is extremely reductive, as if the *Rose* were simply a courtly love poem. The interpretive flattening, however, is precisely the point; it demonstrates the *Rose*'s function as a cultural commonplace for the idea of uncontainable desire. Tracing the same phenomenon in Oton de Granson's *Lai de desir en complainte*, Knox turns to Chaucer's prologue to the *Legend of Good Women*, in which the poet is arbitrarily taken to task by the tyrannical god of love for his poor translation of the *Rose*. Here, Knox suggests, Chaucer is examining the conformist pressures that highly valued 'public texts' place on reading communities in a meditation upon the interpretive flatness observed above.

From here, Knox investigates texts that foreground the *Rose* instead as a site of contest. In Christine de Pizan's *Epistre au dieu d'amours*, the object of Christine's critique is not simply the misogynistic *Rose*. She also takes aim at the courtly reading community that praises the text — reductively — as a paradigm of courtly love and remains indifferent to the damage that it does to its female readers. Christine argues that texts not serving the whole reading community must be expunged from that community so that the community can reform itself around a more suitable shared cultural object. Knox then turns to Thomas Hoccleve's English translation of Christine's work, the *Letter to Cupid*. Unlike Christine, Hoccleve emphasizes the text's openness to wide-ranging interpretations in a general resistance to overly orthodox textual interpretations and in celebration of shared texts' capacity to produce dialogue and debate. In this way, Christine and Hoccleve explore in real life the reading practices illustrated within Chaucer's prologue.

Knox's second chapter focuses on English poets' recognition of the *Rose*'s pivotal role as a philosophical poem in the vernacular. The *Rose*,

Knox contends, 'inaugurates a new period of English literary history. It makes possible philosophical poetry in English' (p. 92). In a series of impressively clarifying readings, Knox walks the reader through some of the thorniest (pun intended) moments in the *Rose* (such as the fountain of Narcissus, the *coilles* episode, and Pygmalion), in which human sexuality is shown to problematize the text's claims to truth and the idea of literary craft itself. Knox then looks at several English texts that each take up the *Rose*'s mantle in this regard: Gower's *Confessio Amantis* and his later poetry; *Cleanness*; Langland's *Piers Plowman*; and Chaucer's *Physician's Tale* and *Pardoner's Tale*. In each text, Knox uncovers key parallels with the *Rose*'s meditations on the challenge posed by human sexuality to natural order and, in turn, to the processes of poetry-making. Particularly standout here for me was the delicate argument that Langland associates deviant sexuality not with gender (as in the famous diatribe of Genius in the *Rose*, inherited from Alain de Lille) but with wasting time. This phenomenon points in turn to the ultimate self-professed time-waster, Will himself as a stand-in for Langland. In this way, as in the *Rose*, deviant sexuality becomes associated with problematic language and writing that preclude the search for truth.

But this second chapter feels different from the aims for the book so carefully outlined by Knox in his introduction and first chapter. I see how Gower, the *Gawain*-poet, Langland, and Chaucer literally form a community in that they are all working with the same complex of ideas lifted from the *Rose*. But methodologically Chapter 2 reads like a more classic vectoral source study because each English text is only being read against the *Rose*. I lost here the book's objective of investigating how the *Rose* becomes a lens through which contemporaries read one another.

This objective reemerges in the superb third and final chapter, where Knox opens with a fascinating discussion of how Laurent de Premierfait and Christine position Dante alongside Jean de Meun in their work, thus reading the *Commedia* and the *Rose* in conversation with one another. Knox goes on to survey how *Rose* manuscripts scribally problematize the poem's complex coauthored status, itself foregrounded so explicitly in the poem's famous midpoint passage. Some late medieval *Rose* manuscripts extend debates about the poem's intentions by anthologizing the *Rose* with the *Testament de Jehan de Meun* and other religious works attributed to de Meun. As Knox astutely argues, such manuscripts codicologically produce a palinodic effect for the *Rose* that goes on to influence the formal use of palinode in authorially designed anthologies: specifically, the placement of the *Parson's Tale* and *Retraction* in Chaucer's *Canterbury Tales*. This argument demonstrates the fruitfulness of material textual analysis when applied to literary analysis in the best traditions of critical bibliography.

The second half of Knox's final chapter turns to the effects of the vexed midpoint of the *Rose*, in which the text meditates on its own coauthorship.

In a nuanced reading, Knox reveals that the seemingly triumphant midpoint instead emphasizes the decay and oblivion of the poets de Meun appears to celebrate as his literary ancestors. In this way, the *Rose* mocks the transitory nature of authorial fame. From here Knox makes a startling move: he asks how the (*non*-Chaucerian) fragment B of the English *Rose* translation, the *Romaunt of the Rose*, might have treated the midpoint of the *Rose*, which is not included in that fragment. To answer this question, Knox turns to other translations and adaptations of the *Rose* that do include the midpoint: Gui de Mori's rewriting of the *Rose*; the Italian *Il Fiore*, possibly authored by Dante; and the Middle Dutch translation by Heinric van Aken. Each author, Knox shows, brings further complexity to this moment: de Mori adds in his own name after Guillaume de Lorris and de Meun; the Italian author replaces de Lorris and de Meun with his own name 'Durante'; and van Aken cursorily mentions a 'Jhan' but asserts his own self as the text's only author. One of the manuscripts of the Dutch work goes a step further and replaces *Jhan* with still another name, 'Mechiel', possibly a scribe. Extrapolating from this evidence, Knox considers how the author of fragment B of the *Romaunt* might have himself used the *Rose*'s midpoint as a vehicle for self-authorization, particularly given that the *Rose* — in at least one section of the *Romaunt* — was already famously translated by Chaucer himself. This section of Knox's book presents an exciting and generative methodology for working with fragments and lacunae. Knox rounds out this chapter with Chaucer's *House of Fame* to bring together the chapter's several argumentative threads concerning de Meun, Dante, poetry, troubled poetic lineages, and the ephemeral nature of fame. The chapter concludes with a towering reading of how Chaucer's work with Dante's *Commedia* in the *House of Fame* is accomplished through both Chaucer's own repeated allusions to the *Rose* and his treatment of Dante's *Rose* echoes.

Knox's monograph offers another crucial addition to Middle English and specifically Anglo-French studies that continues to vastly complicate our understanding of England's self-positioning within a broader European intellectual tradition; I hope it will become required reading. It will be fruitful for *Rose* scholars (particularly in its staggeringly comprehensive and clear outlining of the *Rose*'s ambitions) as well as French medievalists more generally, English medievalists, and scholars working on late medieval philosophy in the vernacular. It will also yield much for manuscript scholars, given the book's sharp attention, in all of its chapters, to material textual evidence; in these moments, Knox's careful analysis especially shines.

Elizaveta Strakhov
Marquette University
yelizaveta.strakhov@marquette.edu

PATRICK OUTHWAITE

Annual Bibliography, 2022

The annual bibliography attempts to cover the year's work on *PPl* and other didactic or allegorical poems in the alliterative tradition (e.g., *Winner and Waster, Parliament of the Three Ages, Death and Life, Mum and the Sothsegger, Pierce the Ploughman's Crede, Richard the Redeless*, and *The Crowned King*) but not alliterative romances or the works of the *Gawain*-poet. The bibliography may occasionally include a selection of books and articles of more general interest to *YLS* readers. Authors should send abstracts of their books (*c.* 800 words) and articles (250–400 words) and details of doctoral dissertations and reviews to Patrick Outhwaite, at p.j.outhwaite@rug.nl.

1. 'Annual Bibliography, 2021', *Yearbook of Langland Studies*, 36 (2022), 165–83.

Sixty-six entries, comprising thirty-seven annotated studies and a catalogue of reviews of twenty-nine books.

2. Baker, Denise N., '*Liberum Arbitrium* and the Tree of Charity in *Piers Plowman*', Yearbook of Langland Studies, 36 (2022), 77–99.

The progression of events culminating in the Tree of Charity (B.15–16.89) has long been recognized, following Mary Carruthers, as the 'cognitive heart' of *PPl*. This essay contends that the episode is also at the 'cognitive heart' of the critical debate about Langland's theology as either 'Augustinian' or 'semi-Pelagian', most prominently articulated by David Aers and Robert Adams. Despite their contrasting interpretations, both scholars identify precisely the issues in the B text that L addresses in his revision by replacing Anima as guide and Piers as guardian of the Tree of Charity with *Liberum Arbitrium* in C.16.156–18.123. By identifying Peter Lombard's discussion of *liberum arbitrium* in *The Sentences* as a plausible source of L's character and exploring the specific meaning of this term as 'free choice' rather than 'free will', this essay demonstrates that L's revisions of B.15–16.89 into C.16.156–18.123 are markedly Augustinian. (DNB)

3. Bergen, Richard Angelo, 'The Nature of Allegory: Spatial Tropes in Medieval and Early Modern Allegorical Narratives' (unpublished doctoral thesis, University of British Columbia, 2022), abstract in <https://dx.doi.org/10.14288/1.0422996>. Abstract available through UBC Theses and Dissertations.

4. Brantley, Jessica, *Medieval English Manuscripts and Literary Forms* (Philadelphia: University of Pennsylvania Press, 2022).

This book aims to provide a general introduction to manuscript studies for readers whose particular interests lie in medieval literature. The field of medieval literary studies has long depended on manuscripts, of course. The nineteenth-century editions that facilitated the widespread study of medieval texts made explicit their dependence on manuscript evidence. But that scholarly tradition was primarily textual and philological, concerned with how to reconstruct readable texts from fragmentary remains in order to develop histories of literature and language. More modern editions have typically moved farther from considering the original forms of the texts they encounter, but it is clearer than ever that manuscripts are important to literary analysis. Medieval books provide indispensable contexts for understanding literary culture, and even for establishing (or questioning) the historical parameters of the 'literary' itself. Bringing the traditional archival strengths of medieval manuscript studies together with the larger, more synthetic, and theoretical achievements of recent approaches to material texts, this handbook aims to ask such big questions. (JB)

5. Bude, Tekla, *Sonic Bodies: Text, Music, and Silence in Late Medieval England* (Philadelphia: University of Pennsylvania Press, 2022).

What is the body when it performs music? And what, conversely, is music as it reverberates through or pours out of a performing body? Bude starts from a simple premise — that music requires a body to perform it — to rethink the relationship between music, matter, and the body in the late medieval period.

Progressing by way of a series of case studies of texts by Richard Rolle, Walter Hilton, Margery Kempe, Geoffrey Chaucer, L, and others, Bude argues that writers thought of 'music' and 'the body' not as separate objects or ontologically prior categories, but as mutually dependent and historically determined processes that called each other into being in complex and shifting ways. These 'sonic bodies' are often unexpected, peculiar, even bizarre, and challenge our understanding of their constitutive parts.

Building on recent conversations about embodiment and the voice in literary criticism and music theory, *Sonic Bodies* makes two major interventions across these fields: first, it broadens the definitional ambits and functions of both 'music' and 'the body' in the medieval period; and second, it demonstrates how embodiment and musicality are deeply and multiply intertwined in medieval writing. Compelling literary subjects are literally built out of musical situations. (TB)

6. (Addendum to the 2021 annual bibliography.) Campbell, Emma, 'The Experience of Listening to Sermons in Late Medieval England' (unpublished doctoral thesis, University of Cambridge, 2021), abstract in <https://doi.org/10.17863/CAM.87160>. Abstract available through Apollo database.

7. Cornelius, Ian, 'Langland Parrhesiastes', in *Medieval Literary Voices: Embodiment, Materiality and Performance*, ed. by Louise D'Arcens and Sif Ríkharðsdóttir (Manchester: Manchester University Press, 2022), pp. 111–30.

The ancient Greek word parrhēsia designates speech that is bold, frank, and free, holding nothing back; a parrhēsiastēs is a person who gives voice to such speech. Although the word was little used in Latin literature and had no precise Latin equivalent, the concept was transmitted to medieval western Europe in rhetorical theory and the New Testament. In this book chapter, Cornelius proposes that the concept of parrhēsia may help to register the irruptive force, pointedness, risks, and complexity of certain acts of saying in *PPl*. For most of this chapter, Cornelius focusses on a single discursive feature of *PPl*: moral admonishment addressed in the second person to audiences outside the represented world of the poem. Cornelius argues that monitory address is an important and well-defined feature of *PPl*, that the poet's confidence in his monitory voice grows during his composition of the poem and that this feature of the poem culminates in Conscience's parrhesiastic addresses to bishops and the king in the C-version Prologue. As a coda to this argument, Cornelius proposes a reading of the dreamer as a figure of wisdom-seeking parrhēsia. (IC)

8. Fonzo, Kimberly, *Retrospective Prophecy and Medieval English Authorship* (Toronto: University of Toronto Press, 2022).

The prescience of medieval English authors has long been a source of fascination to readers. *Retrospective Prophecy and Medieval English Authorship* draws attention to the ways that misinterpreted, proleptically added, or dubiously attributed prognostications influenced the reputations of famed Middle English authors. It illuminates the creative ways in which L, John

Gower, and Geoffrey Chaucer engaged with prophecy to cultivate their own identities and to speak to the problems of their age.

Retrospective Prophecy and Medieval English Authorship examines the prophetic reputations of these well-known medieval authors whose fame made them especially subject to nationalist appropriation. Fonzo explains that retrospectively co-opting the prophetic voices of canonical authors aids those looking to excuse or endorse key events of national history by implying that they were destined to happen. She challenges the reputations of L, Gower, and Chaucer as prophets of the Protestant Reformation, Richard II's deposition, and secular Humanism, respectively.

This intellectual and critical assessment of medieval authors and their works makes the case that prophecy emerged and recurred as an important theme in medieval authorial self-representations. (KF)

9. Galloway, Andrew, 'Long Will and the Scandal of 1385', *Yearbook of Langland Studies*, 36 (2022), 45–76

This essay picks up a cold trail in the search for the author of *PPl*: the name 'William called Long Will', without surname, that Michael Bennett discovered among the names of elite associates of Sir John Holland, half-brother to Richard II, indicted for aiding (or not preventing) Holland's killing of Sir Ralph Stafford in 1385, can be further traced in plea rolls of the case before the King's Bench. Bennett argued that this eccentric name not only parallels the poet's only explicit self-identification but identifies the poet at a late point of his life. The newly discovered and edited records serve as occasion for refuting recent objections to Bennett's claim and for investigating further the figures involved, revealing new reasons to think the poet had a relationship to Holland and others in this group by 1385. Holland, for example, was a major landlord in London's Cornhill area, where the narrator situates himself in the C text; those properties were managed by another of the figures indicted. Moreover, some novel legal stratagems for land transfers used earlier by the Essex and Suffolk priest, William Rokele, currently the most promising candidate for authorship but whose traces vanish after 1369, were adopted by Holland and his agent soon after the events of 1385. Both the legal and poetic evidence is consistent with the theory that the poet went by varying surnames in earlier periods and for different purposes. This essay thus extends the known documentation of the events of 1385 while adding prosopographical information, comparative examples, and discussion of the poem's focus on adopting or relinquishing surnames to confirm the possibility that this William called Long Will could have been the poet of *PPl*, and to articulate some of the implications for his career and the poem. (AG)

10. Irvin, Matthew W., '"A Confidence as Bold": The Rhetorical Construction of Evangelical Authority in Hugh Latimer's "Sermon of the Plough"', *Rhetorica*, 40.3 (2022), 256–96.

Hugh Latimer's 1548 'Sermon of the Plough' is well-known as an example of early English evangelical rhetoric. However, the sermon has often been considered as an effect of, rather than a participant in, evangelical theology. This article reads Latimer's rhetoric, especially his creation of a persona, as fully theological, using Melanchthon's valorization of rhetoric over logic as a model. Latimer's sermon produces an authority that is not limited to Latimer himself, but serves as a reformation of Catholic notions of the authoritative role of the Church, a role based upon the rhetorically effective presentation of the Bible. (MWI)

11. Knox, Philip, *The 'Romance of the Rose' and the Making of Fourteenth-Century English Literature* (Oxford: Oxford University Press, 2022).

The *Romance of the Rose* had a transformative effect on the multilingual literary culture of fourteenth-century England, leaving more material evidence for late medieval English-speaking readers than any other vernacular literary work from mainland Europe. This book examines its decisive effect on English literature of the fourteenth century, and the new literary experiments it provoked from writers such as Geoffrey Chaucer, John Gower, L, and the author of *Sir Gawain and the Green Knight*. Linking the English afterlife of the *Rose* to a host of ongoing cultural developments in mainland Europe, *The 'Romance of the Rose' and the Making of Fourteenth-Century English Literature* reveals the deep interconnectedness of English and European literary culture. Examining courtly, clerical, and classicizing orientations towards the text, it presents new arguments for the place of the *Rose* at the centre of fourteenth-century English literature and explores its rich manuscript history to reveal new evidence about the cultural significance of this love allegory from thirteenth-century France. The chapters avoid an author-centred approach, arranging readings of the *Rose* and its relation with English literature in constellations that reveal complex unfolding inter-relation of the diverse readings of the *Rose* that took place in fourteenth-century England. (PK)

12. McKee, Conor, 'Langland's "Tree of Patience"', *Yearbook of Langland Studies*, 36 (2022), 101–22.

An allegorical tree is presented before Will in B.16 to show him what 'charite is to mene', yet despite the 'Tree of Charity' moniker which follows this passage in critical literature, in the B text L never actually calls the tree itself 'charity' but rather 'patience'. This essay seeks to better understand the interrelation of *caritas* and *patientia* by considering the place of patience in medieval pastoral theology. It draws attention to the use of *patientia* to describe cooperation with grace in pastoral manuals and presents *patientia* as essential to retaining *caritas* after penitence. It also proposes that L prepares us for the tree allegory by highlighting this role of patience as a preparatory virtue through his personification Patience, who takes on a sacramental role in B.14. L's C-text revisions continue to think about cooperating grace by developing the role of *Liberum Arbitrium* in C.18. (CM)

13. Park, Joon, and Eric Weiskott, 'Middle English *araten* and Scenes of Condescension in *Piers Plowman*', *The Explicator* 80/3–4 (2022), 73–77. DOI: 10.1080/00144940.2022.2100239.

Among the English words first recorded in *PPl* is *araten*, 'reprove'. This new, or newly literary, word encapsulates a peculiar quality of *PPl*, its cyclical depiction of verbal combat between opponents with unequal cultural authority. The word *araten* is perfect for *PPl* and plausibly was coined to purpose. This note suggests that *araten* cuts both ways in *PPl*'s multilayered analysis of class, and more broadly that visions of reproof with their political, social, literary, and theological implications were a central form through which L extended the A text into the B and C versions. (JP and EW)

14. Pasnau, Robert, 'Voluntarism and the Self in *Piers Plowman*', in *Gender, Poetry, and the Form of Thought in Later Medieval Literature: Essays in Honor of Elizabeth A. Robertson*, ed. by Jennifer Jahner and Ingrid Nelson (London: Lehigh University Press, 2022), pp. 47–66.

It is often suspected, of various works of fourteenth-century English literature, that they show the influence of philosophical voluntarism in the heightened significance they give to the will and its affective operations. This is an especially tempting thought to have with regard to *PPl*, both because of the poem's explicit engagement with philosophy and theology and because of the poem's choice to make Will its central character. It is Will, in Nicolette Zeeman's vivid phrase, who is the 'single, holistic protagonist, the narrator and motive force of the whole text'. So, although the extent of L's familiarity with the philosophical ideas of his era is a matter of conjecture, it is hard to resist the thought that he is writing under the influence of the fourteenth-century voluntarist movement.

This essay distinguishes among a few claims that might be associated with voluntarism and considers some signs of their presence within *PPl*. A clear understanding of the philosophical character of voluntarism, and its implications for human nature, makes for a compelling case that we should understand the poem as the supreme medieval attempt to imbue an abstract philosophical thesis about the primacy of will with concrete meaning, set within the context of ordinary life. The search for Truth, as L conceives of it, is not chiefly an intellectual journey but rather a volitional one. (RP)

15. Pattenaude, Annika J., 'Undisciplined: Reading Affects in Late Medieval England' (unpublished doctoral thesis, University of Michigan, 2022), abstract in <https://dx.doi.org/10.7302/5951>. Abstract available through ProQuest, 2723415984.

16. Paulson, Julie C., '*Piers Plowman* and the Wisdom of Folly', *Yearbook of Langland Studies*, 36 (2022), 11–43.

This essay considers L's representation of the figure of the fool and what it can teach us about both medieval and current understandings of wisdom and folly. It argues that, in contrast to the deficit-based models of mental and cognitive limitation that are prevalent today, the poem cultivates an understanding of the wisdom of the fool, an understanding that emerges through L's opposition of sinful and holy fools, willed and unwilled forms of folly. Such attention to the poem's representations of folly — and the biblical, literary, and theological sources from which those representations draw — provides a clearer view of L's understanding of the role played by failure, error, and difficulty in the education of the will, with Will's often painful encounters with foolishness (his own and that of others) providing important lessons in humility. In contrast to current models of cognitive deficit and the ideologies of worldly achievement from which they arise, the poem presents a worldview in which foolishness is central to the human experience and the intellectual limitation, marginalization, and suffering associated with it, but also offers generative opportunities for renewal. (JCP)

17. Pigg, Daniel F., 'Words, Signs, Meanings: William Langland's *Piers Plowman* as a Window on Linguistic Chaos', in *Communication, Translation, and Community in the Middle Ages and Early Modern Period: New Cultural-Historical and Literary Perspectives*, ed. by Albrecht Classen (Berlin: De Gruyter, 2022), pp. 209–32.

L's *PPl*, a text written and rewritten between the 1360s and 1390, presents the poet's examination of the way that communication is thwarted in the social world through intentional action of corruption in the way words signify. Through an examination of the B-text *Visio*, readers can see how L's exploration of word and sign corruption can occur at the king's court, in the confessional, and in the all-important action of reading the pardon which Truth has sent to Piers the Plowman. Developing L's poetics of signs through recourse to grammar, rhetoric, logic, biblical interpretation, and analysis of liturgical and para-liturgical components, this essay argues that he crafts a thick description of how communication works in these three areas with the intention of correcting error.

Access to Truth is threatened by a corruption of the process of signification. L shows that while there are attempts to undermine the integrity of the communications model, by and large the court, the confessor in the confessional, and at least Piers in the reading of the pardon manage to keep the system working effectively. L's world, however, is precarious. Desire always threatens to undermine the process of signification. (DFP)

18. Raschko, Mary, 'Storytelling at the Gates of Hell: Narrative Epistemology in *Piers Plowman*', *Studies in the Age of Chaucer*, 44 (2022), 165–92.

This essay investigates the role of collective, reiterative storytelling within *PPl*. More specifically, it characterizes L's Four Daughters' debate in passus B 18/C 20 as a moment of metanarrative reflection that considers the power and limitations of storytelling for knowing God. At the poem's narrative climax, between the Crucifixion and the Harrowing of Hell, L inserts a deliberative pause in which Mercy, Truth, Justice, and Peace attempt to discern what the death of Christ means. While scholars typically read the debate as a discursive exchange, the speakers repeatedly tell stories. Most poignantly, within this larger life of Christ, Mercy, Peace, and the personification Book all narrate new lives of Christ. L presents these nested *vitae Christi* as acts of discernment that integrate select aspects of biblical history and forget or exclude others. By means of narrative selectivity, the speakers render God more legible, while also manifesting ideologies and potentially fostering misunderstanding. Ultimately, the essay argues that L presents any individual *vita Christi* as an insufficient means to know God, but affirms the collective, multivocal project of storytelling as vital to the quest for such knowledge. (MR)

19. Revere, William, 'Life with Concepts: Allegory, Recognition, and Adaptation', *New Chaucer Studies: Pedagogy and Profession*, 3 (2022), 19–30.

This essay examines questions around teaching allegory to undergraduates in a liberal arts setting, with a focus on reading and inviting students to write contemporary adaptations of premodern works. The complexities of literary character are sometimes reflexively disallowed to the personified figures of premodern allegory. A better tack, without assimilating medieval literary modes into modern ones, might have us attend to the variety of ways in which concepts are given embodied, social life in allegory. Adaptation assignments can invite self-involving hermeneutic engagement, analytic rigour, and creative response from students. Branden Jacobs-Jenkins's *Everybody*, a recent adaptation of *Everyman*, is looked to here as a model conversation partner for such a pedagogical approach. (WR)

20. Rhodes, William, 'The Apocalyptic Aesthetics of the List: Form and Political Economy in *Wynnere and Wastoure*', Journal of Medieval and Early Modern Studies, 52 (2022), 119–45.

Lists can suggest both a complete written account and the open-ended accumulation of terms. Their frequent appearance in apocalyptic texts formally mirrors apocalypticism's combination of divinely created order and the chaotic description of catastrophic events. Medieval and early modern poetic prophecies often list local manifestations of disorder and exclude the cosmic frame of divine order, making poems like *Wynnere and Wastoure*, which draws heavily on the tradition of poetic prophecy, seem not particularly apocalyptic. But the list-like passages in *Wynnere and Wastoure* join its focus on economics to the implicit apocalypticism of its prophetic passages. The sense that lists can appear as both an ordered account and a disordered accumulation allows the lists of *Wynnere and Wastoure* to suggest the comforting bounds of an apocalyptic framework while performing its dissolution through a vision of political economy based on endless cycles of winning and wasting. (WR)

21. Rollo-Koster, Joëlle, *The Great Western Schism, 1378–1417: Performing Legitimacy, Performing Unity* (Cambridge: Cambridge University Press, 2022).

The Great Schism divided Western Christianity between 1378 and 1417. Two popes and their courts occupied the see of St Peter, one in Rome, and one in Avignon. Traditionally, this event has received attention from scholars of institutional history. This book, by contrast, investigates the event through the prism of social drama. Marshalling liturgical, cultural, artistic, literary, and archival evidence, it explores the four phases of the Schism: the breach after the 1378 election, the subsequent division of the Church, redressive actions, and reintegration of the papacy in a single pope. Investigating how popes legitimized their respective positions and the reception of these efforts, it shows how the Schism influenced political thought, how unity was achieved, and how the two capitals, Rome and Avignon, responded to events. Rollo-Koster's approach humanizes the Schism, enabling us to understand the event as it was experienced by contemporaries. (JR-K)

22. Russin, Harrison, 'Late-Medieval Catechesis and the Credo', *Journal of the Alamire Foundation*, 14.2 (2022), 199–210.

The period from 1300 to 1500 witnessed an explosion in the composition and popularity of monophonic Creed melodies. The development of this corpus of about seventy such hymns paralleled a growing religious and cultural interest in the Creed. Specifically, this interest was manifest in three primary areas of late medieval religious life: catechism, devotion, and liturgy. This essay focuses on the catechetical dimension of the Creed, arguing that the Creed's role as an object of religious catechesis can help to explain the emergence of the new musical settings, which perhaps aimed to buttress memorization and understanding of the text. Russin examines the changing role of the Creed as an object of catechesis, specifically noting how it became an important marker of faith in the wake of the development of academic theology in the twelfth century. This emphasis by twelfth-century theologians led to ecclesial movements in the thirteenth century that promoted lay participation in the faith through the Creed, which in turn resulted in devotional, artistic, literary, and musical productions of the Creed in the fourteenth century. Highlighting these catechetical and artistic creations that focus on the Creed helps to contextualize the flourishing of its musical settings in the late Middle Ages. (HR)

23. Salisbury, Eve, *Narrating Medicine in Middle English Poetry: Poets, Practitioners, and the Plague* (London: Bloomsbury, 2022).

Exploring medical writing in England in the 100+ years after the advent of the 'Great Mortality', this book examines the storytelling practices of poets, patients, and physicians in the midst of a medieval public health crisis and demonstrates how literary narratives enable us to see a kinship between poetry and the healing arts. Looking at how we can learn to diagnose a text as if we were diagnosing a body, it provides new insights into how we can recuperate the voices of those afflicted by illness in medieval texts when we have no direct testimony. Salisbury considers how we interpret stories told by patients in narratives mediated by others, ways that women factor into the shaping of a medical canon, how medical writing intersects with religious belief and memorial practices governed by the Church, and ways that regimens of health benefit a population in the throes of an epidemic. (ES)

24. Sawyer, Thomas C., 'Bookish Brains and Visionary Learning in the *Apocalypsis goliae episcopi*', *ELH*, 89 (2022), 1–31.

Through a close examination of the *Apocalypsis goliae episcopi* ('The revelation of bishop Goliath'), this essay explores the limitations of human cognition in recording visionary experience. Scholars frequently look to visionary texts for imaginative reflections on the written conditions of memory and identity that characterize the fundamentally bookish cultures of the late Middle Ages. The *Apocalypsis* obsessively describes acts of inscription, announcing throughout its narrative an interest in the complex relationships that emerge between and among books, texts, authors, and readers. Turning on a provocative memorial metaphor — when the dreamer's angelic guide inscribes a record of the vision onto the physical matter of the dreamer's brain — the poem both performs and discloses a bifurcation central to all reading experience. At once parodic and sincere, the *Apocalypsis* suggests that the experience it describes, like all visionary experience, is constituted by someone other than the dreamer of the dream. (TCS)

25. Sisk, Jennifer, 'Langland's Ethical Imaginary: Refuge and Risk in "Piers bern"', *Exemplaria*, 34.3 (2022), 233–39.

Originally imagined as both granary and church writ large, L's Barn of Unity morphs into a space of refuge-in-crisis as it is besieged by Antichrist and the Seven Deadly Sins in *PPl*'s apocalyptic finale. Central to L's imagining is a conundrum at the heart of hospitality, the Latin root of which means not only *guest* and *friend* but also *stranger* and *enemy*. Within Unity, the allegorical figure of Conscience practises hospitality, welcoming others, yet attempting to set conditions for entry to keep his space morally intact. Unity is intended to be a refuge from the violence of sin, but with every act of welcome Conscience risks letting sin in. This essay breaks new ground by interrogating L's representation of these acts of welcome in relation to recent hospitality theory (by Derrida and others) to illuminate how the satirical bent of the ending of *PPl* coexists with reformist idealism. (JS)

26. Somerset, Fiona, 'Speaking in Person', in *Medieval Literary Voices: Embodiment, Materiality and Performance*, ed. by Louise D'Arcens and Sif Ríkharðsdóttir (Manchester: Manchester University Press, 2022), pp. 56–72.

This chapter considers what voice has to do with the ways medieval people thought about personhood. Personification allows medieval authors to round out an abstract quality or thing (whether fitfully or at length) so that it acquires human characteristics and a body, an imagined 'other mind' subject to emotions and sensations, or a role in a narrative, whether very briefly or at more length. As if those rich and complex features of personification were not enough, however, medieval people seem to have found it most necessary to comment on personhood in texts when the person they are imagining has a voice. They populate the moments when someone speaks in the first person, especially if what they say is emotionally difficult or hard to explain, with comments that X is 'speaking in the person of' someone else. Here Somerset considers the interpretative act of disidentification involved in any claim that an 'I' voice speaks in the person of someone else. Why did medieval writers and readers feel the impulse to make up people such as this, sometimes in the most evanescent or fungible way, in order to explain the 'I' voices they fashioned or encountered in texts? (FS)

27. Steel, Karl, 'The Rules of the Game: Wolf-Hunting and the Usefulness of Knights in *Piers Plowman*', *Yearbook of Langland Studies*, 36 (2022), 123–36.

PPl twice attempts to justify aristocratic hunting, first on the half-acre, when Piers tells the knight that his duties include defending his hedges against boars and bucks and his grain against birds, and then again in a new passage in C.9.224–26, which commands knights to protect men, women, and children by hunting wolves. The hunting justifications are unusual. As jealous as they were of their hunting privileges, aristocrats justified it only as practice for martial hardships, and never as serving any common social benefit. For their part, clerics tended to condemn hunting. Not L: as he seeks some purpose for knights in his social imaginary, he reframes one of their chief entertainments as generally useful. The C text even intensifies the justification, with its new threat from wolves. The addition, however, sees L commanding knights to engage in the one form of hunting that could be considered a duty rather than a pleasure, and, moreover, to hunt an animal that was, by L's day, virtually extinct in England. Overall, Piers's hunting justifications tether the utility of hunting, and by extension the utility of knighthood, to an animal too hard to find and too ignoble to be worth the chase. (KS)

28. Steiner, Emily, 'Neck Verse', *New Literary History*, 53.3 (2022), 333–62.

Mitigations in medieval criminal law, designed to prevent or defer execution, have been regarded in a variety of ways: as acts of mercy, as discretionary measures, and as travesties of justice. For post-medieval English and American writers they also represent the past of the law; since at least the eighteenth century they have formed the backbone of legal histories describing the passage from premodern to modern law and from a less to a more equitable distribution of justice. This essay argues that the mitigations inherited from the Middle Ages are 'medievalisms-at-law', serving both as anachronisms — throwbacks to an ostensibly more corrupt or superstitious age — and as touchstones for modernity. When current, they often feel out of time because death is on the line; when obsolete, they abide, both in literature and in law. Seemingly conducive to progressive histories, they threaten to drag modernity back into the Middle Ages. This essay focuses on one such mitigation, the benefit of clergy, which, thanks to its famous 'neck verse', was used not only to obtain mercy for some but also to prevent others from claiming the same benefit. As this essay argues, its potential both to save and exclude is part of what reactivates the benefit of clergy in post-medieval English literature and law. The survival of this legal practice in American slave law, and even in present political discourse, reminds us that old laws never die, nor do they entirely fade away. Instead they go on to create new histories of law, justice, class, and nation. (ES)

29. Strickland, Seth John, 'Rewrite this Book: Compilation and Experimental Literary Practices in *Piers Plowman* and Late Medieval English Book Culture' (unpublished doctoral thesis, Cornell University, 2022), abstract in DAI-A 84/3(E), 2711233300. Abstract available through ProQuest.

30. Strickland, Seth John, 'Piers Plowman', in 'Middle English', *The Year's Work in English Studies*, 101 (2022), 50–56 <https://doi.org/10.1093/ywes/maac003>.

A qualitative bibliographical review of work on *PPl* published in 2020 with some addenda from 2019.

31. Wagner, Kathryn Mogk, 'The Language of Liturgy: Unintelligibility, Translation, and Performance in English Religious Writing, 1350–1550' (unpublished doctoral thesis, Harvard University, 2022). Abstract available through ProQuest, 28964466.

32. Wakelin, Daniel, *Immaterial Texts in Late Medieval England: Making English Literary Manuscripts, 1400–1500* (Cambridge: Cambridge University Press, 2022).

Wakelin's book introduces and reinterprets the misunderstood and overlooked craft practices, cultural conventions, and literary attitudes involved in making some of the most important manuscripts in late medieval English literature. In doing so, he overturns how we view the role of scribes, showing how they ignored or concealed irregular and damaged parchment; ruled pages from habit and convention more than necessity; decorated the division of the text into pages or worried that it would harm reading; abandoned annotations to poetry, focusing on the poem itself; and copied English poems meticulously, in reverence for an abstract idea of the text. Scribes' interest in immaterial ideas and texts suggests their subtle thinking as craftspeople, in ways that contrast and extend current interpretations of late medieval literary culture, 'material texts', and the power of materials. For students, researchers, and librarians, this book offers revelatory perspectives on the activities of late medieval scribes. (DW)

33. Watson, Nicholas, *Balaam's Ass: Vernacular Theology before the English Reformation*, vol. 1 [to 1250] (Philadelphia: University of Pennsylvania Press, 2022).

For over seven hundred years, bodies of writing in vernacular languages served an indispensable role in the religious and intellectual culture of medieval Christian England, yet the character and extent of their importance have been insufficiently recognized. A longstanding identification of medieval western European Christianity with the Latin language and a lack of awareness about the sheer variety and quantity of vernacular religious writing from the English Middle Ages have hampered our understanding of the period, exercising a tenacious hold on much scholarship.

Bringing together work across a range of disciplines, including literary study, Christian theology, social history, and the history of institutions, *Balaam's Ass* attempts the first comprehensive overview of religious writing in early England's three most important vernacular languages, Old English, Insular French, and Middle English, between the ninth and sixteenth centuries. It argues not only that these texts comprise the oldest continuous tradition of European vernacular writing, but that they are essential to our understanding of how Christianity shaped and informed the lives of individuals, communities, and polities in the Middle Ages.

This first of three volumes lays out the long post-Reformation history of the false claim that the medieval Catholic Church was hostile to the vernacular. It analyses the complicated idea of the vernacular, a medieval innovation instantiated in a huge body of surviving vernacular religious texts. Finally, it focuses on the first, long generation of these writings, in Old English and early Middle English. (NW)

34. Weiskott, Eric, 'The Meter of the Ophni and Phineas Insertion in *Piers Plowman*', *Studia Metrica et Poetica*, 9.2 (2022), 117–32.

The C version of *PPl* has yet to earn much attention from metrists relative to the outgrowth of research into fourteenth-century alliterative metre since 1986. L's relationship to metrical tradition is idiosyncratic, a judgement that involves both this author's divergence from conventions characteristic of other alliterative poems and the recognizability of his own metrical habitus across his career. Scansion of an inconsistently alliterating passage new in C (Prol.95–124) illustrates in miniature the unusual problems thrown up by L's metrical practice and suggests that his metrical signature persisted over the years of his writing life. The Ophni and Phineas insertion is of special interest because it has been thought an unfinished draft. (EW)

35. Wood, Sarah, *'Piers Plowman' and its Manuscript Tradition* (York: York Medieval Press, 2022).

The fifty-plus surviving manuscripts of L's *PPl* cast important light on the early public life of this central Middle English work, but they have been relatively neglected by scholarship. This first full study of the subject examines the textual variants, marginal rubrics, and companion texts in the manuscripts. It illuminates a reception quite distinct from the reformist poems written by L's imitators in 'the *PPl* tradition'. It reveals how the earliest scribes devised various traditional forms of presentation that proved remarkably durable in the poem's subsequent reception, even surviving into the age of print. Exploring *PPl*'s appearances in these manuscripts, paired unexpectedly with such genres as romance, hagiography, and travel literature, the book demonstrates the surprisingly affective responses of medieval readers to the represented lives of the narrator Will and the title figure Piers the Plowman. At the same time, it shows that the evidence for individual scribal agendas in particular copies is more ambiguous than often assumed, with each book reflecting the activities of an unknown number of hands and an uncertain mixture of design and accident. By drawing on evidence from textual scholarship as well as codicological and literary approaches, the author offers fresh insight into *PPl*'s place in literary history and proposes new ways of understanding the late medieval manuscript as a multi-layered, collaborative product. (SW)

Book Reviews

36 Aers, David, *Versions of Election: From Langland & Aquinas to Calvin & Milton* (Notre Dame: University of Notre Dame Press, 2022). Rev. by Felisa Baynes-Ross, *Theological Studies*, 83 (2022), 158–60.

37 Ambühl, Rémy, James Bothwell, and Laura Tompkins, eds, *Ruling Fourteenth-Century England: Essays in Honour of Christopher Given-Wilson* (Woodbridge: Boydell, 2019). Rev. by Áine Foley, *Parliaments, Estates and Representation*, 42 (2022), 341–43; James Masschaele, *Speculum*, 97.3 (2022), 776–77.

38 Benson, C. David, *Imagined Romes: The Ancient City and Its Stories in Middle English Poetry* (University Park: Pennsylvania State University Press, 2019). Rev. by Nicholas D. Brodie, *Parergon*, 39 (2022), 220–21; Antonio Paniagua Guzmán, *Literary Geographies*, 8 (2022), 99–102.

39 Breckenridge Wright, Sarah, *Mobility and Identity in Chaucer's 'Canterbury Tales'*, Chaucer Studies 46 (Woodbridge: Brewer, 2020). Rev. by Susan Nakley, *Speculum*, 97.2 (2022), 587–89; Hannah Elizabeth Piercy, *Medium Aevum*, 90.2 (2022), 151–52.

40 Breen, Katharine, *Machines of the Mind: Personification in Medieval Literature* (Chicago: University of Chicago Press, 2021). Rev. by Julie Orlemanski, *Yearbook of Langland Studies*, 36 (2022), 153–57; William Rhodes, *Studies in the Age of Chaucer*, 44 (2022), 382–86.

41 Byron-Davies, Justin M., *Revelation and the Apocalypse in Late Medieval Literature: The Writings of Julian of Norwich and William Langland* (Cardiff: University of Wales Press, 2020). Rev. by Denise N. Baker, *Speculum*, 97.2 (2022), 483–84.

42 Cady, Diane, *The Gender of Money in Middle English Literature: Value and Economy in Late Medieval England*, The New Middle Ages (Cham: Palgrave Macmillan, 2019). Rev. by A. Louise Cole, *Renaissance Quarterly*, 75.4 (2022), 1457–58.

43 Calabrese, Michael, ed. and trans., *Piers Plowman: The A Version* (Washington, DC: The Catholic University of America Press, 2020). Rev. by Tekla Bude, *Digital Philology: A Journal of Medieval Cultures*, 11 (2022), 215–17; Traugott Lawler, *Yearbook of Langland Studies*, 36 (2022), 149–52; Ryan McDermott, *Catholic Historical Review*, 108.4 (2022), 808–09; A. W. Strouse, *Church History*, 91.2 (2022), 389–90.

44 Campbell, Ethan, *The Gawain-Poet and the Fourteenth-Century English Anticlerical Tradition*, Research in Medieval and Early Modern Culture 22 (Kalamazoo: Medieval Institute Publications, 2018). Rev. by Andrew Galloway, *Speculum*, 97.4 (2022), 1171–72.

45 Cré, Marleen, Diana Denissen, and Denis Renevey, ed., *Late Medieval Devotional Compilations in England*, Medieval Church Studies 41 (Turnhout: Brepols, 2020). Rev. by Hans Geybels, *Volkskunde*, 123.2 (2022), 215–16.

46 Da Rold, Orietta, *Paper in Medieval England: From Pulp to Fiction* (Cambridge: Cambridge University Press, 2020). Rev. by Megan L. Cook, *Studies in the Age of Chaucer*, 44 (2022), 386–89; William Noel, *Manuscript Studies: A Journal of the Schoenberg Institute for Manuscript Studies*, 7 (2022), 210–12; David Rundle, *Times Literary Supplement*, 6199 (2022), 21.01.2022; Sebastian Sobecki, *Speculum*, 97.2 (2022), 560–62.

47 Fonzo, Kimberly, *Retrospective Prophecy and Medieval English Authorship* (Toronto: University of Toronto Press, 2022). Rev. by Lerah Tether, *Medieval Review* (2022), 23.08.22.

48 Johnson, Eleanor, *Staging Contemplation: Participatory Theology in Middle English Prose, Verse, and Drama* (Chicago: University of Chicago Press, 2018). Rev. by Barbara Zimbalist, *Journal of English and Germanic Philology*, 121 (2022), 136–39.

49 Katz Seal, Samantha, *Father Chaucer: Generating Authority in 'The Canterbury Tales'*, Oxford Studies in Medieval Literature and Culture (Oxford: Oxford University Press, 2019). Rev. by Thomas Prendergast, *Speculum*, 97.2 (2022), 565–67.

50 Kerby-Fulton, Kathryn, *The Clerical Proletariat and the Resurgence of Medieval English Poetry* (Philadelphia: University of Pennsylvania Press, 2021). Rev. by Wendy Scase, *Yearbook of Langland Studies*, 36 (2022), 158–60; George Shuffleton, *Speculum*, 97.4 (2022), 1217–18.

51 Knight, Stephen, *Medieval Literature and Social Politics: Studies of Cultures and Their Contexts*, Variorum Collected Studies (London and New York: Routledge, 2021). Rev. by Thomas H. Ohlgren, *Arthuriana*, 32 (2022), 96–98.

52 Kraebel, Andrew, *Biblical Commentary and Translation in Later Medieval England: Experiments in Interpretation* (Cambridge: Cambridge University Press, 2020). Rev. by Patrick Hornbeck, *Renaissance Quarterly*, 75.2 (2022), 691–92; James H. Morey, *Journal of English and Germanic Philology*, 121.3 (2022), 413–16.

53 Lears, Adin E., *World of Echo: Noise and Knowing in Late Medieval England* (Ithaca: Cornell University Press, 2020). Rev. by Karen M. Cook, *Sound Studies: An Interdisciplinary Journal*, 8.2 (2022), 254–57; Hannah Skoda, *English Historical Review*, 137.586 (2022), 911–13.

54 Leitch, Megan G., *Sleep and its Spaces in Middle English Literature: Emotions, Ethics, Dreams* (Manchester: Manchester University Press, 2021). Rev. by Jamie C. Fumo, *Yearbook of Langland Studies*, 36 (2022), 145–48; Jamie K. Taylor, *Studies in the Age of Chaucer*, 44 (2022), 412–15.

55 Morton, Jonathan, and Marco Nievergelt with John Marenbon, eds, *The 'Roman de la Rose' and Thirteenth-Century Thought*, Cambridge Studies in Medieval Literature 111 (Cambridge: Cambridge Univer-

sity Press, 2020). Rev. by Christine McWebb, *Speculum* 97.4 (2022), 1237–38.

56 Murton, Megan E., *Chaucer's Prayers: Writing Christian and Pagan Devotion*, Chaucer Studies 47 (Woodbridge: Brewer, 2020). Rev. by Antje Elisa Chan, *Journal of Medieval Religious Cultures*, 48 (2022), 99–102; Joseph D. Parry, *Renaissance Quarterly*, 75.4 (2022), 1436–37.

57 Ormrod, W. Mark, *'Winner and Waster' and its Contexts: Chivalry, Law and Economics in Fourteenth-Century England* (Woodbridge: Brewer, 2021). Rev. by Jennifer Goodman Wollock, *Arthuriana*, 32.2 (2022), 108–10; Jörg Peltzer, *Historische Zeitschrift*, 314.2 (2022), 1130; Michael Prestwich, *Journal of the Historical Association*, 107.374 (2022), 172–73; Thorlac Turnville-Petre, *Yearbook of Langland Studies*, 36 (2022), 161–64.

58 Raschko, Mary, *The Politics of Middle English Parables: Fiction, Theology, and Social Practice* (Manchester: Manchester University Press, 2019). Rev. by Cristina Maria Cervone, *Speculum*, 97.2 (2022), 557–59.

59 Sawyer, Daniel, *Reading English Verse in Manuscript c. 1350–c. 1500* (Oxford: Oxford University Press, 2020). Rev. by Joel Grossman, *Speculum*, 97.2 (2022), 564–65; Elizaveta Strakhov, *Manuscript Studies: A Journal of the Schoenberg Institute for Manuscript Studies*, 7.2 (2022), 381–85.

60 Scott, Anne M., and Michael David Barbezat, ed., *Fluid Bodies and Bodily Fluids in Premodern Europe: Bodies, Blood, and Tears in Literature, Theology, and Art* (Leeds: Arc Humanities, 2019). Rev. by Bettina Bildhauer, *Social History of Medicine*, 35 (2022), 324–26.

61 Smith, D. Vance, *Arts of Dying: Literature and Finitude in Medieval England* (Chicago: University of Chicago Press, 2020). Rev. by Amy Appleford, *Yearbook of Langland Studies*, 36 (2022), 137–39; Wendy A. Matlock, *Journal of Medieval Religious Cultures*, 48 (2022), 102–05.

62 Steiner, Emily, *John Trevisa's Information Age: Knowledge and the Pursuit of Literature c. 1400* (Oxford: Oxford University Press, 2021). Rev. by A. S. G. Edwards, *Yearbook of Langland Studies*, 36 (2022), 140–44; Matthew Boyd Goldie, *Studies in the Age of Chaucer*, 44 (2022), 425–29.

63 Thomas, Arvind, *'Piers Plowman' and the Reinvention of Church Law in the Late Middle Ages* (Toronto: University of Toronto Press, 2019). Rev. by Elizabeth Allen, *Poetics Today*, 43.3 (2022), 587–89; Cristina Maria Cervone, *Irish Theological Quarterly*, 87 (2022), 69–71; Kate Crassons, *English Studies*, 103 (2022), 362–65; Andrew Galloway, *Partial Answers: Journal of Literature and the History of Ideas*, 20.2 (2022), 367–71; Jennifer Garrison, *European Review of History*, 29 (2022), 847–48; David von Mayenburg, *Zeitschrift der Savigny-Stiftung für Rechtsgeschichte: Kanonistische Abteilung*, 108 (2022), 351–53; Ryan McDermott, *Catholic Historical Review*, 108.4 (2022), 808–09; Sarah

McKeagney, *British Catholic History*, 36 (2022), 92–94; Katherine McKenna, *Medieval History Journal*, 25.2 (2022), 292–306; Sharity D. Nelson, *Zeitschrift für Anglistik und Amerikanistik*, 70 (2022), 111–13; Patrick Outhwaite, *University of Toronto Quarterly*, 91.3 (2022), 402–04; Erika Pihl, *Mirator*, 22 (2022), 76–79; Lawrence Scanlon, *Law, Culture and the Humanities*, 18 (2022), 250–68; Zachery E. Stone, *Journal of English and Germanic Philology*, 121.2 (2022), 272–75; Elise Wang, *Modern Humanities Research Association*, 117.4 (2022), 689–99.

64 Turner, Marion, *Chaucer: A European Life* (Princeton: Princeton University Press, 2019). Rev. by Sean Gordon Lewis, *Renaissance Quarterly*, 75.4 (2022), 1435–36.

65 Warren, Nancy Bradley, *Chaucer and Religious Controversies in the Medieval and Early Modern Eras* (Notre Dame, IN: University of Notre Dame Press, 2019). Rev. by Shannon Gayk, *Journal of English and Germanic Philology*, 121 (2022), 144–47.

66 Weiskott, Eric, *Meter and Modernity in English Verse, 1350–1650* (Philadelphia: University of Pennsylvania Press, 2021). Rev. by Molly Clark, *Review of English Studies*, 73.309 (2022), 387–89; Ben Glaser, *Modern Language Review*, 117.3 (2022), 478–80; Nicholas Myklebust, *Arthuriana*, 32 (2022), 103–04; Daniel Sawyer, *English Studies*, 103 (2022), 378–80; Danila Sokolov, *Renaissance Quarterly*, 75.3 (2022), 1113–15.

67 Zeeman, Nicolette, *The Arts of Disruption: Allegory and 'Piers Plowman'* (Oxford: Oxford University Press, 2020). Rev. by Chris Gruenler, *Speculum*, 97.3 (2022), 898–99.